Henry Richard Fox Bourne

**English Seamen**

Under the Tudors. Vol. 2

Henry Richard Fox Bourne

**English Seamen**
*Under the Tudors. Vol. 2*

ISBN/EAN: 9783337006945

Printed in Europe, USA, Canada, Australia, Japan

Cover: Foto ©ninafisch / pixelio.de

More available books at **www.hansebooks.com**

# ENGLISH SEAMEN

UNDER

# THE TUDORS.

BY

H. R. FOX BOURNE,

AUTHOR OF "A MEMOIR OF SIR PHILIP SIDNEY," "ENGLISH MERCHANTS," ETC.

*IN TWO VOLUMES.*

VOLUME II.

LONDON:
RICHARD BENTLEY, NEW BURLINGTON STREET,
Publisher in Ordinary to Her Majesty.
1868.

# CONTENTS OF VOLUME II.

### CHAPTER XI.

QUEEN ELIZABETH'S NAVY AND ITS EARLIER WORK.

[1558—1585.]

PAGE

The English Navy at the time of Henry VIII.'s Death—Its Decline under Mary and Edward VI.—Its Revival under Elizabeth—Her Chief Advisers and Agents; the Howards and Clinton—Cecil's Plan for Naval Improvement—The Strength of the Navy in 1578—The Services of Sir John Hawkins and Sir William Winter—Queen Elizabeth's Irregular War with France and Scotland—Piracy under the Tudors—The Work of the Navy in Checking it . . . . 1

### CHAPTER XII.

THE EARLIER EXPLOITS OF SIR JOHN HAWKINS AND SIR FRANCIS DRAKE IN THE SPANISH MAIN.

[1562—1576.]

"Old William Hawkins" and his Voyages to Brazil—John Hawkins's Training and First Employments—His First West Indian Voyage—His Quarrel with Spain thereupon—His Second West

Indian Voyage—Negro-Hunting in Guinea—Negro-Selling in
the Spanish Main—Hawkins's Exploits at Barbarotta, at Curaçoa,
and at Rio de la Hacha—His Visit to Florida and Return to
England—Queen Elizabeth's Favour and King Philip's Anger
—The Early History of Sir Francis Drake—Hawkins's Third
West Indian Voyage—His Insult to Spain in Plymouth Harbour—His Further Adventures on the African Coast and in the
Spanish Main—His Visit to San Juan de Ulloa, and Great Fight
with the Spaniards there—His Defeat and its Results—The Sufferings of his Comrades in Mexico—The Troubles of his Home-
ward Voyage—Drake's Two First Voyages to the Spanish Main
—His Third Expedition—His Raid on Nombre de Dios—His
Piracies near Cartagena—His Land Expedition towards Panama
—The Fruits of his Piratical Work—The Unfortunate Voyage
of Andrew Barker . . . . . . . . 22

## CHAPTER XIII.

THE VOYAGES OF SIR FRANCIS DRAKE AND THOMAS CAVENDISH TO THE
SOUTHERN SEA AND ROUND THE WORLD.

[1575—1593.]

Drake's Employments in Ireland and England—John Oxenham's
Expedition to the South Sea—Drake's Voyage round the World
—His Ships and their Outfit—His Passage to the African
Coast, and thence to Patagonia—Troubles at Port Saint Julian
—The Execution of Thomas Doughty—The Passage of Ma-
gellan's Strait—A Seven Weeks' Storm and its Work—Drake's
Discovery of Cape Horn—His Piracies off Chili and Peru—His
Capture of the *Cacafuego*—His Passage to California, and
Attempt to find the North West Route—His Kingdom of New
Albion—His Crossing of the Pacific Ocean and Visit to Ternate
—First English Intercourse with the Moluccas—Drake's Escape

*Contents.*

from Shipwreck near Celebes—His Homeward Voyage and his Reception in England—The Results of his Voyage round the World—Enterprises consequent upon it—Edward Fenton's Unfortunate Expedition towards the South Sea—Thomas Cavendish's Voyage round the World—His Passage by way of Africa to the Strait of Magellan—The Story of a Spanish Colonizing Project under Diego Florez de Valdez and Pedro Sarmiento—Cavendish's Discovery of its Ruins—His Passage of Magellan's Strait—His Piracies along the Western Coast of America from Chili to California—His Capture of the *Santa Anna*—His Visit to the Indian Archipelago — His Stay at the Philippine Islands and at Java—His Return to England—His Second Expedition to the South Sea in company with John Davis—His Troubles at Magellan's Strait and off Brazil—His Death on the Way Home—Davis's Passage of Magellan's Strait, and Subsequent Troubles—Davis's Last Work and Death . . 76

CHAPTER XIV.

THE PRELUDE TO THE GREAT ARMADA FIGHT.

[1585—1587.]

The Origin and Progress of England's Quarrel with Spain—Queen Elizabeth's League with the Netherlands, and open War with Philip II.—Lord Charles Howard of Effingham—Sir Francis Drake's and Sir Philip Sidney's Project against Spain—Drake's Expedition to the West Indies—His Visit to the Coast of Galicia and Cape de Verde Islands—His Capture of San Domingo and Cartagena—His Plans for Further Warfare against Philip—His First Expedition to Spain—His Destruction of Spanish Shipping and Spanish Forts at Cadiz and elsewhere along the Coast—His Capture of the *San Felipe*—The Effect of his Work . . . . . . 148

## CHAPTER XV.

### THE GREAT ARMADA FIGHT.

[1588.]

Philip II.'s Preparations for the Invasion of England—English Preparations for Resisting it—The Arguments and Plans of Lord Admiral Howard, Sir Francis Drake, and Sir John Hawkins—Queen Elizabeth's Backwardness—The Voyage of the English Fleet to anticipate the Armada—The Size and Composition of the Armada—The Size and Composition of the English Fleet—The Voyage of the Armada to Plymouth—The First Day's Fighting off Plymouth—Howard's Following of the Armada on its Way to Calais—The Hostile Fleets at Bay—Sir William Winter's Fire-Ships and their Work—The Great Battle off Gravelines—The Retreat and Ruin of the Armada—The Troubles of the English . 201

## CHAPTER XVI.

### THE SEQUEL TO THE GREAT ARMADA FIGHT.

[1588—1603.]

The Consequences of the Overthrow of the Spanish Armada—Schemes for the Further Troubling of Spain—Projects of the Earl of Cumberland and Sir Walter Raleigh—The Great Expedition of Sir Francis Drake and Sir John Norris, in Aid of Don Antonio, against Spain—Their Siege of Corunna—Their Fight with the Spaniards at Puente de Burgo—Robert, Earl of Essex—The End of Drake's and Norris's Expedition—The Earl of Cumberland's First Privateering Voyage—A Fight between English Merchantmen and Spanish Galleys off Gibraltar—Sir John Hawkins's Expedition in Search of Spanish Prizes—The Earl of Cumberland's Second Privateering Voyage—Lord Thomas

## Contents.

Howard's Expedition in Search of Prizes—Sir Richard Grenville's Valiant Fight in the *Revenge*—Sir Walter Raleigh's Share in the War with Spain—His and the Earl of Cumberland's Privateering Expeditions in 1592—The Capture of the *Madre de Dios*—The Progress of Privateering—The War in Brittany—Sir Martin Frobisher's Death—Sir Richard Hawkins's Expedition to the South Sea—His Great Fight with the Spaniards, and Defeat by them off the Coast of Peru—Sir John Hawkins's Last Work at Home—His Expedition to Panama in Company with Sir Francis Drake—The Death of Hawkins—The Death of Drake—Sir Walter Raleigh and his El Dorado Project—Philip II.'s Plans against England—The Great Expedition to Spain under the Earl of Essex and Lord Admiral Howard—Their Fighting in Cadiz Harbour, and Taking of Cadiz—The Last Phase of Tudor Seamanship—Conclusion . . . . . . . 246

# ENGLISH PIRACY, PRIVATEERING AND OPEN WARFARE

UNDER QUEEN ELIZABETH.

# ENGLISH SEAMEN UNDER THE TUDORS.

## CHAPTER XI.

QUEEN ELIZABETH'S NAVY AND ITS EARLIER WORK.

[1558—1585.]

THE great achievements, under Queen Elizabeth, of the seamen who, following the lead of the Cabots, went out in small and ill-constructed vessels to contend with Arctic ice and fog in their search for a north-western passage to Cathay, and who, when they were worsted in that battle, turned aside to begin the colonization of America and the conquest of India, were wholly the result of private enterprise and of prowess which, though sanctioned by the Crown, looked for no reward that it could not win for itself. Private enterprise and prowess unaided by State authority, also, were motives to the famous series of sea-fights and naval expeditions by which England for the first time acquired a right to her proud title of mistress of the sea. The greatest heroes of Elizabeth's great navy, the men who made it possible for her, when the insolence of Catholic

Spain was at its height, to assure the stability of her own kingdom and the liberty of Protestant Europe by vanquishing the Invincible Armada, were private gentlemen and uncommissioned sailors, whose training had been in ways of which the State took no cognizance, or which it recognized chiefly to condemn.

During the thirty years preceding the Great Armada Fight, however, Queen Elizabeth's navy, though its work was insignificant in comparison with the work of men who had no rank in it, made steady progress. The progress resulted from the zeal with which were developed the principles of naval rule that had been adopted by King Henry VIII.

Henry, throughout his reign, had held the French and their allies the Scots at bay. Not satisfied with his possession of Calais, and with the opportunities it afforded for the annoyance of his great enemy, he had taken Boulogne in 1546, and had steadily defended his own realm from the designs of all invaders. But during the ten years following his death there was persistent squandering of the naval reputation that he had won for England. In the brief and unfortunate period of Edward VI.'s reign the royal navy was reduced to half its previous size; and under Mary's shorter and more disastrous sway its fame and influence were yet further diminished.

At the time of Henry's death the royal navy consisted of fifty-three vessels, large and small, with an aggregate burthen of 6,255 tons, and adapted for the employment of 5,136 sailors, 759 gunners, and 1,885 soldiers or strictly fighting-men, making a total, with about 200 officers, of nearly 8,000 men of all sorts. The largest of these was the *Henri Grace à Dieu*, of 1,000 tons' burthen. Two others, the *Peter* and the *Matthew*, were of 600 tons each; two were of 500 tons, four of 450, and three of 400. The rest were of smaller size, some being mere boats, bearing no more than 15 tons apiece.* The governors of Edward VI., inheriting this shipping, put it to a little use in aiding the land attack upon Scotland, which resulted in the battle of Pinkie. In 1547 Leith and most of the Scottish seaports were damaged; the Scottish fleet was routed, and great numbers of merchantmen and other small craft were destroyed.† But in 1548 the English fleet was not able to overthrow the shipping that awaited its return to Scottish waters; and after peace had been made with Scotland and France nothing more of any note was done during Edward's brief reign. At its close the royal ships had been reduced in number from fifty-three to forty-five, and of these only twenty-four were in condition for actual service. Ten, including the *Peter* and the *Matthew*, were in need of thorough repair, and the other eleven were only fit to be broken up and sold for old wood.‡

The sound ships were allowed to fall into decay, and

---

* CHARNOCK, *History of Marine Architecture*, vol. ii., pp. 49, 50. The *Henri Grace à Dieu* was evidently the same, built in 1514, which is described in vol. i., p. 70, and there shown to have been of 1,500 tons burthen. I am unable to explain the discrepancy.

† HOLLINSHED, vol. ii., pp. 990—995.

‡ BRITISH MUSEUM MSS., *Harleian*, No. 354, fols. 90b, 91.

the unsound ones to become perfectly useless during the unworthy reign of Queen Mary. Almost at its commencement, on the 26th of August, 1553, the *Henri Grace à Dieu*, which had been called the *Edward* under Edward VI., and had been re-christened by its older name on Mary's accession, was burnt at Woolwich, " by the negligence of the mariners ;"* and, for any good use to which they were put, the others might also have been burnt. In 1557 Sir John Clere, Vice-Admiral of England, being sent with a fleet of twelve sail to annoy the Scots, was utterly defeated by them ;† and in 1558 Lord Clinton, though his own fleet consisted of all the English fighting-ships that could be brought together, and of thirty Spanish vessels as well, was unable to do any serious injury to the French whom he was ordered to attack upon the coast of Brittany.‡ The only valorous act of this reign was done four years before by Lord High Admiral Howard, on the occasion of his being sent with twenty-eight ships to escort Philip of Spain on his coming to England to be made Mary's husband. Philip was attended by a hundred and sixty Spanish sail, with a Spanish flag floating from the topmast of their admiral's ship. At this Howard was so annoyed that he fired at it, and insisted upon the English colours being substituted before he would pay his respects to Philip, and conduct him into Southampton Harbour.§ That perhaps was

\* HOLLINSHED, vol. ii., p. 1090. † STRYPE, vol. iii., p. 429.
‡ RECORD OFFICE MSS., *Domestic, Mary*, vol. xii., No. 23 ; vol. xiii., No. 61 ; GRAFTON, p. 1361.
§ HOLLINSHED, vol. ii., p. 1118.

the first token of the English jealousy of Spain, which was to issue in very memorable consequences during the next fifty years.

Four years of civil misgovernment and of religious persecution sufficed to make the jealousy strong in the mind of every patriotic Englishman. Elizabeth on her accession found her people heartily disposed but quite unable to exercise it with good effect. Inheriting a kingdom wrecked and wasted in all its parts, the waste and wreck were nowhere more apparent than in her navy. The fate of the *Great Harry*, destroyed " by the negligence of the mariners," had been shared, with differences in the ignoble manner of destruction, by most of the best vessels that should have been preserved for the maintenance of English dignity upon the sea. Through a quarter of a century, harassed by show of friendship with Spain, and by more or less open feud with France and Scotland, Elizabeth had laboriously to bring back the naval strength of England to the condition in which it had been left by Henry VIII. This, and more, she did by prudent exercise of her own abilities, and by yet more prudent use of the abilities of counsellors and agents wiser than herself.

The counsellors in whom most she trusted, and who perhaps best merited her trust, were William and Charles Howard, son and grandson of Lord Thomas Howard, brother and successor, as Chief Admiral of England, of the excellent Sir Edward Howard, and Edward Clinton, afterwards Earl of Lincoln.

Lord William Howard had been a special favourite

with Henry VIII. until the year 1541, when he shared in the disgrace that befel his niece, Queen Catherine Howard. For supposed complicity in her misconduct, he and his wife Margaret, daughter of Sir Thomas Gamage, of Coity, in Glamorganshire, were sentenced to perpetual imprisonment and to be mulcted of their personal property as well as of life interest in their landed estates. But Henry's appreciation of Howard's past services soon led to a remission of this punishment, and under the rule of Henry's three children Howard rose to great distinction. His early zeal in naval affairs appears in his encouragement of the famous enterprise by which Willoughby and Chancelor attempted, in 1553, to find a north-eastern passage to Cathay. He was one of the Company of Merchant Adventurers who fitted out that expedition, and after the expedition had failed, he continued to be a leading member of the Company. Very soon after Queen Mary's accession, on the 11th of March, 1554, he was made a peer of the realm as Lord Howard of Effingham; and on the 20th of the same month he was appointed High Admiral of England and Wales, Ireland, Gascony, and Aquitaine. On the 8th of April following, "in consideration of his fidelity, prudence, valour, and industry," Queen Mary made him " her lieutenant-general and chief commander of her whole fleet and royal army going to sea for the defence of her friends." He had not much to do, either for the defence of friends or for the punishment of foes, under Mary; but the temper in which he applied himself to his work appears in his reception of Philip, in

July, 1554, which has already been noticed. Yet he did all that he could, and, with the better opportunities that came on the accession of Elizabeth, he did better service until his death, on the 12th of January, 1572.*

His service, however, was only such as could be rendered by a vice-admiral, with great influence at Court and with a disposition to use his influence wisely. In the post of High Admiral he had been superseded in April, 1558, by Lord Edward Clinton,† who continued in office until his death, in 1585. It was then conferred upon Lord Charles Howard, and held by him for nearly forty years.

Lord Edward Clinton, who became Earl of Nottingham on the 4th of May, 1572,‡ was Queen Elizabeth's chief official adviser on naval matters during the first half of her reign; but Cecil and all her great statesmen, Gresham and all her great merchants, shared in the advice, and, amid some blunders and follies, helped to make of the English navy a greater power than it had ever been before.

When Elizabeth became Queen, her navy was not considered strong enough to protect the narrow seas against the French, with whom she found herself at war. She had only been three days crowned when, on the 21st of November, 1558, she issued instructions for the bringing together and putting in order of all available ships, and, in order that there might be no lack of

* COLLINS, *Peerage* (1812), vol. iv., pp. 264—267; RECORD OFFICE MSS., *Domestic, passim*.
† RECORD OFFICE MSS., *Domestic, Mary*, vol. xii., No. 69.
‡ *Ibid., Elizabeth*, vol. lxxxvi., No. 35.

mariners, for preventing any one from leaving the kingdom without a license; and these orders were so strictly enforced, that a message had before long to be sent to the Warden of the Cinque Ports, reminding him that the Queen did not wish to imprison all her subjects, but only to have choice of those best fitted to serve her.* In like manner, arrangements were at once made for the fortifying of Dover, Portsmouth, and other defensive standpoints;† and during the ensuing years, every sort of care was taken for enabling the country to withstand any attack that might be made upon it. Elizabeth employed Sir Thomas Gresham in smuggling from Antwerp and other continental towns great quantities of the arms and ammunition in which England was very deficient, and did better in encouraging their manufacture at home. "Very many pieces of great ordnance of brass and iron she cast," says the oldest historian of her reign; "and God, as if He favoured what she undertook, discovered a most rich vein of pure and native brass, which had been a long time neglected, near Keswick, in Cumberland, which abundantly sufficed for that use. And she also was the first that procured gunpowder to be made in England, that she might not both pray and pay for it to her neighbours."‡

One curious expedient for aiding the naval improvement of England was adopted at the instigation of Sir William Cecil. With the renunciation of Popery and

---

* STRYPE, *Annals*, vol. i., p. 6; RECORD OFFICE MSS., *Domestic, Elizabeth*, vol. iv., No. 9.
† CAMPBELL, vol. i., p. 341.  ‡ CAMDEN, *Annals*, p. 56.

Popish fasts, had come a great falling off in the consumption of fish; and, as it was chiefly from the class of fishermen that sailors were recruited, Cecil feared that there would soon be a scarcity of competent mariners. "To build ships without men to man them," he said, "was to set armour upon stakes on the sea shore;" but, except in "the exercise of piracy, which could not last," he saw no chance of obtaining enough men for the ships unless something were done to improve the fisheries.* Therefore, in 1563, an Act of Parliament was passed forbidding the eating of any flesh on Fridays and Saturdays, and of more than half the usual allowance on Wednesdays, with the provision, however, that, "lest any person should misjudge the intent of the statute, which was politicly meant only for the increase of fishermen and mariners and not for any superstition for choice of meats, whoever should preach or teach that eating of fish or forbearing of flesh was for the saving of the soul of man or for the service of God should be punished as the spreader of false news."†

This law was of course inoperative. But, if fewer sailors came to be obtained from the class of fishermen, the deficiency was more than met in other ways. By raising the wages of her seamen, Elizabeth found that she could always obtain as many as she wanted; and such an ardent love of sea adventures was growing up among all ranks of her subjects, that without any inducements in the way of pay, she would have had plenty of recruits.

\* RECORD OFFICE MSS., *Domestic, Elizabeth*, vol. xli., No. 58.
† *Ibid.*, vol. xxvii., Nos. 71, 72.

Every year new ships were built for her; and there was never any trouble about manning them. "The wealthier inhabitants of the sea coast," also, as we are told, "in imitation of their princess, built ships of war, striving who should exceed; insomuch that the Queen's navy, joined with her subjects' shipping, was in short time so puissant, that it was able to bring forth 20,000 fighting-men for sea service."*

In 1578, however, after twenty years of steady growth, Queen Elizabeth's navy appears to have comprised only twenty-four ships, with officers, mariners, fighting-men or soldiers, and gunners numbering in all about 7,000; being less than half the number of ships that were available at the end of Henry VIII.'s reign, and with fewer officers and men by a seventh. These twenty-four vessels were the *Triumph*, of 1,000 tons' burthen; the *Elizabeth* and the *White Bear*, each of 900 tons; the *Victory* and the *Primrose*, each of 800 tons; the *Mary Rose*, the *Hope*, the *Bonaventure*, the *Philip and Mary*, and the *Lion*, each of 600 tons; the *Dreadnought* and the *Swiftsure*, each of 400 tons; the *Swallow*, the *Antelope*, and the *Jeanet*, each of 350 tons; the *Foresight*, of 300 tons; the *Aid*, of 240 tons; the *Bull* and the *Tiger*, of 160 tons; the *Falcon*, of about 100 tons; the *Achates* and the *Handmaid*, of 80 tons; the *Bark of Boulogne* and the *George*, of 60 tons.†

* CAMDEN, p. 56.
† CAMPBELL, vol. i., pp. 355—358. Numerous documents, showing the gradual growth of the navy, are among the RECORD OFFICE MSS. By vol. iii., No. 44 of that series, it appears that in March, 1559, Elizabeth had twenty-one fighting vessels; but many of these were mere

But the changes wrought in the English navy under Queen Elizabeth are only faintly indicated by statistics. Scientific shipbuilding was still in its infancy; but, during this reign, the previous methods were very much improved upon. "Whoever were the inventors," said Sir Walter Raleigh, " we find that every age has added somewhat to ships; and in my time the shape of our English ships has been greatly bettered. It is not long since the striking of the topmasts, a wonderful case to great ships, both at sea and in the harbour, hath been devised, together with the chain-pump, which taketh up twice as much water as the ordinary one did. We have lately added the bonnet and the drabler to the courses; we have added studding-sails, and the weighing anchor by the capstan. We have fallen into consideration of the length of cables, and by it we resist the malice of the greatest winds that can blow. For true it is, that the length of the cable is the life of the ship in all extremities; and the reason is, that it makes so many bendings and waves, as the ship riding at that length is not able to stretch it, and nothing breaks that is not stretched."*

These and other improvements appear to have been adopted chiefly at the instigation of Sir John Hawkins, who succeeded his father-in-law, Benjamin Gonson, as

---

boats, and the five largest were respectively of but 800, 700, 600, 500, and 400 tons burthen. Against that aggregate of 3,000 tons for five ships must be set the aggregate of 8,200 tons for the twelve ships of 400 tons or over in 1578.

* Cited in BELL's continuation of SOUTHEY, *British Admirals*, vol. v., p. 203.

Treasurer or Comptroller of the Navy. Gonson held that office from 1557 till his death in 1578, when it was entrusted to Hawkins, who was perhaps, by reason of his great shrewdness and great experience, the fittest man in all England to be employed as overseer and reformer in all affairs of shipping.* "He was the first," we are told, "that invented the cunning stratagem of false nettings for ships to fight in; and also, in the first year of the Queen, in the wars of France, he devised the chain-pumps for ships, and perfected many defects in the Navy Royal."† The share taken by Hawkins, in conjunction with Sir Francis Drake, in founding the Chest at Chatham, a fund formed of voluntary contributions from prosperous seamen on behalf of their less fortunate brethren,‡ gives evidence of his interest in the welfare of the mariners; and he was no less zealous in seeing that mariners and their captains honestly served their employers, whether those employers were the Queen's ministers, gentlemen-adventurers, or merchants.§

As Treasurer or Comptroller, Sir John Hawkins had to see to the building of new ships, the repairing of old ones, and the fitting out, victualling, and manning of both old and new; in fact, to do everything that was necessary for the preservation and improvement of the

\* RECORD OFFICE MSS., *Domestic, Mary*, vol. x., No. 2; *Elizabeth*, vol. cxxvii., No. 33.
† STOW, *Annals* '1616,, p. 806.
‡ CAMPBELL, vol. i., p. 421.
§ SIR RICHARD HAWKINS, *Observations in his Voyage into the South Sea in* 1593 (Hakluyt Society, 1847., p. 167.

navy.* An annual allowance of 5,714*l*. 2s. 2*d*. was assigned for all these services; but this amount appears to have been every year greatly exceeded, sometimes more than doubled.

With the armament of the navy, Sir John Hawkins had not much to do. This important business was performed, through the greater part of Queen Elizabeth's reign, by Sir William Winter, who was the last Master of the Ordnance of the Navy, the oversight of ships' artillery being afterwards combined with supervision of land ordnance.† The business was certainly as complicated as it was important. About two dozen different kinds of fighting implements were employed in Queen Elizabeth's ships. The cannon generally measured twelve feet, and weighed four tons. The demi-cannon was about a foot longer and a ton lighter. The culverin and demi-culverin were nearly as long, but very much lighter, being adapted for discharging smaller shot. These four were the great ordnance. Sakers, minions, falcons, and falconets were much smaller; and the smallest pieces of ordnance were the fowlers and murthering pieces, generally mounted on the forecastle. Then there were hand-guns; the harquebus, which was generally placed on a rest before aim was taken; the musket, lighter and shorter than the harquebus; and the caliver, which was still less. With these twelve weapons, powder and shot were used. Of more than a dozen miscellaneous and more old-fashioned instru-

---

\* See Monson's *Naval Tracts*, book iii.
† Continuation of Southey, vol. v., pp. 207, 208.

ments, the principal were of course swords and bucklers, bills, pikes, and spears. The musket-arrow, thought much of by Sir John Hawkins, was a very short dart, discharged by a sort of catapult; and fire-arrows were discharged in the same manner. There were also several appliances for shooting "brass balls of artificial fire," which seem to have been miniature bombs, Greek fire, and the like.*

For nearly thirty years Queen Elizabeth's navy, in its relations with foreign powers, at any rate, was chiefly passive. It was absolutely necessary that England should have sufficient force upon the sea to be able to withstand the attacks that were always threatening from France and Spain. But Elizabeth and her wise counsellors abstained as much as possible from actual war. With a few exceptions, the fighting ships, previous to the coming of the Spanish Armada, were occupied chiefly in guarding the coasts and in punishing pirates.

The first exception was in the second year of Elizabeth's reign. Peace with France had been declared in April, 1559; but it was a declaration that deceived no one in England and caused no cessation to French mischief-making in Scotland. An army in disguise was straightway organised in France to be employed in punishing Scottish Protestantism and strengthening the House of Valois in its government of the House of Stuart. Therefore, late in December, a fleet of fourteen ships, the largest that could be brought together, was sent from Gillingham, under Admiral William

* RUNDALL, *Narratives of Voyages to the North-West*, pp. 229—231.

Winter, with orders to proceed first to Berwick and then to the Frith of Forth, there to intercept the French convoys and cause them as much damage as possible. "The principal point in his service," as defined in the instructions issued to Winter, was "to impeach the access of any more succour from France into Scotland, and to facilitate any departure thence towards France." If he found himself strong enough and with any fair chance of success, "war or no war, attacked or not attacked," he was to assail any armed French ships that he could meet with. He was to provoke a quarrel if he did not find one. He was to challenge the right of the French commanders to carry English arms, and to tell them that, as an Englishman, he would not endure it. But all this he was to do ostensibly on his own authority: his commission from Queen Elizabeth was to be a secret.*

Winter obeyed his orders. A storm, which did serious damage to the French fleet under D'Elbœuf, detained him at Lowestoft for a fortnight; but he entered the Forth on the 23rd of January, 1560, to find that a part of the French force had preceded him, but in time to anticipate the rest. Without an hour's delay, he sailed up to two vessels, lying in the harbour, with the French flag at their topmast. Winter showed no flag, and, whe the French admiral sent to ask who he was, he refused an answer. Thereby he gained his object. The angry Frenchmen discharged a shot, and so began the fight. Winter quickly ended it. A well-directed broadside

* RECORD OFFICE MSS., *Dome tic*, vol. vii., Nos. 65, 66

from each of his men-of-war compelled the Frenchmen to surrender. The two fighting ships were captured, and the attendant transports were burnt after the provisions stored in them had been handed over to the people.* After that, Winter kept the Forth from any fresh arrival of Frenchmen, and did good service in Scottish waters until a second and more hopeful peace was signed in July.

It was soon broken; but nothing else of importance was done in the way of avowed sea-fighting with the French. The old breach between England and France was not really healed up during any part of Elizabeth's reign; but the greater hatred of Spain that steadily grew in both nations gradually made them seeming friends. On that account they both, in various degrees, aided the brave Netherlanders in the struggle for independence with which the monarchical principles both of France and of England were in no sort of harmony. The English aid was heartier than the French, because, while the Huguenots who sided with the Netherlanders were proscribed and disgraced, Englishmen in high places, with Elizabeth at their head, as well as common folk, were bound to the sturdy patriots of Holland and Flanders by the strong tie of Protestantism. Hence arose a double, triple, or quadruple course of action, producing an unparalleled confusion in European politics, taxing greatly the abilities of statesmen, and occasioning strange embarrassments in

* RECORD OFFICE MSS., *Scotland, Elizabeth*, vol. ii., Nos. 15, 24, 28—31.

the minds of honest men who had little liking for the tortuous ways of sixteenth-century statecraft. Added to all, were serious difficulties that grew out of the indomitable genius for seamanship and love of bold maritime adventure, with which was joined a hearty love of the gains that were most easily to be acquired by daring exploits on the sea, that characterized every nation not wholly land-locked, and characterized sea-girt England most of all. The product of all these various and confusing factors that here most concerns us was a wonderful development of piracy, which moralists are bound to condemn, and for which abstract rules of justice afford no warrant, but which, practised most of all perhaps by Englishmen, must be recognized as a powerful agent in the well-being of Tudor England.

Piracy was a venerable institution which Christian morality had not yet learnt to reprobate. The annals of mediæval England abound in illustrations of the depredations wrought by the galleys of the Cinque Ports upon the traders of Yarmouth and other places, and of the jealousies and reprisals consequent thereupon; and, when these and others like these were to some extent restrained by the growth of national feeling, similar depredations, causing similar reprisals, were followed with all the more zeal upon the trading vessels of foreign countries. In war-time piracy was openly sanctioned; in peace-time it was only denounced when it seemed likely to issue in fresh and unwelcome war. So it was in Elizabeth's time. Under Elizabeth, indeed, owing to the great increase of seamanship and the great increase of trade, whereby there were always floating upon the seas rich prizes which there were always plenty of men ready to try and make their own in the way of sport, and in the way of business at the same time, piracy became more prevalent. The great enterprises of such men as Hawkins, Drake, and Cavendish, in the Spanish Main and in the Southern Seas, which will presently have to be detailed, were only piracies on a grand scale. Smaller piracies, in English waters, and on the coasts of Scotland, France, and Flanders, practised by the hundred every year, gave occupation not only to lawless men of all sorts, but also to honest gentlemen and honest commoners, who found quieter employments not easy to procure or too tame to be followed with satisfaction. At first they were practised most frequently, and with least condemnation by Queen and statesmen, upon the trading ships of France and Scotland, with which England had been at feud for generations. When the new hatred of Spain rose up, and Protestants began to look upon all possible punishment of Papists as a religious duty, Spanish galleons were hunted down with special zest; and after the Netherlanders had cast off their allegiance to Spain, the English sea-rovers did not trouble to discriminate between the merchant fleets of Antwerp and the merchant fleets of Cadiz. Of course the English were not the only offenders. If they worried the peaceable traders of Scotland, France, Spain, and Flanders, the peaceable traders of England were quite as much worried by Scottish, French, Spanish, and

Flemish marauders; and the sport was keenest when the pirates of one nation met the pirates of another, and fought with fierce earnestness for the mastery.

Thus, while England was at 'seeming peace with all the world, many of its most adventurous subjects were at actual war with the subjects of nearly every European state. It is not, however, necessary to bring together instances of these little wars, as they hardly differed in character from the greater exploits that will be detailed in later pages. All we have here to do is to note the occurrence every year of scores of depredations, fightings, and massacres upon the sea, and, however much we may denounce them upon theoretical grounds, to remember that they were the rough exercises and the tough experiences by which Englishmen were, to a large extent, taught to become great seamen, and to make their mother-country the greatest maritime nation in the world.

Many embarrassments to English statesmen grew out of these piracies, and the chief occupation of Queen Elizabeth's navy, during five-and-twenty years, was in attempting to suppress them. Neither Elizabeth nor Cecil, probably, wholly disapproved of the condemned practices, and more than half the courtiers and statesmen, if not actually sharers in them, participated in the spoils. But there was tolerable piracy and there was intolerable piracy; and that which was intolerable to all honest and honourable men was checked and punished as far as lay within the power of Queen Elizabeth and her deputies. A few instances of this will suffice. In

July, 1562, for example, on the representation of special damage that had been done to some English merchant vessels by Breton rovers, four ships were put to sea under Sir William Woodhouse, with orders "to clear the narrow seas of pirates;"* and, this force being insufficient, two other ships, almost the largest in the navy, were in September commissioned to the same work under Captain George Beston.† In September, 1564, again, Sir Peter Carew was ordered to use two ships in driving from the coasts of Devonshire and Cornwall the pirates who had lately infested them;‡ and in the following year special arrangements were made for punishing the sea-robbers who troubled Norfolk and the other eastern counties, troubling native traders and Dutch fish-dealers alike.§ In May, 1570, was issued a stringent proclamation for repressing pirates and sea-rovers, and prescribing the confiscation of their property.‖ In February, 1572, John Hawkins, George Winter, and others were commissioned to do their utmost in clearing the British seas of pirates and freebooters;¶ and in November, 1575, a like commission was given to Captain William Holstock, two large ships being assigned for the work.** In May, 1576, three vessels were entrusted to Captain Henry Palmer, "for the clearing of the seas of pirates, excepting all ships under the Prince of Orange's commis-

---

\* RECORD OFFICE MSS., *Domestic, Elizabeth*, vol. xxiii., Nos. 64—66.
† *Ibid.*, vol. xxiv., No. 26.  ‡ *Ibid.*, vol. xxxiv., No. 65.
§ *Ibid.*, vol. xxxvii., Nos. 47, 48.  ‖ *Ibid.*, vol. lxix., No. 26.
¶ *Ibid.*, vol. lxxxv., No. 57.  \*\* *Ibid.*, vol. cv., No. 68.

sion."*—a curious exception, indicative of the growing friendship between England and the Netherlanders, whose war with Philip of Spain could still only be carried on under the name of piracy and rebellion. Of the same sort were many other commissions granted in these and later years; and they all resulted in the capture of numerous offenders, who seem to have been treated with equal justice, whether they were Englishmen or foreigners.

Nobler work, however, was preparing for Queen Elizabeth's navy, the preparation being in great part due to the bold seamen who shared in the enterprises that were led by Sir John Hawkins and Sir Francis Drake.

* RECORD OFFICE MSS., *Domestic, Elizabeth*, vol. cviii., Nos. 23, 24.

## CHAPTER XII.

THE EARLIER EXPLOITS OF SIR JOHN HAWKINS AND SIR FRANCIS DRAKE
IN THE SPANISH MAIN.

[1562—1576.]

SIR JOHN HAWKINS was born at Plymouth about the year 1520. His grandfather, John Hawkins, of Tavistock, was a merchant and sea-captain in the service of Henry VIII. between 1513 and 1518.* His father, William Hawkins, is described as a man "for his wisdom, valour, and experience and skill in sea causes much esteemed and beloved by King Henry VIII., and one of the principal sea-captains in the west parts of England in his time." He gave good proof of his wisdom and valour. Having fitted out "a tall and goodly ship of his own," the *Paul of Plymouth*, of 250 tons' burthen, he made in it, in 1530, 1531, and 1532, three several voyages to Brazil, being apparently the first Englishman, with the exception of Sebastian Cabot, who was then in Spanish service, who visited South America.

* BREWER, *Letters and Papers of the Reign of Henry VIII.*, vol. ii., p. 1369. In this chapter I have made use of some of the biographical statements in Chapter VIII. of my *English Merchants* on ' The Hawkinses of Plymouth.'

In each of his voyages, William Hawkins went first to the coast of Guinea, where also he appears to have been the first English trader; and, having there made profitable exchange of his English articles for elephants' teeth and such other commodities as the Negroes had to sell, he crossed the Atlantic, and made further profit by disposing of his newly-acquired goods to the Indians dwelling on the coast of Brazil. "He used such discretion, and behaved himself so wisely with those savage people," we are told, "that he grew into great familiarity and friendship with them." In 1531, it is added, "one of the savage kings of the country of Brazil was contented to take ship with him, and be transferred hither into England; whereunto Master Hawkins agreed, leaving behind in the country, as a pledge for his safety and return again, one Martin Cockeram, of Plymouth." The native chief was brought to London, presented to Henry VIII., and made much of as the first of his race ever seen in England. In 1532 he started to return to his own country with Hawkins; but he died of sea-sickness on the way, and Hawkins expected to get into trouble on account of the disaster. "Nevertheless," says the chronicler, "the savages being fully persuaded of the honest dealing of our men with their prince, restored again the pledge, without any harm to him or any man of the company."*

All we know of old William Hawkins is told in the brief history of those memorable voyages. He had two famous sons, John and William, who, in different moods,

* HAKLUYT, vol. iii., pp. 700, 701.

inherited his seafaring and commercial zeal. William became a great merchant and shipowner in Plymouth and London. John also was a shipowner and merchant, though these callings came to be insignificant in comparison with the other ways in which he served his country.

He was bred a sailor. During his youth and early manhood, we are told, " he made divers voyages to the Isles of the Canaries, and there, by his good and upright dealing, being grown in honour of the people, informed himself of the state of the West Indies, whereof he had received some knowledge by the instructions of his father, but increased the same by the advertisements and reports of that people; and being, amongst other things, informed that Negroes were very good merchandize in Hispaniola, and that store of Negroes might easily be had upon the coast of Guinea, he resolved within himself to make trial thereof."*

That was certainly not a very honourable branch of English commerce. But the discredit lies rather with the age than with Hawkins himself. For generations it had been a custom of the Spaniards and Portuguese to make slaves of their Moorish prisoners and of the African tribes associated with them; and for some time previous Negro slaves had been employed in the Spanish West Indies. This, indeed, had been done partly at the suggestion of the philanthropic Las Casas, who urged the substitution of Negro for Indian slavery on the ground of humanity, never thinking that the cruelty was as great in the one case as in the other.

* HAKLUYT, vol. iii., p. 500; PRINCE, *Worthies of Devon* (1701), p. 389.

Hawkins, therefore, shocked no prejudices and broke no accepted moral law, by participating in the slave-trade. A man of generous nature and high sense of honour would have preferred some other way of enriching himself. But Hawkins was not remarkable for generous or highly honourable conduct. He was a daring voyager, a brave soldier, and one of the first promoters of our country's naval greatness. In other respects he was no better than his fellows.

Hawkins was not quite the first Englishman who traded in Negro slaves. In 1553 Captain John Windham, accompanied by Antonio Pinteado, a Portuguese refugee, who revenged himself for some real or supposed wrongs by enticing others to enter on the African trade that had hitherto been jealously reserved to itself by Portugal, was sent by some London merchants in the track of old William Hawkins to Guinea. Windham's bad management, which caused his own death, and the death of two hundred out of his crew of two hundred and forty, made this voyage altogether disastrous.* But better fortune attended the expedition despatched next year, under Captain John Lock, with young Martin Frobisher for one of its crew.† Elephants' teeth and gold dust were procured in large quantities, also five of the Negroes, whom Lock described as "people of beastly living, without God, law, religion, or commonwealth."‡ There was some difficulty, however, in disposing of these latter commodities in England;

---

\* HAKLUYT, vol. ii., part ii., pp. 11—13.   † See vol. i., p. 121.
‡ HAKLUYT, vol. ii., part ii., pp. 14—23.

and slave-buying seems not to have been repeated until 1562, when Hawkins set out on his first expedition.

In fitting out this expedition he was aided by Lionel Duckett, the great London merchant, by his father-in-law, Benjamin Gonson, the Treasurer of the Navy, and by many other men of influence; and one Thomas Hampton went with him as partner in the undertaking. They left England in October, with a hundred men in three vessels; the *Solomon*, of 120 tons' burthen, the *Swallow*, of 100 tons, and the *Jonas*, of 40 tons, and proceeded quickly to Sierra Leone. There Hawkins, we are told, "partly by the sword, and partly by other means, got into his possession three hundred Negroes at the least, besides other merchandizes which that country yieldeth." These commodities he then conveyed to San Domingo, entering the port with some doubt as to his reception, and with a pretence that he had been driven there by bad weather and want of food. The Spaniards, however, were in need of slaves, and readily bought all Hawkins's cargo. He had "peaceable traffic," says the narrator of the voyage, "trusting the Spaniards no farther than by his own strength he was able to master them." In exchange for his English goods and Negroes he obtained a goodly store of pearls, ginger, sugar, hides, and other native produce. Part of these he conveyed direct to England in September, 1563, in his three English ships, and thereby secured "much gain to himself and the adventurers." The rest he sent, under the care of Thomas Hampton, to Cadiz in two Spanish vessels which had been chartered for the purpose.*

In so doing Hawkins showed that he had no thought of offending Spain or of doing anything more than trading peaceably with its subjects both at home and in the West Indies. Philip II. looked upon the matter very differently. Resenting all English interference with his colonial affairs, he reproved the Governor of San Domingo for sanctioning the trade, confiscated all Hampton's cargo, and nearly subjected Hampton himself to the rough handling of the Inquisition. He sent peremptory orders to the West Indian viceroy that no Englishman, on any pretext, was to be allowed to have any dealings with Spanish subjects, and acquainted the English ambassador at Madrid, that if such a thing were attempted, mischief would result. "Our folks must be narrowly looked to," wrote the ambassador to Queen Elizabeth in June, 1564, "and specially that they enterprise no trade or voyage to the Indies or islands of this King's navigation; which if they do, as already they have intelligence of some that propose it, surely it will breed occasion of much matter to pick."†

Queen Elizabeth did not heed that warning. Hawkins, as soon as he heard of the way in which Hampton and their joint property had been treated, made indignant claim upon the Spanish Government for restitution.

* HAKLUYT, vol. iii., p. 500; RECORD OFFICE MSS., *Spanish*, cited by FROUDE, vol. viii., p. 471.
† FROUDE, vol. viii., pp. 472, 473.

None was made to him, and he thereupon lost no time, with the sanction of the Queen and her Council, in planning retaliation. Elizabeth showed her approval by allowing the *Jesus of Lubeck*, of 700 tons' burthen, one of the largest ships in her navy, to be chartered for 500*l*. for a new voyage.* The Earls of Leicester and Pembroke and other courtiers joined with Hawkins and his City friends in raising money enough for this voyage; and on the 18th of October, 1564, Hawkins left Plymouth with a little fleet of five vessels, the *Jesus*, his old *Solomon* and *Swallow*, and two little barks or sloops, the *Tiger*, of 50 tons, and the *Saint John Baptist*, of 30 tons; the crews of all numbering a hundred and seventy men. "Serve God daily; love one another; preserve your victuals; beware of fire; and keep good company," were the last of the pithy rules which Hawkins drew up for their guidance.†

While Hawkins was preparing for his second expedition, other preparations were being made for a precisely similar enterprise, under a Captain David Carlet, to whom also Queen Elizabeth lent one of her ships, the *Minion*, and who had charge of two smaller vessels, the *John the Baptist* and the *Merlin*, which last ship was blown up soon after its embarkation through an explosion of her powder-store. Carlet appears to have left London only a few days before Hawkins left Plymouth. The parties met in the Channel and kept

---

* RECORD OFFICE MSS., *Domestic*, vol. xxxvii., No. 61.
† The details of this voyage, where no other authority is given, are from a narrative by John Sparke, in HAKLUYT, vol. iii., pp. 501—521.

company for a month. They reached Santa Cruz, one of the Canaries, on the 4th of November. "About this island," says the historian of the voyage, "are certain flitting islands, which have been oftentimes seen, and when men approached near them they vanished; as the like hath been of these islands now known, by the report of the inhabitants, which were not found of long time one after the other; and therefore it should seem he is not yet born to whom God hath appointed the finding of them."

On the 29th of November Hawkins called at Cape de Verde. The inhabitants he found to be of "nature very gentle and loving," and "more civil than any other, because of their daily traffic with the Frenchmen." This did not hinder him from proposing to take some of them as slaves; but, for some reason which is not given, the people of the *Minion* made known to them the designs of Hawkins, " so that they did avoid the snares laid for them." In punishment for that, Carlet was dismissed from the protection of the *Jesus*, and he soon got into such trouble with the Portuguese in Africa that he had to conduct his two vessels back to England without passing on to the West Indies.

In pursuance of his plan Hawkins tracked the African coast for nearly two months, generally going " every day on shore to take the inhabitants, with burning and spoiling of their towns." Many of these inhabitants, perhaps—though that is no justification of the English procedure—did not deserve much better. The Samboses, who lived somewhere beyond Sierra Leone, are described as cannibals living by war and robbery upon their neighbours; "wont not only to eat them that they kill, but also to keep those that they take until such time as they want meat, and then they kill them." The Sapies, their chief victims, we are told, "do not eat men's flesh, unless in war they be driven by necessity thereunto." It is added that "they do jagg their flesh, both legs, arms, and bodies, as workman-like as a jerkin-maker with us pinketh a jerkin." Hawkins did a little jagging of a rougher sort. All that he could, however, he took alive and unhacked, in order to turn them into marketable slaves.

In a fight with the natives of these parts on the 27th of December Hawkins had seven of his own men killed and twenty-seven wounded. On New Year's Day, 1565, he narrowly escaped much greater injury from a great effort made to surprise his men while on shore in a strange place in search of water. "But," says the narrator, pious after his own fashion, "God, who worketh all things for the best, would not have it so, and by Him we escaped without danger—His name be praised for it!"

At length, having collected negroes enough, Hawkins started for the West Indies on the 29th of January. They were becalmed for eighteen days midway, "having now and then contrary winds and some tornadoes amongst the same calm," says the chronicler; "which happened to us very ill, being but reasonably watered for so great a company of Negroes and ourselves. This pinched us all; and, that which was worst, put us in such fear that many never thought to have reached the

Indies without great dearth of Negroes and of themselves; but the Almighty God, which never suffereth His elect to perish, sent us the ordinary breeze."

A desolate part of Dominica was reached on the 9th of March. On the 16th Hawkins touched at Margarita, where he was hospitably entertained, but not allowed to sell his negroes; and at Cumana, which he visited on the 22nd, he also found trade impossible. At Santa Fé, where there were few Spaniards, he was on the following day well received by the Indians. "They came down, presenting meal and cakes of bread, made of a kind of corn called maize. Also they brought down hens, potatoes, and pines, which we bought for beads, pewter whistles, glasses, knives, and other trifles. These potatoes," says the chronicler, concerning an article of food soon to be introduced into England, "be the most delicate roots that may be eaten, and do far exceed our parsnips and carrots." "These Indians," it is added, "surely were gentle and tractable, and such as desire to live peaceably, or else it had been impossible for the Spaniards to have conquered them as they did, and the more to live now so peaceably, they being so many in number and the Spaniards so few."

Some fiercer and more crafty Indians on the American mainland, whom he visited on the 29th of March, invited Hawkins to trade with them. "If it had not been for want of wares to traffic with," we read, "he would not have denied them, because the Indians which he had seen before were very gentle people, and such as do no man hurt. But, as God would have it, he wanted that thing which, if he had had, would have been his confusion; for there were no such kind of people as he took them to be, but more devilish a thousand parts, and are eaters and devourers of any man that they can catch,—bloodsuckers both of Spaniards, Indians, and all that light in their laps; not sparing their own countrymen if they can conveniently come by them."

Having entered on his first voyage with no aversion to the Spaniards, and with the simple object of carrying on a profitable trade in Negroes, Hawkins, on this second voyage, determined only to outreach King Philip, and, in defiance of his inhibitions, to follow out his purpose and win back the wealth of which he considered that he had been robbed when the cargo of hides sent by him to Cadiz was confiscated. He had not yet begun to consider that, if the punishment of Spaniards was not better than commercial gains, it would greatly tend to sweeten them. Therefore, according to an arrangement that he had made with Queen Elizabeth's Council before starting, he attempted to avoid open collision with the colonists. He kept away from San Domingo, and tried, by going only to the smaller and more remote dependencies, to sell his human wares in districts which Philip's prohibitory orders had not reached. With this intent he proceeded to Barbarotta, where he anchored on the 3rd of April, and asked permission to trade with the residents. He was informed that this could not be done, as the residents had been forbidden to have any dealings with foreigners; "wherefore they desired him not to molest them farther, but to depart as he came, for other comforts he might not look for at their hands, because they were subjects, and might not go beyond the law." Hawkins, however, answered that he was an Englishman, with one of Queen Elizabeth's own ships in his fleet, and that he had need of refreshment "without which he could not depart." If they did not allow him to have his way, he said in another message, "he would displease them."

Some profitable trade resulted from his threats, and he remained in Barbarotta until the 4th of May. On the 6th he visited Curaçoa, and there, says the chronicler, "we had traffic for hides, and found great refreshing both of beef, mutton, and lambs, whereof there was such plenty that, saving the skins, we had the flesh given us for nothing; and the plenty thereof was so abundant that the worst in the ship thought scorn, not only of mutton, but also of sodden lamb, which they disdained to eat unroasted." Yet, it is added, "notwithstanding our sweet meat, we had sour sauce there; by reason of riding so open at sea, what with blasts whereby, our anchors being aground, three at once came home, and also with contrary winds blowing, whereby, for fear of the shore, we were fain to haul off to have anchor-hold, sometimes a whole day, and we turned up and down; and this happened not once but half a dozen times in the space of our being there."

From Curaçoa Hawkins passed on, by way of Cape de la Vela, to Rio de la Hacha, on the borders of

Darien. There, arriving on the 19th of May, he requested permission to trade as he had done in Barbarotta, supporting his request by a certificate of good conduct signed by the governor of the latter place. He was told, as he had been told at Barbarotta, that his proposal was in violation of the express orders of King Philip, and could not be assented to. Hawkins repeated his old excuse about bad weather and his need of fresh supplies. "But," he added, "seeing they would, contrary to all reason, go about to withstand his traffic, he would it should not be said by him, that, having the force he had, he was driven from his traffic perforce, but would rather put it in an adventure whether he or they should have the better; and therefore he willed them to determine either to give him licence to trade or else stand to their own harms." That blunt message induced the Spaniards to assent to his trading with them; but after they had inspected the Negroes, they offered only half as much per head as Hawkins had received at Barbarotta. It may be that the best slaves had already been picked out of the gang, and that the Spaniards proposed to give fair value for the remainder. Hawkins did not think so. "Weighing their unconscionable request, he wrote to them a letter, saying that they dealt too rigorously with him, to go about to cut his throat in the price of his commodities, which were so reasonably rated as they could not by a great deal have the like at any other man's hands: but, seeing they had sent him this to his supper, he would in the morning bring them as good a breakfast." The breakfast consisted of a volley of ordnance, followed by the landing of a hundred Englishmen, who, even before they had time to land, put to flight the hundred and fifty Spaniards that came out to meet them. After that, says Hawkins's companion, " we made our traffic quietly." All the remaining Negroes having been disposed of on the English terms, and three boats, " with balls in their noses and men with weapons accordingly," having superintended the settling of accounts, Hawkins left Rio de la Hacha on the 31st of May.

Having thus sold all his Negroes, Hawkins proposed to apply the money he had received for them in purchasing hides and other articles, which, conveyed to Europe for sale, would bring in a second profit. With that view he directed his course to Hispaniola; but bad steering took him instead to Jamaica. The blame of this blunder was laid upon a Spanish merchant whom Hawkins had rescued from the people of Africa and promised to take home to Hispaniola if he would first be an honest guide to his protectors. Even when Jamaica was reached, the Spanish merchant insisted that it was Hispaniola, and identified each creek and headland as they came within sight with similar parts of the larger island. " In the end," says the chronicler, " he pointed so from one point to another, that we were a-leeboard of all places and found ourselves at the west end of Jamaica before we were aware of it; and, being once to leeward, there was no getting up again, so that, by trusting of this Spaniard's knowledge, our captain sought not to speak with any of the inhabitants, which, if he had not made himself sure of, he would have done, as was his custom in those places. But this man was a plague, not only to our captain, whom he made lose, by overshooting the place, 2,000*l.* in hides which he might have got there, but also to himself; for having been three years out of his country and in great misery in Guinea, and now in hope to come to his wife and friends, he could not find any habitation, neither there nor in Cuba, which we sailed all along."

Mistaking Jamaica for Hispaniola, Hawkins also mistook Cuba for Jamaica. He was thus taken out of reach of all the ports at which he might have made profitable purchases of hides. Then he resolved to sail homewards as soon as he had procured the fresh supply of water of which his ships were in sore need. That was not easy. Some they obtained at Pinas, on the 16th of June; and, we are told, "although it were neither so toothsome as running water, by means it is standing, and but the water of rain, and, moreover, being near the sea, was brackish, yet did we not refuse it, but were more glad thereof, as the time then required, than we should have been another time with fine conduit water." Further search for water took the vessels, through a storm in which one of them was nearly wrecked, past Havannah and along the coast of Florida, till they fell in with the Huguenot colony that had been founded there, in 1562, at the instigation of Admiral Coligni. Strife with the Indians and with one another had reduced the colonists from two hundred to forty. Hawkins, in exchange for water, gave them an abundance of food. He also lent them his little *Tiger*, in which to return to Europe, after they had refused his offer of a passage in his own company.

Hawkins started for England on the 28th of July. Contrary winds kept him so long on the way that there was dearth of food. "We were divers times," says the chronicler, " in despair of ever reaching home, had not God, of His goodness, provided for us better than our deserving; in which state of great misery we were provoked to call upon Him by frequent prayer, which moved Him to hear us, so that we had a prosperous wind." The prayer and its consequences took them far to the north, up to the Bank of Newfoundland; but they safely reached Padstow, in Cornwall, on the 20th of September, after just eleven months' absence, " with loss of twenty persons in all the voyage, and with great profit to the venturers, as also to the whole realm, in bringing home both gold, silver, pearls, and other jewels, great store." The profits of the voyage to Hawkins and the friends who helped him to fit it out were reckoned at sixty per cent.

Greater profit came in the favour that was heaped upon Hawkins by Queen and people. "By way of increase and augmentation of honour, a coat of arms and crest were settled upon him and his posterity by a patent thus worded:—'He bears sable on a point wavee, a lion passant gold, in chief three besants; upon his helm a wreath argent and azure, a demi-moor, in his

proper colour, bound and captive, with amulets on his arms and ears, or, mantelled gules double argent.' "*
Hawkins was everywhere applauded for his bold and well-planned seamanship, for his successful opening up of a new line of commerce, and—though this was only spoken of in whispers—for his smart over-reaching of Philip II.'s plans for restraining him.

Hawkins thought it prudent to make light of his victory over the King of Spain. "I have always," he said in a letter to Queen Elizabeth, "been a help to all Spaniards and Portugals that have come in my way, without any form or prejudice offered by me to any of them, although many times in this tract they have been under my power."† "I met him in the palace," wrote the Spanish Ambassador in London to King Philip, in November, "and invited him to dine with me. He gave me a full account of his voyage, keeping back only the way in which he had contrived to trade at our ports. He assured me, on the contrary, that he had given the greatest satisfaction to all the Spaniards with whom he had had dealings, and had received full permission from the governors of the towns where he had been. The vast profit made by the voyage has excited other merchants to undertake similar expeditions. Hawkins himself is going out again next May, and the thing needs immediate attention. I might tell the Queen that, by his own confession, he has traded in ports prohibited by your Majesty, and require her to punish him; but I

* PRINCE, *Worthies of Devon*, p. 389.
† *Cambridge MS.*, cited by FROUDE, vol. viii., p. 478.

must request your Majesty to give me full and clear instructions what to do."*

Philip was not in the habit of giving clear instructions, though full they certainly were, in any case; and here his difficulty was increased by the tact with which Hawkins had so contrived as that any blame which might fall upon him must rebound with much greater force upon Philip's own governors and viceroys in the West Indies. Therefore the Spanish monarch seems to have done little more than grumble, and send out fresh and more stringent orders for the prevention of any further efforts that might be made by Hawkins or other Englishmen at forcing their trade upon the colonies in the Spanish Main.

These did not deter Hawkins; but they had some effect upon Elizabeth and her counsellors. The new expedition, which the Spanish Ambassador spoke of as likely to take place in May, 1566, was postponed till October; and then, when Hawkins was at Plymouth, just ready to embark, letters were sent down by Sir William Cecil strictly forbidding his project of "repairing armed, for the purpose of traffic, to places privileged by the King of Spain."† In consequence, Hawkins was obliged to give his bond, with a penalty of 500*l.*, that he would forbear sending to any of the Spanish possessions the ship which he was fitting out for another slave-trading enterprise.‡ For that, or for some other

* *Simancas MS.*, cited by Froude, vol. viii., p. 479.
† Record Office MSS., *Domestic*, vol. xi., No. 81.
‡ *Ibid.*, vol. xi., No. 99.

reason, he did not accompany the two or three ships that went out in 1566; and of their movements we have no records. All we know is, that they returned to England next summer laden with gold, silver, and fine skins, which Philip's ambassador suspected to have been taken from some Spanish or Portuguese galleon.* It is probable that, lacking the slave-trading tact of Hawkins, their captains applied themselves to the easier work of piracy.

In the meanwhile, Hawkins was not idle. In June, 1567, we find him making estimates concerning the material requisite for setting up a fort on the Guinea coast, if that should be needed for extending his commerce in Negroes.† He was at the same time planning a larger expedition to the West Indies, which the progress of European politics during the previous year again made possible. Elizabeth, having given her countenance to the Netherlanders' insurrection against Spain, could make no serious objection to such work as Hawkins projected. She discreetly abstained from hearing the details of the project; but, knowing its general tenour, she even allowed the *Jesus of Lubeck*, which she had lent to Hawkins in 1564, and the *Minion*, which had been chartered at the same time by Carlet, to be again made use of. Her subjects were not slow in providing money for fitting out the expedition, and in proffering their services as actual sharers in it.

One of these volunteers was young Francis Drake,

* MS. cited by FROUDE, vol. viii., p. 481.
† RECORD OFFICE MSS., *Domestic*, vol. xliii., No. 12.

then about twenty-two years old, but already possessed of many years' experience upon the sea. Drake's father appears to have been a resident in Devonshire of small means, which were made still smaller by the persecution to which he subjected himself through becoming a Protestant in violation of Henry VIII.'s Six Articles. "He was forced," says the old historian to whom Francis Drake told the story, "to fly from his house near South Tavistock in Devon, into Kent, and there to inhabit in the hull of a ship, wherein many of his younger sons were born. He had twelve in all. After the death of King Henry, he got a place among the seamen in the King's navy, to read prayers to them, and soon after he was ordained deacon. But by reason of his poverty he put his son to the master of a bark, with which he used to coast along the shore, and sometimes to carry merchandize into Zealand and France. The youth, being painful and diligent, so pleased the old man that, being a bachelor, at his death he bequeathed his bark unto him."\*

That report of Francis Drake's parentage and early history is partly contradicted by another, almost as old, from which it would seem that his father was a common sailor.† It is clear, at any rate, that the young man rose from obscurity by his own merits, and was a sailor from his boyhood. As soon as he became owner of the coasting-bark which he had previously navigated, he appears to have sold it and applied himself to

---
\* CAMDEN, *Annals*, p. 351.
† In a Memoir of Drake, by CAMPBELL, in the *Biographia Britannica*.

bolder work. He is said to have been purser in a ship trading to the Bay of Biscay in 1563.* In 1565 he went to Rio de la Hacha with a Captain John Lovell, about whose enterprise we have no information, but who evidently was one of the adventurers who followed in the track taken by Hawkins in 1564 to the Spanish Main.† Here he so far distinguished himself as to be entrusted by Hawkins, soon after his return, with the care of one of the vessels appointed for his new expedition.

These vessels were six in all;—the *Jesus of Lubeck*, and the *Minion*, supplied by the Queen, either for hire or on the understanding that her Majesty was to have a share in the profits of the enterprise, and commanded, the one by John Hawkins himself, the other by the John Hampton who accompanied him in 1562; and four others fitted out by Hawkins and his brother William, the *William and John*, under Captain Thomas Bolton, the *Judith*, a bark of 50 tons burthen, entrusted to Captain Francis Drake, the *Swallow*, and the *Angel*. Added to these six was a small pinnace; and the whole fleet is said to have contained, though the number is certainly overstated, fifteen hundred sailors and soldiers.‡ Five hundred is a more probable number. The primary object of the voyage does not seem to have been slave-trading. Two Portuguese refugees had offered to put

* Srow, *Annals*, p. 807.

† *Sir Francis Drake Revived*, published by his Nephew, SIR FRANCIS DRAKE, the Younger, in 1626.

‡ HAKLUYT, vol. iii., p. 521 ; HERRERA, *Historia General*, lib. xix., cap. 18.

Hawkins in the way of loading as many ships as he chose to employ with gold and other wealth belonging to Spain; and perhaps it was intended to use the little fleet, as a first step at any rate, in piratical attack upon galleons in Spanish waters.\* But the Portuguese took fright and ran away before Hawkins was ready to start; and, on the 16th of September, he wrote from Plymouth to Queen Elizabeth, saying he would now take all the management in his own hands, and that he proposed "to lade Negroes in Guinea, and sell them in the West Indies, in truck of gold, pearls, and emeralds."†

On the eve of embarkation a memorable episode occurred. A Spanish galley was passing through the English Channel, with a cargo of captive insurgents from the Netherlands, on its way to Cadiz. Hawkins, glad of an excuse, fired upon the Spanish flag that was hanging from her topmast, and, in the turmoil that ensued while the flag was being lowered, the captives made their escape to the *Jesus*, whence they were sent back to Holland. Elizabeth, formally reproving him for this, was appeased by his assurance that he supposed the Spanish ship had been sent to attack him. But Philip's ambassador was not appeased. "Your mariners rob my master's subjects on the sea and trade where they are forbidden to go," he said in an angry letter to the Queen. "They plunder our people in the streets of your towns. They attack our vessels in your

---

\* HERRERA, lib. xix., cap. 18.
† RECORD OFFICE MSS., *Domestic*, vol. xliv, No. 7.

very harbours, and take our prisoners from them. Your preachers insult my master from their pulpits; and, when we apply for justice, we are answered with threats. We have borne with these things, attributing them rather to passion or rudeness of manners than to any deliberate purpose of wrong; but seeing there is no remedy and no end, I must now refer to my sovereign to learn what I am to do. I make, however, one concluding appeal to your Majesty: I entreat your Majesty to punish this last outrage at Plymouth, and to preserve the peace between the two nations."*

Immediate punishment, if she had wished to effect it, was out of Elizabeth's power. Four days before the ambassador's letter was written, on the 2nd of October, Hawkins had left Plymouth to enter on a course of troubles by which he certainly was punished enough. In a four days' storm off Cape Finisterre the *Jesus* was nearly disabled, and the ship's boats were lost; and when Cape de Verde was reached on the 18th of November, fresh disasters arose. A hundred and fifty men were there landed and sent in search of Negroes. "But," says Hawkins, in his narrative of the voyage,† "we got but few, and those with great hurt and damage to our men, which chiefly proceeded of their envenomed arrows. Although in the beginning they seemed to be but small hurts, yet there hardly escaped any that had blood drawn of them but died in strange sort, with

---

* MSS. cited by FROUDE, vol. viii., pp. 481, 482; RECORD OFFICE MSS., *Domestic*, vol. xliv., No. 13.

† HAKLUYT, vol. iii., pp. 521—525, which is the authority for the following account, when no other is cited.

their mouths shut some ten days before they died, and after their wounds were whole. I myself had one of the greatest wounds, yet, thanks be to God, escaped." Seven or eight Englishmen died of lock-jaw.

At Cape de Verde and on all the coast from Rio Grande to Sierra Leone, where he made tedious search for them until the 12th of January, Hawkins collected only a hundred and fifty slaves; and he thought that sickness and the lateness of the season would compel him to cross the Atlantic, "having yet nothing wherewith to seek the coast of the West Indies." He went a little further, however, and then, to his great satisfaction, was asked by a Negro king to aid him in vanquishing one of his neighbours. All the captives were to go to Hawkins in payment for his services. A hundred and twenty Englishmen were detached for this work. They attacked a town containing eight thousand inhabitants, "strongly paled and fenced after their manner," and, when six of their number had been killed and forty wounded, they had to send to Hawkins for reinforcements. "Whereupon," he says, "considering that the good success of this enterprise might highly further the commodity of our voyage, I went myself, and, with the help of the king of our side, assaulted the town both by land and sea, very hardly with fire—their houses being covered with palm-leaves—obtained the town, and put the inhabitants to flight. We took two hundred and fifty persons, men, women, and children; and by our friend the king on our side there were taken six hundred prisoners, whereof we hoped to have our choice; but the Negro—in which nation is never or seldom found truth—meant nothing less; for that night he removed his camp and prisoners, so that we were fain to content us with those few that we had gotten ourselves."

With his scanty and basely acquired cargo of Negroes Hawkins proceeded to the Spanish Main. Passing Dominica on the 27th of March, and stopping often to trade at the islands on his way, he reached Rio de la Hacha in June. There, as he expected and perhaps hoped, there was opposition to his projects. "The treasurer who had the charge," he says, "would by no means agree to any trade or suffer us to take water. He had fortified his town with divers bulwarks in all places where it might be entered, and furnished himself with a hundred harquebusiers; so that he thought by famine to have enforced us to land our Negroes. Of which purpose he had not greatly failed, unless we had by force entered the town; which, after we could by no means obtain his favour, we were enforced to do, and so, with two hundred men, brake in upon their bulwarks and entered the town, with the loss of only two men of our parts,—and no hurt done to the Spaniards, because, after their volley discharged, they all fled. Thus having the town, with some circumstance, as partly by the Spaniards' desire of Negroes, and partly by the friendship of the treasurer, we obtained a secret trade; whereupon the Spaniards resorted to us by night, and bought of us to the number of two hundred Negroes."

From Rio de la Hacha Hawkins went to Cartagena; but being there forbidden to trade, and having very few Negroes left for any purposes of trade adapted to the port, and being also anxious to get clear of the West Indies before the season of hurricanes set in, he left it peaceably on the 24th of July. He then directed his course to Florida, where on his previous voyage he had been able to obtain fresh supplies of water. When he was westward of Cuba, however, on the 12th of August, a violent storm, lasting four days, sadly troubled the fleet. "It so beat the *Jesus*," says Hawkins, "that we cut down all her higher buildings. Her rudder also was sore shaken; and withal the ship was in so extreme a leak that we were rather on the point to leave her than to keep her any longer. Yet, hoping to bring all to a good pass, we sought the coast of Florida, where we found no place nor haven for our ships, because of the shallowness of the coast. Thus, being in great despair, and taken with a new storm, which continued other three days, we were enforced to take for succour the port which serveth for the city of Mexico, called San Juan de Ulloa."

In that plan Hawkins was overbold, and his prospects were not improved by his capture of three small Spanish vessels which fell in his way, and which he attached to his fleet, hoping that for the hundred prisoners which they yielded he might obtain the requisite supplies by way of ransom. He reached San Juan, which is a rocky island helping to form the harbour of Vera Cruz, on the 16th of September. There he at first adopted a policy of moderation, very rare in him and only here to be explained on the assumption that he had discovered the weakness of his force and the need of propitiating the Spaniards, who now looked upon him as one of their worst enemies. "I found in the same port," he says, "twelve ships which had in them, by report, 200,000*l*. in gold and silver; all which, being in my possession, with the King's Island"—that is, San Juan—"as also the passengers before in my way thitherward stayed, I set at liberty without taking from them the weight of a groat."

The colonists at Vera Cruz at first supposed that Hawkins's ships were a fleet from Spain, for which they were looking out. The chief officers of the port accordingly came on board for the despatches. "Being deceived of their expectation, they were greatly dismayed; but immediately, when they saw our demand was nothing but victuals, they were recomforted." Hawkins kept two of them as hostages, while a message was sent to the governor in Mexico, representing his condition and asking permission to buy such articles as he needed.

That message was despatched on the night of Hawkins's arrival, and in it he exhausted his moderation. "On the morrow," he says, "we saw open of the haven thirteen great ships, and, understanding them to be the fleet of Spain, I sent immediately to advise the General of the fleet of my being there, giving him to understand that before I would suffer him to enter the port, there should be some order of conditions pass between us, for our safe-being there and maintenance of peace." That certainly was haughtier conduct than any that Englishmen had had to complain of at the hands of Spanish captains in British waters. Hawkins himself felt constrained to make some excuse for it. "It is to be understood," he wrote in his history of the enterprise, "that this port is made by a little island of stones not three foot above the water in the highest place, and but a bowshot of length any way, standing from the mainland two bowshots or more. Also it is to be understood that there is not in all this coast any other place for ships to arrive in safety, because the north wind hath there such violence that, unless the ships be very safely moored, with their anchors fastened upon this island, there is no remedy for these north winds but death. Also the place of the haven is so little that of necessity the ships must ride one above the other, so that we could not give place to them, nor they to us. And here I began to bewail that which after followed; for now, said I, I am in two dangers and forced to receive the one of them. That was; either I must have kept out the fleet, the which, with God's help, I was very well able to do; or else suffer them to enter in with their accustomed treason, which they never fail to execute, when they may have opportunity to compass it by any means. If I had kept them out, then had there been present shipwreck of all the fleet, which amounted, in value of our money, to 1,800,000*l.*, which I considered I was not able to answer, fearing the Queen's Majesty's indignation in so weighty a matter. Thus, with myself revolving the doubts, I thought rather better to abide the jutt of the uncertainty than the certainty. The uncertain doubt, I account, was their treason, which, by good policy, I hoped might be prevented; and therefore, as choosing the least mischief, I proceeded to conditions."

Hawkins's "good policy" was no match for the "accustomed treason" of the Spaniards as practised by the commander of their fleet, Francisco de Luxan, and the new Viceroy of Mexico, Don Martin Henriquez, who was on board. This treason, however, was no worse than rough precedents of the age fully sanctioned, and probably no worse than Hawkins himself would have resorted to in like case. Don Martin, when told that the strange ships which opposed his immediate entrance into port were under the command of the hated Hawkins, is reported to have sent a haughty message to him, saying "that he was a Viceroy, and had a thousand men, and therefore he would come in." "If he be a Viceroy," answered Hawkins, "I represent my Queen's person, and I am a Viceroy as well as he; and if he have a thousand men, my powder and shot will take the better place."* Don Martin, knowing that he must enter somehow or run the chance of shipwreck, immediately resolved upon treachery. He sent word that he would comply with any reasonable terms that Hawkins might propose. Hawkins replied that all he wanted was permission to barter certain of his goods, in fair market, for such provisions as were required for his

* Job Hartop, in a narrative printed by HAKLUYT, vol. iii., pp. 187—195.

voyage back to England. "Then the Viceroy," says one of the Englishmen, "yielded to our General's demands, swearing by his King and his crown, by his commission and authority that he had from his King, that he would perform it, and thereupon pledges were given on both parts." Hostages were exchanged—the Spanish hostages being "the basest of their company, in costly apparel,"—and "proclamation was made on both sides that, on pain of death, no occasion should be given whereby any quarrel should grow to the breach of the league."*

Thus the Spaniards entered the harbour, and the Englishmen were at their mercy. After two days of "great amity" Hawkins's suspicions were aroused by seeing that additional guns were placed on the fortifications of the port, and that fresh soldiers were drafted to the ships. A great Spanish hulk, also, was moored beside the *Minion*, and at daybreak Hawkins saw that three hundred men had been smuggled into her in the dark. He bade his men prepare for the worst, and sent Robert Barret, the master of the *Minion*, to ask the Viceroy what all this meant. Barret was straightway put in irons, and a trumpet sounded. That was the appointed signal for an attack upon the English. The three hundred Spaniards had begun to board the *Minion* almost before the trumpet had ceased to blow. "God and Saint George!" shouted Hawkins. "Upon those traitorous villains, and rescue the *Minion*. I trust

* Job Hartop's narrative.

in God the day shall be ours!"* "By God's appointment," he says, "in the time of suspicion we had, which was only one half-hour, the *Minion* was made ready to avoid; and so, loosing her head-fasts and hauling away by the stern-fasts, she was gotten out. Thus, with God's help, she defended the violence of the first brunt of these three hundred men. The *Minion* being passed out, they came aboard the *Jesus;* which also, with very much ado and the loss of many of our men, kept them out. There were also two other ships that assaulted the *Jesus* at the asme instant, so that she had hard getting loose; but yet, with some time, we had cut our head-fasts. Now, when the *Jesus* and the *Minion* were gotten about two ships' lengths from the Spanish fleet, the fight began so hot on all sides that, within one hour, the admiral† of the Spaniards was supposed to be sunk, their vice-admiral burnt, and one other of their chief ships believed to be sunk; so that the ships were little able to annoy us."

But this first triumph was brief. Hawkins had to face an overwhelming force on shipboard and all the artillery of San Juan and Vera Cruz. Let the sequel be told in the words of Job Hartop, one of the combatants. "We cut our cables, wound off our ships, and presently fought with them. They came upon us on every side, and continued the fight from ten of the clock until it was

---

* Job Hartop's narrative.

† In those days the chief fighting ships were generally called the Admiral and the Vice-Admiral; the titles of the chief officers on shipboard, as on land, were General and Lieutenant-General.

night. They killed all our men that were on shore in the island saving three, which, by swimming, got aboard the *Jesus of Lubeck*. They sunk the *Angel*, and took the *Swallow*. The Spaniards' admiral had above three score shot through her. Many of her men were spoiled. Four other of their ships were sunk. There were in that fleet, and that came from the shore to rescue them, fifteen hundred. We slew of them five hundred and forty, as we were credibly informed by a note that came to Mexico. In this fight the *Jesus of Lubeck* had five shot through her mainmast: her foremast was struck in sunder, under the hounds, with a chain-shot, and her hull was wonderfully pierced with shot. Therefore it was impossible to bring her away. They set two of their own ships on fire, intending therewith to have burnt the *Jesus of Lubeck*, which we prevented by cutting our cables in the hawse and winding off by our stern-fast. The *Minion* was forced to set sail and stand off from us, and come to an anchor without shot of the island. Our General courageously cheered his soldiers and gunners, and called to Samuel his page for a cup of beer, who brought it him in a silver cup; and he, drinking to all his men, willed the gunners to stand by their ordnance like men. He had no sooner set the cup out of his hand but a demi-culverin shot struck away the cup, and a cooper's plane that stood by the mainmast, and ran out on the other side of the ship. Which nothing dismayed our General; for he ceased not to encourage us, saying, 'Fear nothing; for God, who hath preserved me from this shot, will also deliver us from these traitors and villains.'. Then Captain Bland, meaning to have turned out of the port, had his mainmast struck overboard with a chain-shot that came from the shore. Wherefore he anchored, fired his ship, took his pinnace with all his men, and came on board the *Jesus of Lubeck* to our General; who said unto him that he thought he would not have run away from him. He answered that he was not minded to have run away from him, but his intent was to have turned up, and to have laid the weathermost ship of the Spanish fleet aboard and fired his ship, in hope therewith to have set on fire the Spanish fleet. He said, if he had done so, he had done well. With this, night came on. Our General commanded the *Minion*, for safeguard of her masts, to be brought under the *Jesus of Lubeck's* lee. He willed Master Francis Drake to come in with the *Judith* and to lay the *Minion* aboard, to take in men and other things needful, and to go about; and so he did. At night, when the wind came off the shore, we set sail, and went out, in despite of the Spaniards and their shot, when we anchored with two anchors under the island, the wind being northerly, which was wonderful dangerous, and we feared every hour to be driven with the lee shore."*

* The above details, ill-arranged and differing somewhat from the other narratives extant, are yet the best we have. They agree, in the main, with Hawkins's shorter and also confusing account, and with another account, by Miles Philips (HAKLUYT, vol. iii., pp. 469--487). HERRERA, whose report is certainly not more favourable to his countrymen's good faith, says that the fight was begun on shore by Spaniards, with arms concealed, who invited some Englishmen to drink, and then set upon them. He reports that the Spanish hostages left with

Thus dismally, though gloriously, ended Hawkins's great fight with the Spaniards at San Juan de Ulloa on the 23rd of September, 1568. But the troubles of the Englishmen were not here ended. Drake, in his little *Judith*, crowded with his own men and several who had escaped from the other ships, proceeded at once to England, thereby incurring serious blame, and reached Plymouth after a tardy voyage, a day or two before the 20th of January, 1569.* The *Jesus of Lubeck*, the *William and John*, the *Angel*, and the *Swallow* had been wrecked or taken by the Spaniards, many of their crews being drowned or captured, and only so many as could make their escape in boats being able to take refuge in the *Minion*. " The men on board the *Minion*," says Hawkins, " without either the captain's or the master's consent, set sail in such hurry and confusion, that it was not without great difficulty I was received on board."

The Englishmen taken by the Spaniards had no mercy from them. " It is a certain truth," it was said in 1582, " that they took our men and hung them up by the arms, upon high posts, until the blood burst out of their fingers' ends. Of which men so used there is one Copstone and certain others yet alive, who, by the merciful providence of the Almighty, were long since arrived here in England, carrying still about with them, and shall to their graves, the marks and

---

Hawkins testified to the generous treatment they received at his hands. —*Historia General*, lib. xix., cap. 18.

* RECORD OFFICE MSS., *Domestic*, vol. xlix., Nos. 36, 37.

tokens of those their inhuman and more than barbarous cruel dealings."*

Of those who escaped in the *Minion*, about two hundred in all, many fared no better. "We were now left alone," says Hawkins, "with only two anchors and two cables, our ship so damaged that it was as much as we could do to keep her above water, and a great number of us with very little provisions. We were besides divided in opinion what to do. Some were for yielding to the Spaniards; others chose rather to submit to the mercy of the savages; and again, others thought it more eligible to keep the sea, though with so scanty an allowance of victuals as would hardly suffice to keep us alive. In this miserable plight we ranged an unknown sea for fourteen days, till extreme famine obliged us to seek for land. So great was our misery that hides were reckoned good food. Rats, cats, mice, and dogs, none escaped us that we could lay our hands on. Parrots and monkeys were our dainties. In this condition we came to land, on the 8th of October, at the bottom of the Bay of Mexico, where we hoped to have found inhabitants of the Spaniards, relief of victuals, and a proper place to repair our ship. But we found everything just contrary to our expectation; neither inhabitants, nor provisions, nor a haven for the repair of our ship. Many of our men, nevertheless, being worn out with hunger, desired to be set on shore, to which I consented. Such as were willing to land I put them apart, and such as were desirous to go home-

* Miles Philips's narrative, in HAKLUYT, vol. iii., p. 473.

wards I put apart; so that they were indifferently parted, a hundred on one side, and a hundred on the other side. These men we set a-land with all diligence in this little place; which being landed, we determined there to take in fresh water, and so with our little remains of victuals to take the sea."

Hawkins's excuse for thus abandoning half his men to the scant mercies of Indians and Spaniards in a Mexican morass is in the certainty that, without some such measure, the whole party must have perished of starvation on ship-board; and he is not greatly to be blamed for adding to the many who desired to be thus left a few of mutinous disposition who, having at first insisted upon being put on land, had in the end to be coerced thereto. "When we were landed," says one of the number, "he came unto us, where, friendly embracing every one of us, he was greatly grieved that he was forced to leave us behind him. He counselled us to serve God and to love one another, and thus courteously he gave us a sorrowful farewell, and promised, if God sent him safe home, he would do what he could that so many of us as lived should by some means be brought into England, and so he did."*

The melancholy history of these hundred men must be briefly told. Their troubles began as soon as they were landed, when many of them were made ill by the quantity of water which they drank and the unwholesome nuts which they ate. At night time their only bed was the damp ground. They wandered through

* Job Hartop's narrative, in HAKLUYT, vol. iii., p. 491.

marshes for some days, until they met a wandering
tribe of man-eating Indians who, supposing them to be
Spaniards, fiercely assailed them, and, after they had
begged by signs for mercy and shown by their speech
that they were not of the hated race, stripped all who
wore coloured clothes, and left only the black raiment
to be divided among them. Only eight Englishmen
were slain in this meeting. The others divided into
two parties, half going northwards along the shore, and
half going to the west, in a route pointed out by the
Indians. This latter company forced their way for a
fortnight through marshes overgrown with grass five
or six feet high, interspersed with bramble-covered
clumps of ground on which their naked limbs were
torn at every step. Many were killed by Indians who
shot at them unawares. Those who escaped from the
Indians' arrows were plagued almost to madness by
mosquitoes and other stinging flies. At length they
reached the river Panuco, and saw Spaniards on the
other side, who crossed over in boats and so conveyed
them to the town of Panuco. There, upon telling their
story, the Governor threatened to hang them all for
treacherous villains, and, when sued for mercy, put them
for three days into " a little hogsty," where they were
fed upon pigs' food and nearly poisoned by foul smells.
At the end of the three days, they were bound two and
two together and marched over ninety leagues of road
to the city of Mexico. They were kindly used at some
of the halting-places, and one of the two officers to
whom they were entrusted did what he could to

lessen their sufferings; but the other "carried a javelin in his hand," says Miles Philips, one of the two who has told the story, "and sometimes, when as any of our men with very feebleness and faintness were not able to go so fast as he required them, he would take his javelin in both his hands, and strike them with the same between the neck and the shoulders so violently that he would strike them down: then would he cry and say, 'March, march on, you English dogs, Lutherans, enemies to God.'" At last they reached Mexico, and there they were put into a vile prison, in company with many of the comrades from whom they had parted a few weeks before, and many others who had been taken prisoners at San Juan de Ulloa; the whole body of prisoners being about a hundred. After they had been in gaol for four months, they were taken out and distributed as servants among the Spanish colonists, who generally employed them as overseers of their Indian and Negro slaves. That state of things lasted six years, and most of them fared well during that time. But in 1575 the Inquisition was introduced into Mexico, and then "their sorrows began afresh." On the eve of Good Friday all were dressed for an auto da fè, and paraded through the streets. A few were burnt: others were sent to the galleys: those who had kind friends escaped with short imprisonment and two or three hundred lashes apiece. Miles Philips, one of the most fortunate, served five years in a monastery, and then, having made friends with some Indian fellow-slaves and learnt their language, managed to make his escape to Guatemala, and thence, professing that he was a Spaniard, to work his way to England in February, 1582. Another of the party, Job Hartop, who was soon taken to Spain, thus sums up a long narrative of his long troubles: "I suffered imprisonment in Mexico two years; in the Contratation House in Seville, one year; in the Inquisition House in Triana, one year. I was in the galleys twelve years; in the Everlasting Prison Remediless, with the coat with Saint Andrew's Cross on my back, four years; and, at liberty, I served as a drudge Hernando de Loria three years; which is the full complement of twenty-three years."* Hartop returned to Portsmouth in 1590, and a few others reached England at various times; but most of the hundred men left by Hawkins on the Mexican coast died of the hardships inflicted upon them by the Spaniards.

Death came more quickly to most of the hundred who left the Mexican coast with Hawkins on the 16th of October, 1568. While the division of the men was being made, the *Minion* had been very nearly wrecked in a violent storm that lasted for three days. But "God again had mercy on them." The disconsolate voyagers had fair weather as they sailed out of the Gulf of Mexico and past the Bahamas, although through lack of food they were hardly able to manage the sails. A great many died of starvation. The rest slowly worked their way across the Atlantic, and finding themselves near the coast of Spain, put in at Pontevedra,

* HAKLUYT, vol. iii., pp. 469—487, 487—495.

in Galicia, on the 31st of December. There and at
Vigo, whither they went on hearing that they were
identified, and that steps were being taken for their
arrest, they obtained supplies of food and the assistance
of twelve English sailors, who navigated the ship for
them. They themselves nearly all died of the "miserable diseases" which came upon their weakened bodies
through the "excess of fresh meat," which they procured in Spain. Hawkins and a few others, however,
survived and reached Mount's Bay, in Cornwall, on the
25th of January, 1569. " All our business hath had
infelicity, misfortune, and an unhappy end," he said in
a letter addressed on that day to Sir William Cecil.
" If I should write of all our calamities, I am sure a
volume as great as the Bible will scarcely suffice."*

When the story of these calamities was made known,
a new thrill of hatred against Spain and all Spaniards
ran through England. Spaniards had been too often
ill-used by Englishmen, and especially by Hawkins
himself, for their bad faith to be made a ground of
serious complaint by Queen Elizabeth to King Philip;
but the recollection of this occurrence was treasured up
until a future time as one of the many cogent reasons
for the carrying on of open war between England and
Spain. In the meanwhile it gave a new impetus to the
private warfare that had already been in progress for
ten years or more.

* RECORD OFFICE MSS., Domestic, vol. xlix., No. 40. A whole
volume (liii.) of this collection is occupied with the reports, evidence of
witnesses, and the like, presented to a Commission of Inquiry, to which
Hawkins's case was referred, in July, 1569.

Hawkins applied himself to the prosecution of that warfare with persistent zeal. But he had suffered too much in purse, as well as in health, by the misfortunes of his last voyage to be hasty in entering upon another. The task of fighting with the Spaniards in the Spanish Main he left to others, and his most famous follower was young Francis Drake.

Having lost, in the expedition of 1567, all his little savings, Drake determined to win back all that had been taken from him, and in doing so to seize as much more as he could lay hands on. And he set about the business in a business-like way. "Finding that no recompense could be recovered out of Spain by any of his own means or by her Majesty's letters," we are told, "he used such help as he might by two several voyages into the West Indies, to gain such intelligence as might further him to get some amend for his loss." The first of these voyages was undertaken in 1570, in two little vessels, the *Dragon* and the *Swan*. The second was undertaken in 1571 in the *Swan* alone. About neither expedition is much more recorded than that in them "he got such certain notice of the persons and places aimed at as he thought requisite."*
They were small trading and piratical voyages made

---

\* *Sir Francis Drake Revived*, by PHILIP NICHOLS—"reviewed also by Sir Francis Drake himself before his death, and much holpen and enlarged, by divers notes with his own hand, here and there inserted" (1626)—which is my chief authority for the account of the voyage of 1572. Some other details are from a SLOANE MS. in the British Museum made use of by BARROW, in his *Life, Voyages, and Exploits of Sir Francis Drake* (1843).

probably at other people's expense, and used by Drake for earning money, as well as for acquiring information, both being alike needful to the work he had in view.

In 1572 Drake entered upon this work in good earnest. On the 24th of May he left Plymouth, in company with his brother John — another brother, Joseph, being also of the party — with two barks, the *Pascha*, of 70 tons burthen, and the *Swan*, of 25 tons, well supplied with food and all fighting implements, "especially having three dainty pinnaces made in Plymouth, taken asunder all in pieces, and stowed aboard, to be set up as occasion served." His entire crew comprised seventy-three men and boys. With this force he purposed to despoil Nombre de Dios, on the north side of the Isthmus of Darien, then "the granary of the West Indies, wherein the golden harvest brought from Peru and Mexico to Panama was hoarded up till it could be conveyed into Spain."

Drake proceeded at once to a little bay in the Gulf of Darien, which he had discovered in a previous voyage, and named Port Pheasant, "by reason of the great store of those goodly fowls, which he and his companions did there daily kill and feed on in that place." This seems to have been a haunt of English voyagers who amused themselves with West Indian piracy, already practised by many. In it Drake found upon a tree a communication from a John Garret of Plymouth, who had been previously associated with him, warning him that the Spaniards had discovered the hiding-place, and that it was no longer safe to use it.

Drake, however, remained a few days, long enough to set up the three pinnaces that he had taken from England, and also to welcome one James Rouse, who had also been previously connected with him, and who now seems to have come to the place by appointment. Rouse brought his little bark, with a crew of thirty men, and a Spanish caravel and shallop which he had captured on the way out. It was arranged that he should stay at Port Pheasant with the three barks and the caravel, while Drake went to plunder Nombre de Dios with the three pinnaces and the shallop, manned by fifty-three of his own men and twenty of Rouse's.

The bold little company reached Nombre de Dios at three o'clock in the morning of the 23rd of July. In the dark they sped into the port, and all landed without opposition from the single gunner who was on the watch. "On landing on the platform," says one of the freebooters, "we found six great pieces of ordnance mounted upon their carriages, some demi, some whole, culverins. We presently dismounted them. The gunner fled: the town took alarm, as we perceived not only by the noise and cries of the people, but by the bell ringing out, and drums running up and down the town. Our captain sent some of our men to stay the ringing of the alarm-bell, which had continued all this while, but the church being very strongly built and fast shut, they could not without firing, which our captain forbade, get into the steeple where the bell hung." The first firing came from the Spaniards, who discharged a volley of shot upon the invaders, and wounded

Drake in the leg, but they were driven off by the English arrows. John Drake and seventeen others— the most notable of whom was John Oxenham of Plymouth, at first a common sailor and cook, but already high in favour as a daring buccaneer—were sent to get possession of the King's Treasure House; and twelve men were left in charge of the pinnaces. With the other forty-three Drake rushed into the market-place, causing as much noise as possible to be made with trumpets and drums and as much glare as possible with fire-pikes and torches, so as to deceive the sleepy inhabitants concerning the number of their assailants. In a smart skirmish with the Spaniards he drove them back, with the exception of two or three whom he forced to lead him at once to the Governor's House. The door was open, and Drake hurrying in, discovered a great heap of silver bars, which he guessed to be seventy feet long, ten broad, and twelve high, and worth about 1,000,000*l*. Leaving here a strong guard, Drake hastened to the Treasure House, where a yet greater store of gold was thought to be, telling his comrades "that he had now brought them to the mouth of the treasury of the world, which if they did not gain, none but themselves were to be blamed." They did not gain it, however, and the blame, if any, was with Drake himself. Of the wound which he had received almost at landing he had made light, "knowing that, if the general's heart stoops, the men's will fall, and that, if so bright an opportunity once setteth, it seldom riseth again." But blood dropped from his leg at every step, and while he was before the Treasure House, directing his men as to the best way of forcing an entry, says the narrator, "it soon filled the very prints which our footsteps made, to the great dismay of all our company, who thought it not credible that one man should lose so much blood and live." Drake lived, but he fainted, and his men were so disconcerted thereat, that they could do nothing but bind up his wound with his scarf, and then bear him back to the pinnaces. Many of them picked up a goodly quantity of plunder as they went, and in the harbour they despoiled a Spanish ship of several kegs of wine. But, with very little of the booty that they hoped for, they had to retreat to a small island some six miles off, called by them the Island of Victuals, and there spend two days in attending to the wounds which many others, besides Drake, had received. The wine which they had captured proved very serviceable; and other refreshment, "no less strange than delicate," was procured from the gardens and farmhouses in the fruitful Island of Victuals.*

While Drake was there lying, a Spanish hidalgo from Nombre de Dios, in seeming friendship, came to visit him. He asked whether the captain was the same Drake who had troubled the coast on two previous years, and, seeing how sorely the Spaniards had been hurt, whether the English poisoned their arrows, and how the wounds could be healed. Drake haughtily replied "that he was the same Drake they meant;

* A slightly different account of this raid, by Lopez Vaz, a Portuguese, is in HAKLUYT, vol. iii., pp. 525, 526.

that it was never his custom to poison arrows; that their wounds might be cured with ordinary remedies; and that he wanted only some of that excellent commodity, gold and silver, which that country yielded, for himself and his company; and that he was resolved, by the help of God, to reap some of the golden harvest which they had got out of the earth and then had sent into Spain to trouble the earth."

On the 25th of July Drake left the little Island of Victuals and returned to Captain Rouse and his barks. Rouse feared pursuit, and therefore, receiving his share of the small spoil, departed to follow his own way of piracy. Drake, thereupon, sent his brother John to make fresh observations of the approaches to the river Chagres, a little to the west of Nombre de Dios, which he had seen in 1571, but about which, a new plot being in his mind, he desired some further information. The information appears to have been unsatisfactory and the plan abandoned.

Drake then sailed towards Cartagena, and almost in its harbour, on the 13th of August, boarded and plundered two Spanish ships, one of them of 240 tons burthen. In the evening, leaving his two barks among some barren islands a little to the south, he took the three pinnaces into the harbour itself, heard that the colonists had been warned, by a flying pinnace from Nombre de Dios, of his approach, and, in cool defiance, sailed up to a great ship of Seville which was to start next morning for San Domingo. "Every pinnace, according to the captain's order, one on the starboard bow, the other on the starboard quarter, and the captain in the midships on the larboard side, forthwith boarded her, though all had some difficulty to enter, by reason of her height. But, as soon as all entered upon the decks, they threw down the gratings and spar-decks, to prevent the Spaniards from annoying them with their close fights; who then, perceiving the English were possessed of their ship, stowed themselves all in the hold with their weapons. Having cut their cables at the hawse, with the three pinnaces they towed her about the island into the sound right afore the town. Meanwhile the town, having intelligence hereof by their watch, took the alarm, rang out their bells, shot off about thirty pieces of great ordnance, put all their men in a readiness, horse and foot, came down on the very point of the wood, and discharged their calivers in going forth." While all that stir was being made, Drake was in safe retreat.

His hardiness, which would have been foolhardiness in any one of less skilful and persistent daring, had now brought him into what might seem to be a desperate state. The fortifications at Nombre de Dios and Cartagena, the two strong gates of the Gulf of Darien, had put out all their strength to withstand him, and stout galleys were looking out for him in the intermediate waters. Therefore, fearing nothing, he determined to resort to a bold expedient. Trusting most to his fleet pinnaces, and not having men enough for all his five vessels, he set on fire his little *Swan*, and turned the *Pascha* into a store-ship, to be lodged in a remote corner of the

bay. In that corner, which he reached on the 21st of
August, he made friends of the native Symerons or
Maroons, a race of Indians, with Spanish blood among
them, formed, or at any rate augmented by fugitives from
the slavery enforced by the Spanish conquerors of America, and thus imbued with fierce hatred against them.
These Symerons helped Drake's followers to clear a plot
of ground and build enough huts for them to live in,
thus providing very convenient head-quarters for the adventurers during the next few months.

From this temporary residence Drake made more
piratical expeditions than need be here detailed. During
one little cruise, with two of the pinnaces, he took six
Spanish frigates—frigates in those days being small
pinnaces of only 5, 10, or 15 tons burthen—laden with
" hogs, hams, and maize," of which useful articles he
put the greater part into two of the captured boats,
discharging the Spaniards in the other four. More
than once he passed within gun-shot of Cartagena, and
even landed in its neighbourhood. On the 20th of
October two frigates were sent out thence, in hopes of
decoying him into the harbour. He burnt one and
sunk the other, within sight of two armed ships despatched to take him, and then retired without waste
of powder. On the 3rd of November, says the quaint
narrator, " we espied a sail plying to the westward to
our great joy, who vowed together that we would have
her, or it should cost us dear. Bearing with her, we
found her to be a Spanish ship of above 90 tons, which,
being hailed by us, despised our summons and shot off

her ordnance at us. The sea went very high, so that it was not for us to attempt to board her, and therefore we made fit small sail to attend upon her and keep her company, to her small content, till fairer weather might lay the sea. We spent not past two hours in our attendance, till it pleased God, after a great shower, to send us a reasonable calm, so that we might use our pieces and approach her at pleasure, in such sort that in short time we had taken her, finding her laden with victual, well powdered and well dried, which at that present we received as sent us of God's great mercy."

Drake's God was not altogether merciful. His brother John was killed, in November, in a fight with a Spanish frigate, and his other brother Joseph died, in the following January, of a disease brought on by drinking brackish water.* By the 3rd of February, twenty-eight of his seventy-three comrades had died in one way or another.

On that day Drake started on a famous land adventure. With seventeen Englishmen and thirty Symerons he began to journey towards Panama, on the south side of the Isthmus of Darien, the rich capital of the district fitly named Castila del Oro, or Golden Castile. On the road he attempted to waylay a treasure-party pro-

* "That the cause might be better discerned, and consequently remedied to the relief of others, by our Captain's appointment, he was ripped open by the surgeon, who found his liver swollen, his heart as it were sodden, and his guts all fair. This was the first and last experiment that our Captain made of anatomy in this voyage."—SLOANE MS.

ceeding to Nombre de Dios; but one of his men, being drunk, made so much noise that the Spaniards were alarmed too soon, and the Englishmen had to save themselves with some rough fighting, which they carried up to the gates of Venta Cruz, and ended by sacking that town. Shortly afterwards he met another treasure-party, which he successfully attacked and robbed of 300 pounds of silver and some bars and wedges of gold. This booty, however, was soon lost. Drake buried it in the sand, intending to pick it up on his return; but one of his followers, having been taken by the Spaniards, was compelled by torture to reveal the hiding-place, and so it was restored to its rightful owners.

Yet this expedition had a memorable issue. In 1513, Vasco Nuñez de Balboa, wandering among the steep mountains of the Isthmus of Darien, had ascended one of the highest, and thence obtained that view of the Pacific Ocean, the first enjoyed by Europeans, which had been a great incentive to the Spanish conquest of South America and treasure-seeking along the shores of the Southern Sea. Just sixty years afterwards Drake was led by his Symeron friends to what appears to have been the same mountain, at the summit of which was "a goodly and great high tree," revered by the natives, and twisted, at its upper part, into "a convenient arbour, wherein twelve men might sit." He ascended it and beheld the Pacific, and then, says the old historian, who probably invented for Drake the melodramatic imitation of Vasco Nuñez's behaviour, "being influenced with ambition of glory and hopes of wealth, he was so vehemently transported with desire to navigate that sea, that falling down there upon his knees, he implored the Divine assistance that he might, at some time or other, sail thither and make a perfect discovery of the same; and hereunto he bound himself with a vow."*

That resolution may have hastened Drake's return to England. After an absence of two or three months, he went back to his little settlement on the Gulf of Darien, and, loading his bark and pinnaces with the abundant treasure that he had collected, set sail in June. After a prosperous voyage he entered Plymouth Harbour on Sunday, the 9th of August, 1573. It was sermon-time when the news of his arrival got abroad, and we are told that all the congregation hurried out of church to welcome him, "all hastening to see the evidence of God's love and blessing towards our gracious Queen and country, by the fruit of our captain's labour and success."

He was not welcomed by his fellow-townsmen of Plymouth alone. All praised him for his successful enterprise against the Spanish colonies, and none blamed him for the lawless ways in which that enterprise had been often carried through. In his eight-and-twentieth year, Drake found himself rich in fame as well as in money. He had not succeeded in his raid on Nombre de Dios, and in some other treasure-winning projects he had failed; yet, as we are told, "he had gotten a pretty store of money, by playing the seaman and the pirate."†

\* CAMDEN, *Annals*, p. 249. † *Ibid.*

His piracy must be judged by sixteenth-century principles of morality; his seamanship by a standard of courage that is unchangeable.

The many kindred undertakings which were contemporaneous and subsequent to this famous voyage need not here be chronicled. It will suffice briefly to describe one which may at the same time afford further illustration of the hatred growing among Englishmen against Spain and all Spaniards, and show how grievous was the failure which came to enterprises conducted by men who had no share in the wit and prowess possessed by Drake.

The manager of this particular enterprise was Andrew Barker, a merchant of Bristol. Having successfully traded for some years with the Canaries, a cargo belonging to him, worth nearly 2,000*l*., was, in 1575, seized by the Inquisition. Knowing that "no suit prevaileth against the Inquisition of Spain," Barker determined to reimburse himself by a season of piracy in the Spanish Main, after the method made famous by Drake. He accordingly fitted out two barks, the *Ragged Staff*, in which he himself went as captain, with Philip Roche for master, and the *Bear*, entrusted to Willian Coxe. He left Plymouth early in June, 1576, and proceeded by way of Cape de Verde to the Spanish Main. At Trinidad he had some trade with its Indian inhabitants. At Margarita he captured a small Spanish ship; and in the Gulf of Darien, fifty miles beyond Cartagena, he seized a larger ship, containing 500*l*.'s worth of gold and silver, and, among other treasure, "certain green stones called emeralds, whereof one, very great, being set in gold, was found tied secretly about the thigh of a friar." A third Spanish vessel was taken near Veragua, and to it were transferred the crew of the *Ragged Staff*, which was no longer seaworthy and had to be sunk. Barker could hardly so dispose of those of his comrades who were unseaworthy; but he quarrelled and fought with them. In a duel with Roche, at Veragua, he was wounded in the cheek; and in the Bay of Honduras he was also wounded in another duel. The crew of the *Bear*, turning mutinous in a body, took him out of his own ship and placed him, with those who still supported him, upon the island of San Francisco. They promised to take him on board again, on his agreeing to their terms; but before that could be done a party of Spaniards landed secretly at San Francisco, and killed Barker and eight other Englishmen. Thereupon Coxe took the command of the expedition. The *Bear* being unfit for further service, he caused it to be sunk, and built a new frigate in the Bay of Honduras. This alone returned to England, the Spanish frigate, in which was most of the booty, having been wrecked with more than half of its crew. "Divers of our company, upon our arrival at Plymouth," says one of the party, " were committed to prison at the suit of Master John Barker, of Bristol, brother unto our captain, Master Andrew Barker, as accessories to our captain's death and betrayers of him unto the enemy; and, after straight examination of many of us, by letters of direction from her Majesty's Privy Council, the chief malefactors were only chastised with long imprisonment, where indeed, before God, they had deserved to die; whereof some, although they escaped the rigour of men's law, yet could they not avoid the heavy judgment of God, but shortly after came to miserable ends."*

* HAKLUYT, vol. iii., pp. 528—530.

## CHAPTER XIII.

THE VOYAGES OF SIR FRANCIS DRAKE AND THOMAS CAVENDISH TO THE SOUTHERN SEA AND ROUND THE WORLD.

[1575—1593.]

CAPTAIN FRANCIS DRAKE had no sooner returned from his successful expedition to the Spanish Main than he began to plan a new voyage in the direction of the Southern Sea, of which he had had a distant view in 1573. But "he was prevented from setting forth," according to his old biographer, "partly by secret envy at home, and partly by being employed in his prince and country's service in Ireland."* The report of his daring insults to the Spaniards probably led Queen Elizabeth to forbid at any rate immediate renewal of his distant voyaging, and to give him work which was less likely to bring her into trouble with foreign powers. In the autumn of 1573, by the Queen's permission, we are told, "he furnished, at his own proper expense, three frigates with men and munition, and served voluntary in Ireland under Walter, Earl of Essex, where he did excellent service both by sea and land, at

* PRINCE, *Worthies of Devon*, p. 487.

the winning of divers strong forts."* About that "excellent service," which must have been fierce butchery at the best, we have no precise details. It was of short duration, as the Earl of Essex's Quixotic attempt at the colonization of Ulster was short-lived. After a year or two of Irish adventure, Drake appears to have spent another year or two in attendance at Court, where, as the favourite of Queen Elizabeth's new favourite, Sir Christopher Hatton, and as a humble sharer in the royal smiles, he was able to lay the foundations of his future advancement.

For four years, at any rate, though he was "privately brooding over his new design," he was not openly active in its furtherance; and through that delay his project was in part anticipated by one of his most zealous followers in the exploits of 1572 and 1573. John Oxenham had not only distinguished himself in the raid upon Nombre de Dios; he had also been Drake's chosen companion in ascending the tree on the mountain-summit in Castila del Oro whence the Pacific Ocean had been seen, and when Drake had vowed that one day he would sail thereon, "if it would please God to grant him that happiness," Oxenham had declared that, unless he were forcibly hindered, "he would follow him by God's grace." To this resolution he adhered, after their return to England, until, says the old biographer, "having waited Drake's leisure for two years, and not knowing how much longer it would be, if at all, ere his occasions would permit him so to do, he thought him-

* STOW, Annals.

self disobliged from his promise; and so he undertook something himself."*

In the Spanish Main, under Drake, says the same biographer, Oxenham "had gotten among the seamen the name of captain for his valour, and had privily scraped together a good store of money." In 1575, he put both money and name to good use in fitting out a small expedition for piracy and searching in the Southern Sea. In a ship of 140 tons burthen, with seventy men on board, he sailed to the shores of the Isthmus of Darien, westward of Nombre de Dios. There he entered a narrow creek, and, drawing his ship on the shore, covered it and his provisions and great guns with boughs. With the crew and six Symeron guides he crossed the Darien mountains and, by the side of a stream running into the Pacific, built a little pinnace, "which was five-and-forty foot by the keel." Thus he was able, first of Englishmen, to sail on the Pacific Ocean. He proceeded to the Pearl Islands, there to watch for Spanish treasure-ships on their way to Panama. After ten days' waiting he captured a small bark, bringing 60 pounds of gold from Quito and an abundance of food, which was of more present value than the gold. Six days later he seized another little vessel, coming from Lima with 100 pounds of silver among its stores. He also found a few pearls on the Pearl Islands. Then he returned to the river in the Bay of Panama whence he had started, and dismissed the captured barks.

\* PRINCE, *Worthies of Devon*, p. 187.

Then good fortune left him. Immediately after his departure from the Pearl Islands the Indians sent information to Panama of his presence in the Southern Sea. Four barks and a hundred soldiers were thence despatched under Juan de Ortega to search for him, and they met the Spanish vessels which had just been let loose from the mouth of the river. Thither Ortega at once went. He followed Oxenham up the river and, after searching for four days, found his pinnace lying on the shore, with six Englishmen in charge of it. In a scuffle with them one was killed, and the other five ran off to tell Oxenham of the danger. It seems that the Englishmen had quarrelled about the spoil they had won. Oxenham wished without delay to take it back to the ship on the other side of the Isthmus, and there store it for future division. Some of his followers claimed their shares at once, and the dispute was only settled by its being temporarily lodged in a hut half a league from the spot where the pinnace had been left; and there, while Oxenham was a little way off, Ortega found it. A fight ensued in which, with loss of seven of his own men, Ortega killed five and captured eleven of Oxenham's, putting the rest to flight. With some difficulty and without their treasure, these made their way back to the place in which they had concealed their ship. But the Spaniards in Nombre de Dios, informed from Panama of Oxenham's movements, had discovered and seized it. With only such refuge as the Symerons could give them, many of them ill and others faint-hearted, with little food and less material for fighting or working, Oxenham and his fifty men had to wander about until they could find some way of improving their forlorn condition. This they never found. A hundred and fifty soldiers were sent from Nombre de Dios in search of them and, with the assistance of some Negroes or Symerons, they were soon captured and taken to Panama. Oxenham was asked if he had Queen Elizabeth's authority for entering the dominions of the King of Spain. Being able to produce none, he and all his followers, with the exception of two or three boys, were executed as pirates. "Thus," says the old historian, " miscarried this great and memorable adventure."*

Its fate was very different from that of the greater and more memorable adventure in which Drake engaged soon after. Whatever " secret envy " and personal ambition had deterred him from it through four years were removed by the summer of 1577, and then Drake applied himself heartily to the carrying out of his old plan. The growing quarrel between England and Spain, weakening every day Elizabeth's fear of too much offending Philip, led her to withdraw her prohibition of the undertaking. It is even said that she openly expressed her approval of it, and gave Drake an implied commission thereto in presenting to him a sword and saying, " We do account that he which striketh at thee, Drake, striketh at us." At any rate, she offered

* CAMDEN, *Annals*, pp. 251, 252; HAKLUYT, vol. iii., pp. 526, 527; BURNEY, *Chronological History of the Discoveries in the South Sea*, vol. i., pp. 295—299.

no opposition to the active preparations which during some months were being openly made, though their precise object was kept secret, for an armed expedition against the possessions of Spain.*

This expedition was fitted out partly at Drake's own expense, partly with the assistance of his friends, Elizabeth herself being one of them. It comprised five vessels; the *Pelican*, to which was afterwards given the famous name of the *Golden Hind*, a ship of 100 tons, commanded by Drake himself, the *Elizabeth*, a bark of 50 tons, under John Winter, the *Marigold*, a bark of 30 tons, under John Thomas, the *Swan*, a fly-boat of 30 tons, under John Chester, and the *Christopher*, a pinnace of 15 tons, under Thomas Moon. The crews of these vessels numbered in all a hundred and sixty-four, officers, sailors, and soldiers; and they were supplied with four pinnaces taken to pieces and adapted for speedy putting together whenever they were needed for use, as well as with "such plentiful provision of all things necessary as so long and dangerous a voyage seemed to require." "Neither did he omit," it was said of Drake, "to make provision for ornament and delight, carrying to this purpose with him expert musicians, rich furniture—all the vessels for his table, yea, many belonging to the cook-room, being of pure silver—with

---

\* *The World Encompassed by Sir Francis Drake;* "carefully collected out of the Notes of Master FRANCIS FLETCHER, preacher in this employment, and divers others his followers in the same," and published by Sir Francis Drake, the younger; re-issued, with copious notes and additions from MSS. in the British Museum by the Hakluyt Society (1854) This is my authority for the ensuing details, where no other is cited.

divers shows of all sorts of curious workmanship, whereby the civility and magnificence of his native country might, among all nations whither he should come, be the more admired."

All these preparations were completed by the 15th of November. On that day Drake started from Plymouth. But a storm which overtook the little fleet near Falmouth did so much damage that it had to be taken back for repairs. A second and successful start was made on the 13th of December. At Mogadore, off the coast of Morocco, Drake halted on the 25th, and there put up one of his pinnaces. There were no people on the island, but the Moors from the mainland crossed over to trade and exchange presents with him. Leaving Mogadore on the last day of the year, he seized three fishing-boats and three caravels, all belonging to the Spaniards, on the way to Cape Blanco, which he reached on the 16th of January. There he dismissed two of the captured fishing-boats, and gave the *Christopher* in exchange for the third, which was a stout little bark of 40 tons burthen. He also released two of the caravels. Four days were passed in trade with the miserable inhabitants of Cape Blanco, who eagerly bartered gums and other valuable commodities for some of Drake's provisions. Near Cape de Verde Islands and the adjoining coast, where Hawkins and other slave-traders had made hateful the name of Englishmen, he was very differently received. All the inhabitants fled on his arrival, first filling the wells with salt and doing all else in their power to hinder his gaining the refreshment of which he was in need. Refreshment was obtained in that neighbourhood, however, by the capture of a Portuguese ship, laden with wine and other articles. Drake gave to her crew the little pinnace that he had put together at Mogadore, and placed in her twenty-eight of his own men, under the command of Thomas Doughty.

That arrangement was unfortunate. Doughty had only been in charge a few days when he was accused of having purloined some of the Portuguese stores, with intent "to rob the voyage and deprive the company of their hope and her Majesty and other adventurers of their benefit, to enrich himself and make himself greater to the overthrow of all others.' Drake, on examination, found in Doughty's possession only a few old coins, a ring, and some other articles of trifling value, which were proved to have been given to him by one of the Portuguese sailors. Thinking that Doughty was thus falsely accused, he placed him in temporary command of his own ship, the *Pelican*, and himself remained for a few days to arrange matters in the prize-ship. In the *Pelican*, however, Doughty fell into fresh disgrace: "he was thought to be too peremptory and exceeding his authority, taking upon him too great a command." Drake had to make a fresh investigation, and the issue of this, though we are not told on what grounds, was Doughty's removal into the *Swan* as "a prisoner, with utter disgrace." Thus were sown the seeds of much future trouble.

In the meanwhile Drake's little fleet was crossing the

Atlantic. Quitting the African coast on the 2nd of February, and crossing the equator on the 17th of the same month, it came within sight of Brazil, about two hundred miles north of the Rio de la Plata, on the 5th of April, sixty-three days having been passed without sight of land. On their approach the ships were seen by the natives of the district, who thereupon, we are told, " made upon the coast great fires for a sacrifice to the devils, about which they use conjurations, making heaps of sand and other ceremonies, that, when any ship shall go about to stay upon their coast, not only sands may be gathered together in shoals in every place, but also that storms and tempests may arise, to the casting away of ships and men."* Not hindered by the report of those incantations, Drake attempted to land; but he could find no suitable harbour, and he accordingly sailed on to the mouth of the La Plata, where he anchored his ships on the 14th of April. Nearly a fortnight was spent in halting for refreshment and in exploring the river. There and along the more southern coast, seals and ostriches were used as food, greatly to the satisfaction of the voyagers.

On the 12th of May Drake reached the Gulf of Saint George, in Patagonia. On the way thither, seeking vainly for a good place of shelter, he had lost sight of the *Swan* and the Portuguese prize-ship, which had been named the *Mary*. Only this vessel was found during his fortnight's stay in the Gulf of Saint George, and in later coasting both north and south in search

* HAKLUYT, vol. iii., p. 732.

of the *Swan*, the *Christopher*—the fishing-bark exchanged for the smaller *Christopher*, to which its name had been transferred—was also lost. The *Mary*, too, soon proved unseaworthy, and had to be unloaded and broken up. Thus the fleet was reduced to three vessels, the *Pelican*, the *Elizabeth*, and the *Marigold*, besides the pinnaces.

While coasting up and down Drake made a memorable stay at Port Saint Julian, between the 19th of June and the 17th of August. Both here and in the Gulf of Saint George he came into contact with the aborigines of Patagonia. "Magellan," says the chronicler of the voyage, "was not altogether deceived in naming them giants; for they generally differ from the common sort of men, both in stature, bigness, and strength of body, as also in the hideousness of their voice; but yet they are nothing so monstrous or giant-like as they are reported, there being some Englishmen as tall as the highest that we could see." Later travellers have found that they are hardly as tall as ordinary Englishmen. To early voyagers, however, always looking out for marvels, their curious customs gave a semblance of great height and inordinate bulk. On their bodies they wore little but paint, and they delighted in huge headgear. Their arms and legs were daubed over with different colours: on a white back would be a black sun, and a black stomach would be ornamented with a white moon. Immense and parti-coloured horns, spikes, and the like, were fastened to their crowns. Their manners also were peculiar.

"They fed on seals and other flesh, which they ate nearly raw, casting four or six pounds weight into the fire, till it was a little scorched, and then tearing it in pieces with their teeth like lions, both men and women." The Patagonians carried on some trade, chiefly in seals and other food, with the English, and showed even too much readiness to imitate their customs. "One of the giants," we are told, "standing with our men when they were taking their morning draught, showed himself so familiar that he also would do as they did; and, taking a glass in his hand, being strong canary wine, it came no sooner to his lips than it took him by the nose, and so suddenly entered his head that he was so drunk, or at least so overcome, that he fell on his bottom, not able to stand, yet he held the glass fast in his hand, without spilling any of the wine; and when he came to himself he tried again, and, tasting, by degrees got to the bottom. From which time he took such a liking to the wine, that, having learnt the name, he would every morning come down from the mountains with a mighty cry of 'Wine! wine! wine!' continuing the same until he arrived at the tent."

The intercourse with the Patagonians at Port Saint Julian was not wholly either amusing or profitable. On the 20th of June, one of Drake's party, anxious to show his skill in archery to the natives, pulled his bow-string so violently that he snapped it. They, taking fright in some way, immediately wounded him mortally with arrows. Thereupon the only other Englishman on the spot discharged his musket upon the assailants, and

his shot was answered by an arrow, which brought him
to the ground. Drake himself, being within sight, then
came up, and dispersed the crowd by shooting the
ringleader, who died with "so hideous and terrible a
roar, as if ten bulls had joined together in roaring."
The Patagonians made no fresh attack, and the bodies
of the two unfortunate Englishmen were buried "with
such honours as in such case martial men use to have
when they are dead, being both laid in one grave, as
they were both partakers of one manner of death, and
ended their lives together by one and the self-same
kind of accident."

"To this evil, thus received at the hands of the
infidels," adds the narrator, "there was adjoined and
grew another mischief, wrought and contrived closely
among ourselves, as great, yea, far greater and of far
more grievous consequence than the former, but that it
was, by God's providence, detected and prevented in
time, which else had extended itself not only to the
violent shedding of blood, by murdering our general,
and such other as were most firm and faithful to him, but
also to the final overthrow of the whole action intended
and to divers other most dangerous effects." The
offender, real or fancied, was the same Thomas Doughty,
who had been put in charge of the Portuguese prize-
ship taken off Cape de Verde. He had been an old
acquaintance of Drake's, and a man well esteemed
before the departure of the fleet from England. Drake's
first liking of him is shown in his appointing him to the
care of the Portuguese vessel, and that Drake shared in

the growing opposition to him appears from his sanctioning of his speedy degradation. Then or at some later time he was informed that, even before leaving Plymouth, Doughty had proposed that, as soon as convenient, Drake should be got rid of, and he himself should take command of the whole expedition. Drake is reported to have at first disbelieved this charge, but to have been ultimately convinced. At any rate, a sort of court-martial was held at Port Saint Julian, and by it Doughty was adjudged guilty of mutiny, and condemned to death. According to one account, he confessed his guilt, and, when Drake offered to leave him in Patagonia or to send him back to England in one of the pinnaces, he is said to have chosen a death by which that guilt would in part be expiated. According to another account, "he utterly denied it upon his salvation, at the hour of communicating the sacrament of the body and blood of Christ, at the hour and moment of his death, affirming that he was innocent of such things whereof he was accused, judged, and suffered death for."* It is not easy to believe that he really was guilty; but it is still harder to believe that Drake, to gratify his own or others' spite—one scandal being that this was done out of compliment to the Earl of Leicester, whom Doughty had accused of murdering the Earl of Essex†—would have sanctioned his punishment without being convinced that it was right and neces-

---

* Both statements are given in full, with much illustrative matter and much argument in disparagement of Drake, in Mr. VAUX's edition of *The World Encompassed*, published by the Hakluyt Society in 1854.
† CAMDEN, *Annals*, p. 251.

sary. At any rate, Doughty was executed at Port Saint Julian with the approval of nearly all his comrades, followed by that of nearly all Englishmen at home when the story was told to them.

Port Saint Julian had only once before been visited by Europeans, the first visit being made by Magellan in 1519. On that occasion, also, a man had been executed for mutiny, and the gibbet used for the purpose was still standing in Drake's time. "Of the wood of which gibbet," says the chronicler, "our cooper made tankards or cans for such of the company as would drink in them; whereof, for my own part, I had no great liking, seeing there was no such necessity."

There was more need of food than of vessels in which to put it. "Our stay being longer than we purposed," it is recorded, "our diet began to wax short, and small mussels were good meat, yea, the seaweeds were dainty dishes. By reason whereof we were driven to seek corners very narrowly for some refreshing, but the best we could find was shells instead of meat. We found the nests, but the birds were gone; that is, the shells of the cockles upon the sea-shore, where the giants had banqueted; but could never chance with the cockles themselves in the sea. The shells were so extraordinary that it would be incredible to the most part; for a pair of shells did weigh four pounds, and what the meat of two such shells might be may be easily conjectured."

Drake left Port Saint Julian on the 17th of August. Three days' quick sailing to the south brought him to

Cape Virgin Mary, at the entrance to the Strait of Magellan. "We found the strait," says one of his comrades, "to have many turnings and, as it were, shuttings up, as if there were no passage at all; by means whereof we had the wind often against us, so that, some of the fleet recovering a cape or point of land, others should be forced to turn back again and to come to an anchor where they could. There be many fair harbours, with store of fresh water, but yet they lack their best commodity; for the water is there of such depth that no man shall find ground to anchor in, except it be in some narrow river or corner, or between some rocks; so that, if any extreme blast or contrary winds do come, whereunto the place is most subject, it carrieth with it no small danger. The land on both sides is very huge and mountainous; the lower mountains whereof, although they be monstrous and wonderful to look upon for their height, yet there are others which exceed them in a strange manner, reaching themselves above their fellows so high that between them did appear three regions of clouds. These mountains are covered with snow. The strait is extremely cold, with frost and snow continually. The trees seem to stoop with the burden of the weather, and yet are green continually; and many good and sweet herbs do very plentifully grow and increase under them."*

Drake was Magellan's first follower in the passage of this dangerous channel. On entering it, "in homage to the Queen's Majesty, he caused his fleet to strike

* HAKLUYT, vol. iii., p. 734.

their topsails upon the bunt; and withal, in remembrance of his honourable friend and favourer, Sir Christopher Hatton, he changed the name of the ship which himself went in from the *Pelican* to be called the *Golden Hind*." Sixteen days were spent in traversing it, part of the time being occupied in a little exploration of the islands, and, on one of these islands, in much useful hunting of penguins. Three thousand of these birds were caught in one day. "They have no wings," says the quaint describer of them, " but short pinions, which serve their turn in swimming. Their colour is somewhat black, mixed with white spots under their belly and about their necks. They walk so upright that, afar off, a man would take them to be little children. If a man approach anything near them, they run into holes in the ground, which be not very deep, whereof the island is full ; so that to take them we had staves with hooks fast to the end, wherewith some of our men pulled them out, and others being with cudgels did knock them on the head, for they bite so cruelly with their crooked bills that none of us were able to handle them alive."* With the human inhabitants of these islands, also, Drake's party had some slight dealings. In the Strait of Magellan, they considered, there was " nothing wanting to make a happy region, but the people's knowing and worshipping the true God."

They were again in the open sea, and Drake's long-cherished project was at length realized, on the 6th of September. He proposed at once to sail northwards,

* HAKLUYT, vol. iii., p. 752.

both to relieve his people from the cold which had oppressed them in Magellan's Strait, and to attempt the spoliation of the rich Spanish possessions in Peru, which was a leading object of his voyage; and before the close of the following day he had easily traversed some seventy leagues of water. But then a terrible tempest arose, followed by other storms hardly less violent, in the course of which the ships were driven southwards, below Cape Horn, and westward for more than six hundred miles. Then, on the 30th of September, finer weather returned, though, in the violent winds that still oppressed them, a week was occupied by the *Golden Hind* and the *Elizabeth* in getting back to land, and during that week the little *Marigold* was blown out of sight, never to be again heard of.

Soon Drake was left quite alone with the *Golden Hind*. The two remaining ships, having approached a little bay near to the western opening of Magellan's Strait, on the 7th of October, there sought for shelter, "it being a very foul night, and the seas sore grown." But the *Golden Hind* had only been anchored for a few hours when her cable broke and she was driven out to sea again. Next morning the *Elizabeth* took refuge in the strait, "hardly escaping the danger of the rocks." She waited at the entrance for ten days, and then retired to a sound a little further in, where two weeks more were spent in waiting. At the end of that time, John Winter, her captain, determined to go home. On the 1st of November, we are told, " by Captain Winter's compulsion, full sore against the mariners' minds, they gave up their voyage." Without much difficulty they made their way back to England, where they arrived on the 2nd of June, 1579, and spread the report that Drake had been wrecked.*

But Drake was fortune's favourite. The storm that took him out to sea on the 7th of October forced him southwards. On the coast of Tierra del Fuego he took shelter for two days, when he was again driven from his anchorage and parted from his brave little pinnace, of four or five tons burthen, which up to this time had clung to the *Golden Hind.* Eight men were on board this pinnace, with only one day's supply of victuals. They struggled on to the last. Four of them were killed by the natives of a little island, whither they went in search of food, and two others afterwards died of wounds received at that time. The pinnace also was wrecked, and the two survivors, after two months' waiting, had to paddle across to the mainland on a single plank, about ten feet long, spending three days in the passage. "On coming to land," says Peter Carder, who has told the story, "we found a rivulet of sweet water; when William Pitcher, my only comfort and companion, although I endeavoured to dissuade him, being before pinched with extreme thirst, overdrank himself and, to my unspeakable grief, died within half an hour, whom I buried as well as I could in the sand." Carder made friends with some Patagonians, lived with them for some years, and returned to England in 1587.†

\* HAKLUYT, vol. iii., p. 752.
† PURCHAS, vol. iv., p. 1188; BURNEY, vol. i., p. 368.

Drake and the forty or fifty men in the *Golden Hind* thus came to be the only representatives of the fleet that had left England nearly a year before. They began to regret that they had changed the name of their ship, seeing that she was now verily "a *Pelican* alone in the wilderness." Their case indeed seemed desperate. "The violence of the storm without intermission," says the chronicler of the voyage, "the impossibility to come to anchor, the want of opportunity to spread any sail, the most maddened seas, the lee shore, the dangerous rocks, the contrary and most intolerable wind, the impossible passage out, the desperate tarrying there, and the inevitable perils on every side, did present so small a likelihood to escape present destruction that, if the special providence of God Himself had not supported us, we never could have endured that woful state, as being environed with most terrible and most fearful judgments round about."

The series of storms, which lasted almost without intermission for fifty-one days, had, however, one good result. On the 28th of October, the last day of storm, Drake "fell in with the uttermost part of the land towards the South Pole, without which there is no main or island to be seen to the southward, but the Atlantic Ocean and the South Sea meet in a large and free scope." He landed at the edge of Cape Horn, called by him—in opposition to the old term Terra Incognita—Terra Nunc Bene Cognita, and, standing upon its farthest limit, was able to boast, as often he did in later years, that he had been upon more southern land than any other man alive.*

On the 30th of October, having satisfied himself with his exploration of Cape Horn and its neighbourhood, and being at last favoured with fair weather, Drake turned northward. He was anxious to return to the coast of Peru, where, according to the instructions he had given in anticipation of their being parted, he hoped to meet the *Elizabeth*, perhaps also the *Marigold*. He found neither, and, on the way past Tierra del Fuego, he was very nearly killed. Landing with a boat's crew of eight at a little island on the way, where he hoped to obtain fresh water, he was, after some show of friendship, fiercely attacked by the natives. Two Englishmen were killed, and every one of the other seven was wounded, Drake himself being struck by arrows under his right eye and on the crown of his head. They had great difficulty in returning to the ship, and regarded as miraculous both that and their subsequent cure; "for," it is said, "our chief surgeon being dead, and the only remaining one absent in the *Elizabeth*, and so being left to the care of a boy who had little experience and no skill, we were little better than altogether destitute of such cunning and helps as so grievous a state of so many wounded bodies did require."

This accident caused some delay; but by the 30th of November Drake had reached the Bay of San Felipe.

* Sir Richard Hawkins, cited by Southey, vol. iii., p. 142.

He there had friendly intercourse with the natives, and by one of them he was led back, some six leagues, to Valparaiso. At Valparaiso he easily despoiled its two or three dozen Spanish colonists of everything possessed by them which was useful to his ship, and from a Spanish vessel in the port he took a goodly quantity of wine, with some gold, pearls, and other articles. Other booty, and water, which just then was more needed than the richest treasure, he tried to get at Coquimbo on the 19th of December; but there more than a hundred Spaniards were prepared to receive him, and, after losing one man, he retired to a little bay about a hundred miles further north, where there were no Spaniards to quarrel with him.

In that bay he waited for nearly a month, partly to build a new pinnace, partly to watch for his missing ships upon the sea, and to make inquiries concerning them from the Indians on the shore. Departing thence about the middle of January, he proceeded slowly along the coast, still looking for the *Elizabeth* and the *Marigold*, taking a few small prizes, and robbing a few Spaniards in the settlements which he passed. On the 15th of February he reached Callao, the port of Lima, and there had less ignoble exercise of his skill in piracy.

When near the entrance to the harbour, Drake captured a Portuguese bark. He offered to release her, on condition that the captain should safely pilot him into the harbour. This was done at night time, so secretly that he was in the midst of seventeen trading-vessels before any alarm was given. "The masters and merchants here were most secure," we are told, " having never been assaulted by enemies." Therefore they were quite unprepared for Drake's attack, and the seventeen ships were plundered by him without the loss of even a charge of powder and shot.

The plunder, though valuable, was not as much as Drake had hoped for, being chiefly silk, linen, and other merchandize. He asked where the silver was lodged, and was informed that part of it still lay in the strong house in the town, but that a goodly store had lately been despatched to Panama in a large treasure-ship, "the great glory of the Southern Sea," named the *Cacafuego*. Thereupon, cutting the cables of the ships he had just rifled, in order to hinder them in any pursuit that might be attempted, he hurried off before morning in quest of the *Cacafuego*. Ten days were spent in eager pursuit. From one Spanish vessel which they met, but did not choose to waste time in despoiling, they heard that the treasure-ship had been seen three days before. Another vessel which was spoken with had passed her two days before. Drake saw that he was gaining on her, and used every effort to overtake her before she could reach Panama. He promised his chain of gold to the man who should first descry her. At length, on the 25th of February, sixty or seventy miles north of the equator, and within two days' sail of Panama, his object was gained. It was even facilitated by a mistake made by the captain of the *Cacafuego*. Seeing a vessel behind him, he slackened speed, intending to ask her destination, and to offer her protection. He had no suspicion that the *Golden Hind* could belong to any nation but his own. Drake, however, soon undeceived him. Approaching the *Cacafuego*, he challenged her to submit. The astonished captain asked what he meant thereby. In answer, Drake " shot her mast overboard with a great piece, and, having wounded the master with an arrow, the ship yielded." He took from her an abundance of jewels and precious stones, eighty pounds of gold, twenty-six tons of raw silver, and thirteen chests of silver coin, the whole being valued at little short of 90,000*l*.\*

By this capture, following those at Callao, the *Golden Hind* was filled to the utmost with valuable property. Drake had made as much profit by piracy in the Southern Seas as was possible with the tonnage to which his expedition had been reduced. According to the plan with which he had left England, it was now his business to return to it, as quickly and easily as he could. But he found that there was no quick or easy way open to him. Toilsome and perilous as his outward voyage had been, the toil and peril of the homeward voyage would necessarily be very much greater. The Spanish colonists and traders along nearly the whole western side of South America, whom he had hitherto taken by surprise, would now be watching and planning for his overthrow. He was therefore induced to take a new course.

\* HAKLUYT, vol. iii., pp. 734, 735, 746—748; HERRERA, cited by SOUTHEY, vol. iii., pp. 147—157.

Little inducement from fear was needed where there was a prospect of fresh glory; and the project which seems now first to have occurred to him promised glory without limit if it could be successfully accomplished. When he started on his expedition, England was full of interest in the scheme, to which Frobisher's three famous voyages had been devoted, for reaching the Indies by sailing along the northern limits of America, from east to west. Drake considered that the work in which Frobisher had failed would be excellently done by him, if, after sailing up to the north-western corner of America, he could reach home by sailing round its northern shores, from west to east. Accordingly, as soon as the plundered *Cacafuego* had been dismissed, somewhere near the equator, and not far from the Galapagos Islands, he announced his project to his hardy little crew, now numbering about fifty men. "All of us," says one of the number, "willingly hearkened to our General's advice, which was, first, to seek out some convenient place to trim our ship, and store ourselves with wood and water and such provisions as we could get; and, thenceforward, to hasten on our intended journey for the discovery of the said passage, through which we might with joy return to our longed homes."

That bold resolution having been taken, Drake sailed due north, leaving Panama on his left, towards the coast of Nicaragua. Reaching a convenient bay in that neighbourhood on the 16th of March, he spent a week or ten days in making preparations for their projected voyage, and seeing that the *Golden Hind* was fit to enter upon it. Then, plundering a few ships that came in his way, and stopping once to ransack a Spanish settlement in the Gulf of Tehuantepec, he proceeded with all possible speed upon his new enterprise. Quitting the Mexican coast on the 16th of April, he sailed westward into the open sea for some fifteen hundred miles, and thence, for about two thousand, in a northern direction. He was thus, on the 2nd of June, brought very near to the most northern shore of California, in 42 degrees of latitude. But on that day a sudden change of temperature so frightened many of his followers, who appear to have already grown tired of the prospect, that he was forced to abandon his projected Arctic voyaging. "The night following," says one of the number, evidently exaggerating, "we found such an alteration of heat into extreme and nipping cold, that our men in general did grievously complain thereof; some of them feeling their healths much impaired thereby. Neither was it that this chanced in the night alone; but the day following carried with it not only the marks, but the stings and force of the night going before. Our meat, as soon as it was removed from the fire, would presently in a manner be frozen up; and our ropes and tacklings in a few days were grown to that stiffness that what three men before were able to perform now six men, with their best strength and utmost endeavours, were hardly able to accomplish, whereby a sudden and great discouragement seized upon the minds of our men, and they were possessed with a great mislike and doubt of any good to be done that way."

It is clear that the sailors, accustomed to exciting piracy in tropical waters, were weary of their monotonous sailing in a colder region, and therefore made much of a trifling spring-frost: other than trifling it could not be, in the same latitude as New York, on the 3rd of June. Drake did his best to encourage them, and addressed arguments that strengthened their faint hearts for a few hours. "As well by comfortable speeches of the Divine Providence and of God's loving care over His children, out of the Scriptures, as also by other good and profitable persuasions, adding thereto his own cheerful example," we are told, "he so stirred them up to put on a good courage, and to acquit themselves like men to endure some short extremity to have the speedier comfort, and a little trouble to obtain the greater glory, that every man was thoroughly armed with willingness, and resolved to see the uttermost, if it were possible, of what good was to be done that way."

The willingness and the resolution lasted for two days, and took them very nearly up to Vancouver's Island. "The 5th day of June," says the fear-stricken chronicler, "we were forced by contrary winds to run in with the shore, which we then first descried, and to cast anchor in a bad bay, the best road we could for the present meet with; where we were not without some danger by reason of the many extreme gusts and flaws that beat upon us; which, if they ceased and were still at any time, immediately upon their intermission there followed such vile, thick, and stinking fogs, against which the sea prevailed nothing, till the gusts of wind again removed them, which brought with them such extremity and violence when they came that there was no dealing or resisting against them. In this place was no abiding for us, and to go further north the extremity of the cold—which had now utterly discouraged all our men—would not permit us."

Very much to the satisfaction of Drake's crew and, though very much to his own annoyance, doubtless in the end to the good of all, a strong and steady north wind set in, and " commanded them to the southward, whether they would or no." In the course of twelve days they traversed nearly seven hundred miles of coast-line, and on the 17th of June " it pleased God to send them into a fair and good bay," which appears to have been what is now the harbour of San Francisco.

There Drake remained five weeks, repairing some damage that had been done to his ship, and having much friendly intercourse with the natives. After two days of cautious exchanging of presents and other tokens of mutual kindliness, the English, who were in tents, with their ship on dry land, saw, with some fear, that the Indians were gathering in the distance in large numbers. " Presently," says our chronicler, "came down from the country a great multitude, and among them a man of goodly stature and comely personage, who was the King himself, accompanied by many tall and warlike men. Before his Majesty advanced, two ambassadors presented themselves to the General to announce his approach, and continued speaking for about an hour, at the end of which the Hioh, or King, making as princely a show as he possibly could, with all his train came forward; in the course of which they cried continually, after a singing manner, with a lusty courage. As they drew nearer and nearer unto us, so did they more and more strive to behave themselves with a certain comeliness and gravity in all their actions." The "comeliness and gravity" were of a curious sort. The men sang and danced as they approached; the women "tore themselves till the face, breasts, and other parts were bespattered with blood." As they bore no arms, save a few quaintly-ornamented clubs hanging from the necks of the chief persons, Drake made no opposition to their coming. "Then they made signs to our General to have him sit down. To whom, both the King and divers others made several orations, or rather, indeed, if we had understood them, supplications that he would take the province and kingdom into his hand and become their king and patron, making signs that they would resign unto him their right and title in the whole land and become his vassals; which, that they might make us indeed believe that it was their true meaning and intent, the King himself, with great reverence, joyfully singing a song, set the crown upon his head, enriched his neck with chains, and, offering unto him many other things, honoured him with the name of Hioh. They added thereto, as it might seem, a song and dance of triumph, because they were not only visited of the gods, for so they still judged us to be, but that the great and chief god was now become their god, their king and patron, and themselves were become the only happy and blessed people in the world. Which thing our General thought not meet to reject, because he knew not what honour and profit it might be to our country. Wherefore, in the name and to the use of her Majesty, he took the sceptre, crown, and dignity of the said country in his hands, wishing that the riches and treasure thereof might so conveniently be transported to the enriching of her kingdom at home."

To the district of which he was thus crowned king, Drake gave the name of New Albion. He little thought that in its precincts, hidden only by a thin coating of earth, was Californian gold rivalling in value the fancied wealth that Spaniards sought for and all Europe craved after, in the fabled El Dorado of the south.

King Drake, during the ensuing month, saw much of his Indian subjects. "They are a people of a very tractable, free, and loving nature, without guile or treachery," we are told. "Their bows and arrows would do no great harm, being weak, and fitter for children than for men; and yet the men were so strong of body, that what two or three of our people could scarcely bear, one of them would take upon his back, and, without grudging, carry it up hill and down hill an English mile together." The women, who wore clothes, while the men went nearly naked, were praised for being "very obedient and serviceable to their husbands." "The common sort of the people," says another of the voyagers, "leaving the King and his guard with our General, scattered themselves, together with their sacrifices, among our people, taking a diligent view of every person; and such as pleased their fancy, which were the youngest, they, enclosing them about, offered their sacrifices unto them, with lamentable weeping, scratching and tearing the flesh from their faces with their nails, whereof issued abundance of blood. But we used signs to them of disliking this, and stayed their hands from force, and directed them upwards to the living God, whom only they ought to worship. Every third day they brought their sacrifices unto us, until they understood our meaning, that we had no pleasure in them. Yet they could not long be absent from us, but daily frequented our company to the hour of our departure; which departure seemed so grievous unto them that their joy was turned into sorrow. They entreated us that, being absent, we would remember them, and by stealth provided a sacrifice, which we misliked."\*

Drake left New Albion and the coast of America on the 23rd of July. Having been hindered, seven weeks before, by contrary winds and the fears of his sailors from pursuing his design of going home by the icy seas to the north of North America, he determined to follow the lead of Magellan, and circumvent the world by passing through the Southern and the Indian Seas into the Atlantic Ocean. This he did in exactly a year, and with skilful and heroic seamanship, which rivalled, if it did

\* HAKLUYT, vol. iii., pp. 441, 442.

not surpass, that shown by Magellan; but it was not marked by many very memorable incidents.

After sixty-eight days of straight and quick sailing, he reached what seem to have been the Pelew Islands, in Polynesian waters, on the 30th of September. These, from the way in which he was treated by the natives, he called the Islands of Thieves. He sighted the Philippines on the 16th of October, and the Moluccas on the 3rd of November. There he made a famous beginning of English intercourse with the East Indies. He was preparing to anchor at Tidore, when some natives, who could speak Portuguese, came in a boat to tell him that the Portuguese tyrants, having been driven out of Ternate, had now settled in Tidore, and that, if he would go to the former place, its King would join him in altogether expelling their common enemies from the East. Drake had had fighting enough since he left England, and now only wished to reach home safely and quickly. But he went to Ternate and exchanged courtesies with its King.

Of this King's state and costume, which was all that, during their hasty visit, the English were able to observe closely, we have ample details. "Four great and large canoes" were sent out to meet him, "in every one whereof were certain of his greatest states that were about him, attired in white lawn of cloth of Calicut, having over their heads, from the one end of the canoe to the other, a covering of thin perfumed mats, borne up with a frame made of reeds for the same use, under which every one did sit in his order, according to his dignity; divers of whom, being of good age and gravity, did make an ancient and fatherly show. There were also divers young and comely men attired in white, as were the others. The rest were soldiers, which stood in comely order round about on both sides; without whom sat the rowers in certain galleries, which, being three on a side all along the canoes, did lie off from the side thereof three or four yards, one being orderly builded lower than another, in every of which galleries were the number of fourscore rowers. These canoes were furnished with warlike munition, every man, for the most part, having his sword and target, with his dagger, besides other weapons, as lances, calivers, darts, bows and arrows; also every canoe had a small cast cannon mounted at the least one full yard upon a stock set upright." These messengers conducted Drake into the harbour on the same evening, and there he sumptuously entertained the King of Ternate. Next morning, himself staying on shipboard, he sent some of his followers to Court. "The King being yet absent, there sat in their places sixty grave personages, all which were said to be of the King's Council. There were besides four grave persons, apparelled all in red down to the ground, and attired on their heads like the Turks; and these were said to be Romans,* and liegers there to keep continual traffic with the people of Ternate. There were also two Turks, liegers in this place, and one Italian. The King at last came in, guarded with twelve lances,

---

* This is probably a misprint. They were evidently traders from some Asiatic state.

covered over with a rich canopy, with embossed gold. Our men rising to meet him, he graciously did welcome and entertain them. He was attired after the manner of the country, but more sumptuously than the rest. From his waist down to the ground was all cloth of gold, and the same very rich. His legs were bare, but on his feet were a pair of shoes made of Cordovan skin. In the attire of his head were finely wreathed hooped rings of gold, and about his neck he had a chain of perfect gold, the links whereof were great and one gold double. On his fingers he had six very fair jewels, and, sitting in his chair of state, at his right hand stood a page with a fan in his hand, breathing and gathering the air to the King. The fan was in length two foot, and in breadth one foot, set with eight sapphires, richly embroidered, and knit to a staff three foot in length, by which the page did hold and move it."*

More important than these exhibitions of wealth was a treaty for trade and mutual protection which Drake made, on behalf of Queen Elizabeth, with the King of Ternate. He did not take much account of it; but in later years it became a famous precedent for English commerce with the East.

The *Golden Hind*, with plenty of fresh provisions and some cloves, the first bought by Englishmen in the Moluccas, left Ternate on the 9th of November. On the 11th she halted at a little island eastward of Celebes, and there four weeks were spent in strengthening her for the long sea voyage which was to bring her

* HAKLUYT, vol. iii., pp. 739, 740.

back to England. All that strength was needed on the 9th of January, 1580, when, after more than three weeks of rough beating about among the dangerous currents and more dangerous shoals in the neighbourhood of Celebes, she struck on a rock. "Here," says the quaintest of all quaint historians, "they struck; having ground too much and yet too little to land on, and water too much and yet too little to sail in. Had God, who, as the wise man saith, holdeth the winds in His fist, but opened His little finger and let out the smallest blast, they had undoubtedly been cast away. But there blew not any wind all the while. Then they, conceiving aright that the best way to lighten the ship was first to ease it of the burthen of their sins by true repentance, humbled themselves by fasting under the hand of God. Afterward they received the communion, dining on Christ in the sacrament, expecting no other than to sup with him in Heaven. Then they cast out of the ship six pieces of great ordnance, threw overboard as much wealth as would break the heart of a miser to think on't, with much sugar, and packs of spices; making a caudle of the sea round about. Then they betook themselves to their prayers, the best lever at such a dead lift indeed, and it pleased God that the wind, formerly their enemy, became their friend."* Perhaps it would have been more devout to have prayed before working, but Drake and

---

* FULLER, *Holy State*, p. 127. Fuller's version is not quite correct in the details. Drake threw overboard eight, not six guns, and certainly sacrificed no part of his golden cargo.

his comrades knew when to be pious and when to be prudent. Yet in this case neither piety nor prudence helped them. Their ship stuck fast in spite of both, until at low tide, by a lucky accident, she slipped off the rock and floated in fair water.

Saved from that imminent peril, they endured no other throughout the remainder of their voyage. After refreshing themselves at Java and another island in the East Indian archipelago, they crossed the Indian Ocean, and, with rare freedom from storms, passed the Cape of Good Hope, which they considered "a most stately thing, and the fairest cape they had seen in the whole circumference of the earth."* Then they traversed the western coast of Africa, calling at Sierra Leone for two days; and at length, on the 26th of September—"which," says the chronicler, "was Monday in the just and ordinary reckoning of those that had stayed at home, but in our computation was the Lord's day or Sunday"—they anchored in Plymouth Harbour.

There were no bounds to the joy of Drake's fellow-townsmen, who, from John Winter's report of his disappearance near Magellan's Strait, had learnt to think of him as long since dead, when he once more trod their streets and talked with them of his exploits and escapes. But he only remained in Plymouth a few days. In his little *Golden Hind* he hastened up to Deptford, and there, leaving the ship in safe keeping, proceeded to make personal report of his achievements to Queen Elizabeth, then keeping Court at Richmond. It appears

* HAKLUYT, vol. iii., p. 741.

that he was not at once permitted to make this personal report. "The people generally," it is recorded, "with exceeding admiration, applauded his wonderful long adventures and rich prize;" but "the Queen paused," and statesmen and courtiers, following her instructions, likewise held aloof.*

There was good reason for this, and no unkindness to Drake in it. Early in the year there had been great stir in the law courts and among diplomatists about the comparatively small quantity of treasure taken from the Portuguese by Drake, which Winter had brought home in the *Elizabeth*. The Portuguese ambassador had angrily claimed restitution, and restitution had only been withheld through the convenient tardiness of the Court of Admiralty.† And now Drake had come home with fifty times as much treasure, acquired by piracy upon Spanish ships and in Spanish waters. The Spanish ambassador stormed and raged, demanded instant punishment of Drake, and immediate compensation for his evil deeds.‡ Elizabeth had learnt to think lightly of Spanish threats and Spanish claims. She saw that war with Spain was inevitable, and was, in her own slow way, and according to the scanty powers of her Exchequer, steadily preparing for it. But there were many weighty reasons for avoiding an immediate rupture, and she considered that an immediate rupture would very likely follow her public approval of Drake's pro-

* STOW, *Annals*, p. 807.
† RECORD OFFICE MSS., *Domestic*, vol. cxxxix., Nos. 5, 24.
‡ *Ibid.*, vol. cxliv,. No. 1.

ceedings. Therefore she and her statesmen allowed it to go forth that they "misliked and reproached him," and that arrangements were being made for "all possible disgraces against the master thief of the unknown world."* She gave orders on the 24th of October, only a few days after his arrival at Deptford, that all the treasure he had brought home was to be sent up to London, and be placed in the Tower for safe keeping, for equitable distribution in due time among its proper owners.†

That much was made public. It was kept private that this arrangement was made with the full concurrence of Drake himself, and that from the treasure, before its removal to London, 10,000*l*.'s worth was to be left in Drake's hands, "the leaving of which sum in his hands was to be kept most sacred to himself alone."‡

Thus, though it was prudently kept secret, Queen Elizabeth's implied approval of Drake's conduct was prompt and clear. It was soon shown yet more clearly in public. Her special reasons for keeping on good terms with Spain soon became less urgent, and then, when the Spanish ambassador again made claim for Drake's punishment and the restitution of his prizes, she haughtily replied, "that the Spaniards, by their ill-treatment of her subjects, to whom, contrary to the law of nations, they had prohibited commerce, had drawn these mischiefs upon themselves; that Drake should be

---

\* Stow, p. 807.
† Record Office MSS., *Domestic*, vol. cxliii., No. 30; vol. cxliv., No. 17.
‡ *Ibid.*

forthcoming to answer according to law, if he were convicted by good evidence and testimony of having committed anything against law and right; and that the goods in question were purposely laid by that satisfaction might be made to the Spaniards, although the Queen had spent a greater sum of money than Drake had brought in against those rebels whom the Spaniards had raised and encouraged against her, both in Ireland and in England."* And Queen Elizabeth herself was then no longer backward in showing that she considered Drake had both law and right on his side. On the 4th of April, 1581, she went down to Deptford, there to be entertained by him at a sumptuous banquet on board the *Golden Hind*, and on that occasion knighted him for his famous prowess and its famous consequences.† That was a signal for universal heaping of favour upon him. Cautious statesmen and jealous courtiers forgot their caution and their jealousy in the

* CAMDEN, *Annals*, p. 255.
† STOW, p. 807. The *Golden Hind*, by Queen Elizabeth's orders, was preserved at Deptford, till it could be preserved no longer, "for a monument to all posterity of that famous and worthy exploit of Sir Francis Drake." It was afterwards taken to pieces, and the best parts of the wood were made into a chair, and lodged in the University of Oxford; whereupon Cowley wrote these lines:—

"To this great ship, which round the globe has run,
And matched in race the chariot of the sun;
This Pythagorean ship, (for it may claim,
Without presumption, so deserv'd a name,)
By knowledge once, and transformation now,
In her new shape this sacred port allow.
Drake and his ship could ne'er have wished from fate
A happier station or more blest estate;
For lo! a seat of endless rest is given
To her in Oxford, and to him in Heaven."

utterance of his praises. Merchants and men of science applauded him as one of the greatest friends of commerce and promoters of geographical knowledge ever sent to bless the world; and every English patriot thanked God that so mighty a champion of his country's honour, so daring a punisher of foreign insolence, had been suffered to rise up among them.*

The admiration with which Drake's skill and prowess were regarded was in no way lessened by the great pecuniary gains attendant upon them. Besides the 10,000*l.* secretly reserved for Drake, and the great quantity of jewels, precious stones, and other costly articles of which no account is given, the bullion lodged in the Tower was worth about 60,000*l.*; and, after some money had been paid to the Spanish ambassador in partial compensation for the injuries done by Drake to private individuals—which money, being intercepted by Philip II., was used by him in meeting some of the expenses of his war in the Netherlands—the various courtiers and merchants who contributed to the fitting out of the expedition received 47*l.* for every 1*l.* advanced by them.†

* One of the thousand compliments to Drake appeared on the signboard, long standing, of the Queen's Head Tavern :—

"O Nature! to Old England still
Continue these mistakes;
Still give us for our King such Queens,
And for our **Dux** such **Drakes**."

—BARROW, *Memoirs of the Naval Worthies of Queen Elizabeth's Reign*, p. 116.

† RECORD OFFICE MSS., *Domestic*, vol. cxliv., No. 60; LEWES ROBERTS, *Merchant's Map of Commerce* (1638); BARROW, *Life of Drake*, pp. 175–177.

This success, of course, added to the eagerness with which Drake and others applied themselves to projects for carrying on the work of voyaging in the Southern Seas which he had made so famous. He had only been in England a month or two before it was suggested, apparently by Sir Francis Walsingham, to form "a company of such as should trade beyond the equinoctial line," with Drake for its life-governor.* A few months later, in April, 1581, proposals were submitted to Elizabeth's Government for the fitting out of an armed expedition of eight ships and six pinnaces, under Sir Francis Drake, Edward Fenton, and others, which should have for its "first enterprise" the attacking of Spanish galleons in the West Indies and other parts near at hand; and for its "second enterprise" the establishment of her Majesty's right to trade with India and the spice islands in the Indian Archipelago, to which Portugal, now annexed to Spain, had hitherto laid exclusive claim.†

Neither of these enterprises, however, was at once adopted; and in the voyage next undertaken in supplement to Drake's exploits Drake adventured nothing but his money. There was still a show of peace with Spain, and it was not just then thought prudent openly to engage in further defiance of Philip II. Therefore the defiance was entered upon in an underhand way, by the perversion from its original purpose of the voyage by which, as we have seen, it was at first proposed to

* RECORD OFFICE MSS., Domestic, vol. cxliv., No. 44.
† Ibid., vol. cxlviii., Nos. 43–47.

send Martin Frobisher upon a fourth search for the north-west passage to Cathay.* How or why this original purpose was modified we are not told; but it is easy to understand that, when the failure of Frobisher's three previous voyages was contrasted with the brilliant success of Drake's achievements, the subscribers of 11,600*l.* should prefer to speculate in the new instead of in the old direction, especially when Drake himself had subscribed 1,000*l.*, and was a principal adviser in the undertaking. At any rate, in the revised instructions issued to Frobisher a few weeks before his intended departure, this clause was inserted:—" We will this voyage shall be only for trade, and not for discovery of the passage to Cathay."† Soon after that Martin Frobisher's name was, in the instructions, replaced by that of Edward Fenton, and in the further instructions added thereto, it was oddly said, " You shall take your right course to the isles of the Moluccas for the better discovery of the north-west passage."‡

This voyage was excellent in intention. " We will," it was said in the instructions, " that you deal altogether in this voyage like good and honest merchants, trafficking and exchanging ware for ware, with all courtesy to the nations you shall deal with, as well ethnicks as others; and for that cause you shall instruct all those that shall go with you that, whensoever you or any of you shall happen to come in any place to con-

* See vol. i., pp. 175, 176.
† British Museum MSS., *Cotton*, Otho E. viii., fols. 87-92.
‡ Hakluyt, vol. iii., pp. 754-757.

ference with the people of those parts, in all your doings and theirs, you so behave yourselves towards the said people, as may rather procure their friendship and good liking by courtesy than move them to offence or misliking; and especially you shall have great care of the performance of your word and promise to them." They were also "straightly enjoined, as they would answer the contrary by the laws of the land, that, neither going, tarrying abroad, nor returning, they should spoil or take anything from any of the Queen's friends or any Christians, without paying justly for the same, nor use any manner of violence or force against any such, except in their own defence."*

Catholic Spaniards being looked upon by Protestant Englishmen as neither Queen's friends nor Christians, they easily turned those orders into a licence for piracy against 'Spain. Fenton himself seems not to have taken that view altogether; but it was the view taken by the most enterprising of his comrades and by the most zealous of his employers. "I wish all the King of Spain's gold in their bellies, to temper the pride of such a tyrant," was the sentiment of one of the principal setters out of the expedition.†

The expedition consisted of four ships, the *Leicester*, with Edward Fenton for admiral, William Hawkins, apparently a nephew of Sir John Hawkins, for lieutenant, and Christopher Hall, Frobisher's old comrade, for master, and a hundred and twenty other officers and

* HAKLUYT, vol. iii., pp. 754-757.
† BRITISH MUSEUM MSS., *Cotton*, Otho E. viii., fol. 121.

men; the *Edward Bonaventure*, under Luke Ward, with a crew of eighty-two; the *Francis*, of which John Drake, Sir Francis Drake's brother, was captain, having seventeen sailors; and the *Elizabeth*, under Thomas Skevington, with sixteen sailors.* They left Plymouth on the 1st of June, 1582. On the day of starting began "great grudging and choler," through Fenton's intentional or accidental leaving behind of William Hawkins, John Drake, and some others of the company. They soon overtook the main body of the fleet; but, says Hawkins, "I had not from that time till my coming home any good countenance."† Quarrels and jealousies lasted all through the voyage, and helped to bring it to an early end; although, for any good or honourable issue that it had, it might better have been ended much earlier. Fenton loitered about the African coast, apparently looking out for Spanish prizes but finding none, between the 26th of June and the middle of October. He had been ordered to go round to the East Indies, by the way of the Cape of Good Hope. Instead of that he crossed the Atlantic, and on the 1st of December he reached the Brazilian coast. There he loitered about for a further period, until the 24th of January, 1583, when he fell in with three great Spanish ships of 600, 500, and 400 tons burthen respectively.

* BRITISH MUSEUM MSS., *Sloane*, No. 2146, fols. 72, 73. A very curious and copious history of this voyage and its preliminaries, from Jan. 14, 1582, by Richard Madox, the chaplain of the *Leicester*, is in the BRITISH MUSEUM among the *Cotton* MSS., Appendix xlvii.; and *Titus*, B viii., fols. 171-121.
† *Ibid.*, *Cotton*, Otho E. viii., fol. 201.

With these he fought, and they were driven off, with the loss of a hundred or more Spaniards against six or eight Englishmen; but Fenton was not active enough to turn his victory to any advantage. Perhaps this was partly due to the weakness of his own men, many of whom suffered severely from scurvy and other diseases. In the *Leicester* alone about forty died during the voyage, and the sickness was as great in the other ships. He therefore returned to England, sorely against the wishes of his comrades, who openly taunted him with ignorance and cowardice.

On one occasion he told Hawkins, who seems to have been the leader of this half-mutinous opposition, that Sir Francis Drake had only made himself rich and famous by playing the thief and pirate. "Do you think *I* will?" he added; "nay, I know how to make my voyage without any of your evil advices." "When we come home," answered Hawkins, "if you call Sir Francis thief, I will see how you can justify it; for when we came both forth we were gentlemen alike." Thereto Fenton angrily exclaimed, "Thou shalt not be so good as I so long as thou livest." "What make you of me then?" said Hawkins. "A knave, a villain, and a boy," answered Fenton. "If I were at home, I would not be afeard to follow you in any ground in England," replied Hawkins, anxious, if possible, to keep down his anger; "but here, in this place, for quietness' sake, I let it pass, and will bear every wrong, be it ever so great." "Wilt thou so?" said Fenton. To which Hawkins answered, "Yea, truly." "Then," it is added, "the General would have drawn his long knife and have stabbed Hawkins; and, intercepted of that, he took up his long staff, and was coming at Hawkins, but the master, Mr. Bannister, Mr. Cotton, and Simon Fernandes stayed his fury."*

Fortunately that altercation occurred in the Downs, only a few days before the return of the unfortunate and ill-managed fleet on the 29th of June, 1583.† On that day Fenton wrote up to Lord Treasurer Burghley and to the Earl of Leicester to excuse himself and explain the causes of the disasters;‡ but he fell into disgrace, which nothing but his favour at Court prevented from being his utter ruin.

Many other futile attempts were made in later years to follow in Drake's track; and in 1586 an attempt was made, which was by no means futile, by Thomas Cavendish. Cavendish, born about 1556, was the scion of an old Suffolk family, long resident at Trimley Saint Martin, near Ipswich. He is reported in a few years to have squandered most of his patrimony " in gallantry and following the Court." Then, like many other adventurous noblemen and gentlemen, he took to piracy as a means of money-making.§ He certainly became a

* This is from Hawkins's own report.—BRITISH MUSEUM MSS., Otho E. viii., fol. 205.

† Very full accounts of this luckless expedition are in HAKLUYT, vol. iii., pp. 757–768 (by Luke Ward), and among the BRITISH MUSEUM MSS., *Cotton*, Otho E. viii., fols. 179–200 (by John Walker), besides the narratives of Hawkins and Madox already cited.

‡ RECORD OFFICE MSS., *Domestic*, vol. clxi., No. 16; BRITISH MUSEUM MSS., *Cotton*, Otho E. viii., fols. 157–159.

§ SIR WILLIAM MONSON's *Tracts* in Churchill's Collection, vol. iii., pp. 368, 369.

fierce and skilful pirate. His first schooling in seamanship was as a volunteer, with a ship of his own, in the expedition led by Sir Richard Grenville, under Sir Walter Raleigh's directions, for establishing the luckless colony of Virginia in 1585.* Having landed the colonists he shared with Grenville in some successful piracy, and, immediately after his return to England, prepared to embark next year in a much greater undertaking, modelled closely upon the example of Sir Francis Drake.

Entirely at his own expense, as it would seem, he fitted out a little fleet which consisted of two vessels built for the purpose, the *Desire*, of 120 tons burthen, and the *Content*, of 60 tons, and of the *Hugh Gallant*, of 40 tons, which had seen some previous service. The crews of the three numbered a hundred and twenty-three persons, and they took with them enough provisions to last two years. John Brewer—who had accompanied Drake in his great voyage, and who was captain of the *Content*, Cavendish himself having command of the *Desire*—was their chief guide and pilot.†

They left Plymouth on the 21st of July, and, after a small fight with five Spanish ships which they met near the coast of Spain on the 26th, proceeded to the African shore. Calling at Sierra Leone, they destroyed one of the Negro towns and took what little spoil they could find, apparently out of mere love of mischief.

---

\* See vol. i., p. 212.
† The following details are derived chiefly from the narrative of Francis Pretty, in HAKLUYT, vol. iii., pp. 803–825.

Then, between the 6th of September and the 1st of November, they sailed across the Atlantic, and on the latter date anchored off Brazil, near the Island of San Sebastian. Halting there to set up a pinnace, and also at a harbour which they discovered lower down, and called Port Desire, they reached Magellan's Strait on the 6th of January, 1587.

Anchoring for the night at the entrance to the Strait, they saw signal-lights on the shore, and next morning Cavendish went in a boat to see where they were and what they meant. He found that here were twenty-three Spaniards, the miserable remnant of a force of thirty-five hundred that, on the report of Drake's achievements, had gone out to build a fort and oppose the passage of the Strait by any other English ships.

This expedition had been altogether disastrous. Of the twenty-three ships that quitted Seville in September, 1581, under Diego Flores de Valdez as leader of the fleet, and Pedro Sarmiento as governor of the intended colony, five of the largest, with eight hundred men on board, were wrecked almost before the Spanish coast was out of sight. The others were driven back to Cadiz, and two were so much damaged as to be of no further use. The remaining sixteen started again in December, and a hundred and fifty men died of sickness on the way to Rio Janeiro. The survivors, weak and out of heart, stayed in Brazil until November, 1582, while De Valdez and Sarmiento quarrelled as to which of them was master of the expedition during this delay in the voyage. Another ship had then to be broken up as unserviceable, and before Magellan's Strait was reached another and the largest that remained, containing three hundred and fifty persons and a great quantity of stores, was utterly wrecked. That misfortune so frightened De Valdez that he returned to Brazil, losing yet another ship on the way. There he heard of Fenton's cruising in the neighbourhood, but had neither courage nor power to go in pursuit of him. The three ships which Fenton attacked in January were three which, finding them too rotten to be of further use to him, De Valdez had sent homewards with a cargo of three hundred sick and unserviceable Spaniards. Perhaps it was fear of Fenton that drove those who stayed behind, about a thousand men in ten ships, to proceed at last towards their destination. They started again with this object in January, 1583, and after coming within sight of the Strait were again driven back. Another ship was wrecked, and three were detached with some of the company, who wished to try and work their way separately up to Chili. When De Valdez returned to Brazil and anchored off Rio Janeiro, however, he found there four fresh ships laden with stores that had been sent from Spain with assistance for the colony. With them and with some of his followers he returned to Spain, leaving Sarmiento to make further trial of the colonizing project, with five ships and five hundred and thirty persons. Sarmiento was a somewhat better leader. After wintering in Brazil, he started on the 2nd of December for the

Strait. He reached it on the 1st of February, 1584, and, though deserted on the same evening by the crews of three ships, after the colonists had been landed, he found himself at the head of a company of four hundred men and thirty women. With these he founded a city called Nombre de Jesus on the northern corner of the Strait, and a town of San Felipe a little way in the channel; but in crossing from the one settlement to the other, he was driven out to sea with his ship and a scanty crew by a storm that lasted twenty days. At the end of that term he found that he had been beaten back to the neighbourhood of Rio Janeiro. Some of his followers said that this was according to his wishes. If so, he suffered for his treachery. His ship was wrecked, and when, after long waiting, he was on his way to Spain in another, he was captured by three ships belonging to Sir Walter Raleigh and taken prisoner to London, to be introduced to Queen Elizabeth, who, as he stated, honourably received him, and sent him home with a present of 1,000 crowns.*

That was about the time of Cavendish's departure for the South Sea. The colonists whom Sarmiento left behind had been left to live or die as best they could; and when Cavendish discovered them he found that all had died with the exception of twenty-three or twenty-four, whose life must have been worse than death. "It seemed unto us," says one of the English voyagers, "that their whole living for a great space was altogether upon mussels and limpets; for there was not anything

\* BURNEY, vol. ii., pp. 45–57.

else to be had, except some deer which came out of the mountains down to the fresh rivers to drink. During the time that they were there, which was two years at the least, they could never have any thing to grow or in any wise prosper. And on the other side, the Indians oftentimes preyed upon them, until their victuals grew short, so that they died like dogs in their houses and in their clothes, wherein we found them still at our coming; until that in the end, the town being wonderfully tainted with the smell and the savour of the dead people, the rest which remained alive were driven to forsake the town and to go along the sea-side and seek their victuals to preserve them from starving. And so they lived for the space of a year and more with roots, leaves, and sometimes a fowl which they might kill."

The name of this miserable town of San Felipe—he did not visit Nombre de Jesus, but it seems before that time to have come to utter ruin—Cavendish changed into Port Famine. He stayed there several days and took on board one of the miserable colonists, Tomé Hernandez by name. Neither friends nor foes in his own day charged him with any inhumanity in leaving the others to their dismal fate.

The Strait of Magellan was safely passed through by the 24th of February. Cavendish then proceeded northwards in the track of Drake, but with freedom from such storms as made havoc of Drake's fleet. Along the coast of South America, he and his comrades amused themselves with some fighting with the natives.

But they found no Spanish barks or galleons to capture; and when, on the 30th of March, they approached Valparaiso, there to use Hernandez as an agent in treating for the purchase of provisions, their plan came to nothing through the cleverness of Hernandez, who ran away, "notwithstanding all his deep and damnable oaths that he would never forsake them, but would die on their side before he would be false."

Hernandez did worse than that. On the following day, while the English were searching for water and other refreshment a few miles out of Valparaiso, he assisted the Spaniards in attacking them. In some sharp skirmishing twelve Englishmen were killed or taken, apparently without any successful retaliation on the part of their countrymen.

Cavendish sailed northward, vainly seeking for prizes until the 23rd of April, when, near Arica, he captured a small bark, full of wine. The crew escaped in a boat, and the bark, christened the *George*, was added for a short time to the little fleet. On the same day Cavendish seized a larger ship, and another fell into his hands on the 25th of the month; but both these, being nearly empty and of no use, were set on fire. Other prizes then came frequently in his way, and he rivalled Drake for the boldness with which he plundered ships and ransacked towns with a force so small that it was only saved from certain destruction by the rapidity of its movements and the smartness with which it avoided the elaborate efforts made for its overthrow. Unlike Drake, Cavendish was sometimes over bold. Having lost twelve men at Valparaiso on the 1st of April, he lost twelve more at Puna, an island in the Gulf of Guayaquil, on the 2nd of June. Twenty Englishmen were carelessly searching the district for sheep, fowls, and the like, when a formidable body of Spaniards attacked them with such energy that only eight escaped. This time, however, Cavendish had his revenge. "The selfsame day," says the curt chronicler, glorying in his cruelty, "we went on shore again with seventy men, and had a fresh skirmish with the enemies, and drave them to retire, being a hundred Spaniards serving with muskets and two hundred Indians with bows, arrows and darts. This done, we set fire on the town and burnt it to the ground, having in it to the number of three hundred houses, and shortly after made havoc of their fields, orchards and gardens, and burnt four great ships which were in building on the stocks."

Piracy, which was too brave and romantic as practised by Drake to deserve much blame, wore its proper shape of ugliness in Cavendish's hands. Yet Cavendish was better than many of his fellows. He thought, like Drake, that he was a chosen messenger to pour out the vials of God's wrath upon the devil-inspired Spaniards, and that all the booty he took upon earth was only a foretaste of the heavenly reward which he was earning.

This foretaste was considerable during Cavendish's seven months' cruize in the waters extending from Chili up to Mexico. On the 5th of June, when he set sail from Puna, he found he had not men enough to manage all his ships. Therefore he sunk the *Hugh Gallant*. In the other two vessels, leaving the Quito and Panama districts to his right, he then proceeded almost in a straight line to the Mexican coast. Near Acapulco he captured, on the 9th of July, two ships, one of which being just as large as the *Desire*, furnished her with a very serviceable supply of new sails and rigging, besides other valuables. On the 23rd of the month he landed at a town called Guatulco, which he sacked before burning its hundred houses. Among the treasure taken were six hundred bags of indigo, worth 40 crowns apiece, and four hundred bags of cocoa berries, worth 10 crowns apiece. "These cocoas," it is said, "go among them for meat and money. A hundred and fifty of them are in value one real of plate in ready payment. They are very like an almond, but are nothing so pleasant in taste. They eat them, and make drink of them."

At Guatulco, Cavendish brought upon himself the special wrath of pious Catholics by burning a church. The church was very old, and very sacred by reason of a great wooden cross which Saint Andrew was believed to have planted there when he preached Christianity to the Aztecs of Mexico. The story goes that Cavendish, in excess of sacrilegious spite, smeared this cross with pitch and heaped it round with reeds to make it burn the brighter; but that, after the reeds and the pitch had been burning for three days, the Spaniards, returning to their ruined home, found it, not only uninjured, but even shining with a celestial lustre. "The report of its miraculous preservation spread far and wide, and from all parts devotees came to visit it and to carry away fragments, the smallest splinter of which, if cast into a sea, stilled a tempest; if thrown into a fire, quenched the flames; and, if put in water, changed it into a sovereign medicine. When about a fifth part only was left, the Bishop of Antiguera removed it to his city, built a chapel for it, and enshrined it there with all possible honours."*

As far as Cavendish was concerned, however, its miraculous powers were used only in its own preservation. Cavendish left Guatulco unharmed, and continued his piracies without restraint. When prizes were not to be found on the sea he went inland in search of plunder, making his name terrible in the district for two centuries to come.

He waited on the coast longer than he had intended, because he heard that a great galleon, the *Santa Anna*, of 700 tons burthen, was expected to arrive with a cargo of spices and other rich treasure from the Philippine Islands. With this vessel he fell in, a little below the northern promontory of California, on the 4th of November. In a sudden effort to board her, he was driven off with a loss of two killed and five wounded men. "But," says the chronicler, "we new trimmed our sails and fitted every man his furniture, and gave them a fresh encounter with our great ordnance, and also with our small shot, raking them through and through, to the killing and wounding of many of their men. Their captain still, like a valiant man, with his company, stood very stoutly into his close-fights, not yielding as

* Torquemada, cited by Southey, vol. iii., p. 264.

yet. Our General, encouraging his men afresh with the whole voice of trumpets, gave them the other encounter with our great ordnance and all our small shot, to the great discouragement of our enemies. They, being thus discouraged and spoiled, and their ship being in hazard of sinking by reason of the great shot which were made, whereof some were under water, within five or six hours' fight, set out a flag of truce and parleyed for mercy, desiring our general to save their lives and take their goods, and that they would yield presently. Our General, of his goodness, promised them mercy, and called them to strike their sails and to hoist out their boat and come aboard, which news they were full glad to hear of; and presently one of their chief merchants came on board, and falling down upon his knees, offered to kiss our General's feet and craved mercy. Our General most graciously pardoned both him and the rest, upon promise of their true dealing with him and his company concerning such riches as were in the ship; and he sent for the captain and the pilot, who, at their coming aboard, used the like duty and reverence that the former did. The General, of his great mercy and humanity, promised their lives and good usage."

Cavendish thought that, if he released the *Santa Anna*, she might reach some Spanish port in time to give information, and cause him to be troubled with pursuers. He therefore led her into a bay near by, and there discharged her crew and passengers, numbering a hundred and ninety in all, with a fair allowance of food and furniture, advising them, in his "great mercy and humanity," to build a new bark for themselves in lieu of the *Santa Anna*, which he partly burnt. Then he proceeded to arrange his booty, consisting of 122 pounds of gold, and of "rich silks, satins, and damasks, with musk and divers other merchandize and great store of all manner of victuals, with choice of many conserves of all sorts for to eat, and of sundry sorts of very good wines." This lasted thirteen days, and was attended with some trouble. "In division of the treasure," we are told, "many of the company fell into a mutiny against our general, especially those in the *Content*, which, nevertheless, were after a sort pacified for the time." As Cavendish sailed out of the harbour, however, on the 19th of November, the *Content* lagged behind, and during the ensuing night was lost sight of for ever. It was supposed that her crew parted from their comrades by design, and attempted to reach England alone. This they never did.

Cavendish, like Drake, was thus left to complete the voyage round the world in a single ship. He performed the rest of the circuit in nearly five months less than the time which had been occupied by Drake. This he was enabled to do not only by use of Drake's experience, but by the assistance of a Spanish pilot whom he had taken from the *Santa Anna*, and who was well acquainted with the passage across the Pacific Ocean and the intricacies of the Indian Archipelago.

On the 3rd of January, 1588, Cavendish arrived at Guahan, one of the Ladrones, where the natives so troubled him with proposals for trading, that, in the hard spirit that always marked his conduct, he fired at them. " They were so yare and nimble," it is recorded, " that it could not be seen whether they were killed or not, so ready were they at falling backward into the sea and diving." Not stopping to inquire into their fate, he sailed on to the Philippine group, and, on the 15th of January, called at a little island called Capul.

There he was willing to trade, and during nine days he made observations which, when the account of them reached England, greatly encouraged others to follow in his track. Already thriving commerce had been begun by Spaniards and Portuguese with the people of this island and the larger ones adjoining it, with Manilla for their head-quarters. The inhabitants were described by one of Cavendish's party as " of great genius and invention in handicrafts and sciences, every one so expert, perfect, and skilful in his faculty, as few or no Christians are able to go beyond them in that they take in hand. For drawing and embroidery upon satin, silk, or lawn, either beast, fowl, fish, or worm, for liveliness and perfectness, both in silk, silver, gold, and pearl, they excel."

On the 23rd of January, Cavendish invited the chiefs of Capul " and of a hundred islands more" to wait upon him on board the *Desire*. They came, bringing tribute in the shape of pigs, poultry, cocoa-nuts, and potatoes, of the sort they had been taught to yield to the Spaniards, for such they thought Cavendish and his comrades to be. " He then," says the chronicler, " made himself and his company known that they were Englishmen, and enemies to the Spaniards, and thereupon spread his ensign and sounded up the drums, which they much marvelled at. They promised, both for themselves and all the islands thereabout, to aid him whensoever he should come again to overcome the Spaniards. Also our General gave them money back again for all the tribute which they had paid; which they took marvellous friendly, and rowed about our ships, to show us pleasure, marvellous swiftly. At the last, he caused a saker to be shot off, whereat they wondered, and with great contentment took their leave of us."

Cavendish's short stay at Capul was marked by one ugly incident. His Spanish pilot had hitherto been very serviceable to him, though his prudent navigation was doubtless caused only by regard for his own safety. In leading the English to the Philippine Islands and acquainting them with the wealth which Spain and Portugal desired to keep to themselves, he was guided only by treachery. No sooner had he arrived than he prepared a letter to the Spanish governor at Manilla, which, if it had not miscarried, would have been almost certain to end in Cavendish's overthrow and the restitution of the treasures he had taken from the *Santa Anna*. His plot, however, was betrayed; and Cavendish, thereupon, " willed that he should be hanged, which was accordingly performed."

On the 28th of January, when near Manilla, Cavendish fell in with a Spanish vessel which had lately left that port. His pursuit of her was unsuccessful, and he only captured one Spaniard. Him, after some questioning, he released with a message to the Spanish governor, to the effect that he should come again with ample force in a few years' time, when he should expect the enemies of God and man to have ready an abundant store of wealth for him to seize.

At present he was anxious to get home. He hurried past the Moluccas, near which several of his men sickened, and one died " by reason of the extreme heat and untemperateness of the climate." Sailing north, he reached the eastern side of Java on the 5th of March, and there halted for eleven days, making friends with the natives, and giving his men the rest of which they were in great need. He was highly pleased with the Javans, who were described as " the bravest race in the south-east parts of the globe;" and even more pleased with some Portuguese residents, who, faithful to the cause of Don Antonio, and resenting Philip II.'s aggression in their country, seem to have sought peace and happiness by making Java their home. " They were men of marvellous proper personage." we are told, " each in a loose jerkin and hose, which came down from the waist to the ankle. Because of the use of the country, and partly because it was a time for doing of their penance, they had on each of them a very fair and white lawn shirt with falling bands on the same, very decently, only their bare legs excepted. These Portuguese were no small joy to our General and all the rest of our company; for we had not seen any Christian that was our friend for a year and a half before. Our General entreated them singularly well with banquets and music. They told us they were no less glad to see us than we to see them, and inquired of the state of their country, and what was become of Don Antonio their King, and whether he were living or no. for they had not of long time been in Portugal, and the Spaniards had always brought them word that he was dead. Then our General satisfied them in every demand, assuring them that their King was alive and in England, and had honourable allowance from our Queen, and that there was war between Spain and England, and that we were come under the King of Portugal into the South Sea, and had warred upon the Spaniards there, and had fired, spoiled, and sunk all the ships along the coast that we could meet withal, to the number of eighteen or twenty sail. With this report they were sufficiently satisfied. They told us that if their King, Don Antonio, would come unto them, they would warrant him to have all the Moluccas at command, besides China, Ceylon, and the Isles of the Philippines, and that he might be sure to have all the Indians on his side. They took their leave with promise of all good entertainment at our return."

Leaving Java on the 16th of March, Cavendish spent two months " in traversing that mighty and vast sea between the island of Java and the main of Africa, observing the heavens, the stars, and the fowls, which are marks unto seamen." He passed the Cape of Good

Hope on the 18th of May, halted at St. Helena from the 9th to the 20th of June, and thence, in eighty-one days of direct sailing, as he said, " God suffered him to return to England." On the 3rd of September, from a Flemish ship which he met not far from Lisbon, he heard, " to his singular rejoicing and comfort," of the great triumph that had been attained by England in the overthrow of the Invincible Armada. The storm which wrought the final ruin of the Armada met him in the English Channel and threatened to wreck his ship, even when home was in sight; but at length on the 9th of September, " by the merciful favour of the Almighty, they recovered their long-wished-for port of Plymouth." Thence Cavendish wrote to Lord Chamberlain Hunsdon, requesting him to inform the Queen of his achievements. "As it hath pleased God," he said, " to give her the victory over part of her enemies, so I trust ere long to see her overcome them all; for the places of their wealth, whereby they have maintained and made their wars, are now perfectly discovered, and, if it please her Majesty, with a very small power she may take the spoil of them all."*

This was partly done by Queen Elizabeth, and done in yet greater part by her successors. But Cavendish had no further share in the spoil. Having returned to England in the autumn of 1588 with wealth "enough to buy a fair earldom," and with fame which, notwithstanding the turmoil produced just then by other famous achievements, was second only to that of Drake in

* HAKLUYT, vol. iii., p. 873.

1580, for a time he seems to have settled down to the enjoyment of his wealth and fame. When tired of that he entered upon another expedition, the history of which, bringing to a close his brief career, it will be best to detail at once, though in violation of the strict order of chronology.

The expedition was projected early in 1591; and unfortunately, as it happened, Cavendish, wishing that it should be in keeping with other huge enterprises which by that time had become popular, allowed other adventurers to join with him in fitting it out. The arrangements were thus left in unworthy hands, and of the money which Cavendish himself contributed, we are told, a sum of 1,500*l.* was stolen by the agents to whom it was intrusted. "These varlets, whom the justice had before sought with great diligence," says Sir Richard Hawkins, "I saw, within a few days after his departure, walking the streets of Plymouth without punishment." Even without that money, however, a larger fleet was prepared than Cavendish proved able to manage. On the 26th of August, 1591, he sailed out of Plymouth Harbour with three good ships and two barks. The chief of these was the *Leicester Galleon*, the same in which Edward Fenton had made his unfortunate expedition in the same direction nine years before, and which, being the property of the Earl of Leicester, was probably furnished by him as one of the adventurers. Of it Cavendish himself was captain. The others were, his old ship the *Desire*, commanded by John Davis, the famous Arctic navigator, who had just returned from a voyage to the East Indies as pilot to a Dutch fleet,* the *Roebuck*, under Captain Cook, the *Black Pinnace*, and the *Dainty*, which was contributed by Adrian Gilbert. John Jane, who had accompanied Davis in two of his Arctic voyages, went as merchant and chronicler of the enterprise.† The crews of this expedition numbered nearly four hundred men in all.

It was unfortunate from first to last. The fleet was becalmed for twenty-seven days near the equator, and in consequence many died of scurvy before reaching the coast of Brazil. When near that coast, on the 2nd of December, Cavendish plundered a Portuguese vessel, and, reaching land on the 5th, he pillaged a small settlement near Rio Janeiro. An attack upon Santos, on the 16th, was ruined through the carelessness of Captain Cook; and in consequence the voyagers suffered sorely for want of provisions. Worse trouble came on the way to Magellan's Strait, when, on the 8th of February, the ships were parted by a storm. The little *Dainty* returned to England. The *Desire* and the *Roebuck* reached Port Desire, which had been the meeting-place appointed by Cavendish in case of separation, on the 6th of March. The *Black Pinnace* arrived on the 16th and the *Leicester* on the 18th. All the four ships had suffered greatly, the *Roebuck* and the *Leicester* most of all, and the troubles in the latter ship were aggravated by quarrels that arose between

---

* See vol. i., pp. 289, 290.

† HAKLUYT, vol. iii., pp. 842—852. This, and a letter from Cavendish to Sir Tristram Gorges (PURCHAS, vol. iii., pp. 1194–2000), are the authorities for the ensuing paragraphs.

Cavendish and his crew. In consequence of them Cavendish removed from the *Leicester* to the *Desire*, soon to quarrel with its crew also. Lacking the energy and perseverance that he showed during his former voyage, he seems to have offended all by his haughty tone, and to have thus greatly helped on the disputes by which the whole enterprise was brought to ruin.

Leaving Port Desire late in March he reached Magellan's Strait on the 8th of April. "Such," he says, "was the adverseness of our fortunes, that in coming thither we spent the summer, and found the Strait in the beginning of a most extreme winter, not durable for Christians." He entered it on the 14th of April, and after a week of slow sailing was brought to a standstill by bad weather. For three weeks the ships had to take shelter in a little bay from, according to Cavendish's statement, "such flights of snow and extremity of frosts as, in all his life, he never saw any to be compared with." "Many of our men," says Jane, "died of cursed famine and miserable cold, not having wherewith to cover their bodies, nor to fill their bellies, but living by mussels, water, and weeds of the sea, with small relief from the ship's stores of meal sometimes." That suffering begat cruelty. "All the sick men in the *Galleon* were most uncharitably put ashore in the woods, in the snow, rain, and cold, when men of good health could scarcely endure it, where they ended their lives in the highest degree of misery."

In this trouble Cavendish went to Davis for advice. Davis, who, after his Arctic experiences, saw no great hardship in the snow and frost of Magellan's Strait, urged patient waiting till they could pass out into the South Sea, and thence seek warmer waters. Others of the party also desired that they should "stay God's favour for a wind." Cavendish, however, wished to turn back and seek the East Indies by way of the Cape of Good Hope; and, after quarrelling with Davis and all the bravest of his company, he so far prevailed upon them that, aided by a west wind, they passed out of the Strait in three days, and attempted to go to Santos in search of refreshment. But no sooner were they in the Atlantic again than fresh storms arose, by which the *Desire* and the *Black Pinnace* were parted from the *Leicester*, to which Cavendish, after his quarrel with Davis, had returned, and the *Roebuck*. They, also, were separated for a time; but, meeting again, with difficulty took shelter in a bay somewhere south of Rio Janeiro.

Loitering about the coast of Brazil in hopes that Davis would join him, and made desperate by his misfortunes, Cavendish insured his ruin. He sent out marauding parties in search of food, by which his already too scanty crews were utterly wasted. One party of twenty-five was wholly lost. Out of another party of eighty, sent to attack three Portuguese ships at Spirito Santo, thirty-eight were killed and forty were wounded. The survivors quarrelled with him. The crew of the *Roebuck*, regardless of his protestations, set sail for England and were wrecked on the way. Cavendish besought those who stayed with him to make another attempt at reaching the South Sea. "My persuasions," he says, "took no place with them; but most boldly they all affirmed that they had sworn they would never again go to the Strait; neither by no means would they." At length he consented to go back to England.

On the passage, apparently in July, 1592, he died of a broken heart. Our last view of him is in a pathetic letter to his executor, Sir Tristram Gorges, from which some sentences have been already cited. "Most loving friend," he said, "there is nothing in this world that makes a truer trial of friendship than at death to show mindfulness of love and friendship, which now you shall make a perfect experience of; desiring you to hold my love as dear, dying poor, as if I had been most infinitely rich. The success of this most unfortunate action, the bitter torments whereof lie so heavy upon me, as with much pain I am able to write these few lines, much less to make discourse to you of all the adverse haps that have befallen me in this voyage, the least whereof is my death." He did manage, however, to discourse much of his misfortunes. "My greatest grief," he said, after detailing other griefs perhaps as great or greater, "was the sickness of my dear kinsman, John Lock, who by this time was grown in great weakness, by reason whereof he desired rather quietness and contentedness in our course than such continual disquietness, which never ceased us. And now by this, what with grief for him and the continual trouble I endured among such hell-hounds, my spirits were clean spent, wishing myself upon any desert place in the world, there to die, rather than thus barely to return home again; which course I had put in execution, had I found an island which the cards make to be eight degrees to the southward of the line. I swear to you I sought for it with all diligence, meaning, if I had found it, to have there ended my unfortunate life. But God suffered not such happiness to light upon me, for I could by no means find it; so as I was forced to go towards England, and having gotten eight degrees by north the line, I lost my most dearest cousin. And now consider whether a heart made of flesh be able to endure so many misfortunes, all falling upon me without intermission. I thank my God that, in ending of me, He hath pleased to rid me of all further trouble and mishaps." Then he spoke of his private affairs. "I have made my will, wherein I have given special charge that all goods, whatsoever belong unto me, be delivered into your hands. For God's sake, refuse not to do this last request for me. I owe little that I know of, and therefore it will be the less trouble; but if there be any debt that of truth is owing by me, for God's sake see it paid." Whatever was left he assigned to his sister. "To use compliments of love, now at my last breath, were frivolous; but know that I left none in England whom I loved half so well as yourself, which you in such sort deserved at my hands as I can by no means requite. I have now no more to say; and take this last farewell, that you have lost the lovingest friend that ever was lost by any. No more. But, as you love

God, do not refuse to undertake this last request of mine. Bear with this scribbling; for I protest I am scarce able to hold a pen in my hand."

The pen dropped, and the hand dropped, and one of the most truly representative of Tudor Englishmen, bold, brave, strong in love and strong in hate, too zealous in the achieving of any object to which he set himself, to consider whether it was wise, honest, or generous, closed a life that had been attended by some rare circumstances of glory in bitter pangs of grief and broken words of tenderness.

Blaming in that letter nearly all his comrades in his unfortunate voyage, Cavendish blamed John Davis more than most. "That villain," he said, "hath been the death of me and the decay of this whole action. His only intent was utterly to overthrow me, which he hath well performed." There is no evidence of any such intent, and it is altogether inconsistent with everything that we know of Davis's character. When separated from Cavendish by the storm that befel them on passing out of Magellan's Strait, Davis went with all speed to Port Desire, believing that there he would be joined by Cavendish. He waited and watched for nine weeks and more. Then, believing that the *Leicester* and the *Roebuck* were either lost or had gone, according to Cavendish's plan, towards the Cape of Good Hope, he started with the *Desire* and the *Black Pinnace* in the direction originally appointed. Using well his large experience in seamanship, he had employed the interval in refitting his ships and storing them with salted penguins. He was thus able to brave the dangers of the Strait, and, after first, on the 14th of August, discovering the Falkland Isles, he traversed it, and entered the South Sea on the 2nd of October.

He was only able to stay in it a week. He fell among storms as great as those by which Drake had been harassed in 1578. On the 4th of October the *Black Pinnace* was wrecked, and on the 5th the *Desire* was barely saved, " the storm continuing beyond all description in fury, with hail, snow, rain, and wind, such and so mighty as that in nature it could not possibly be more, the sea such and so lofty with continual breach that many times they were doubtful whether the ship did sink or swim." The storm lasted for four days more. "The 10th of October," says Jane in his narrative, " being, by the account of our captain and master, very near the shore, the weather dark, the storm furious, and most of our men having given over to travail, we yielded ourselves to death without further hope of succour. Our captain sitting in the gallery very pensive, I came and brought him some rosa solis to comfort him; for he was so cold, he was scarce able to move a joint. After he had drunk and was comforted in heart, he began, for the ease of his conscience, to make a large repetition of his forepassed time, and, with many grievous sighs, he concluded in these words: 'O most gracious God, with whose power the mightiest things among men are matters of no moment, I most humbly beseech Thee that the intolerable burden of my sins may, through the blood of Jesus Christ, be taken from me, and end our days with speed, or show us some merciful sign of Thy love and our preservation.'" Hardly had the good man's prayer been uttered, than, as if in answer to it, the sun broke through the clouds.

Thereby Davis was able to calculate his exact position, and, through that and the following day, there was just enough abatement of the storm to enable him to lead his ship back into the Strait. He sailed through it with great difficulty, and with great difficulty proceeded homewards. He was not troubled by storms alone. In the Isle of Penguins he laid in a store of dried penguins for food during the long voyage, and after a time, we are told, "ugly, loathsome worms of an inch long were bred in them." "This worm," it is added, "did so mightily increase and devour our victuals, that there was in reason no hope how we should avoid famine, but be devoured of the wicked creatures. There was nothing that they did not devour, iron only excepted—our clothes, hats, boots, shirts, and stockings. And for the ship, they did eat the timbers; so that we greatly feared they would undo us by eating through the ship's side. Great was the care and diligence of our captain, master, and company to consume these vermin; but the more we laboured to kill them, the more they increased upon us, so that at last we could not sleep for them, for they would eat our flesh like mosquitoes." This new horror, added to the old ones, drove some of the sailors mad. Many others died; and at length the whole company of the *Desire* was reduced, from the seventy-six men with whom it quitted Plymouth, to sixteen, and of these sixteen only five had strength and wit remaining to enable them properly to work the ship. This, however, they managed to do, and they reached Ireland in June, 1593.

John Davis, as we have seen, made some other famous voyages. He went as pilot in the first Dutch expedition to the East Indies in 1598, and he was second in command of the first expedition fitted out by the English East India Company in 1601.* He died in harness. A trading and piratical enterprise by Sir Edward Michelborne, in rivalry of the East India Company, having received the countenance of King James, Davis was employed in it as captain of the *Tiger*, a ship of 240 tons burthen. The expedition left the Isle of Wight on the 5th of December, 1604, and reached the neighbourhood of Sumatra on the 19th of July, 1605. Five months were spent in trading with the natives of Acheen, Bantam, and other parts, and in chasing Spanish and Portuguese ships in the neighbouring waters. At length, on the 27th of December, Michelborne fell in with a little vessel in which ninety Japanese pirates, having lost their own ship, had taken refuge. For a day or two there was much show of friendship between the two races, and accordingly Davis, who had been ordered to take their weapons from the Japanese when they came into English company, neglected to use this precaution. Thereby he was the first to suffer. The Japanese, anxious to repair the loss of their own ship, took advantage of what

see vol. i., pp. 289, 292.

seemed an opportunity for murdering the English and taking possession of the *Tiger*.* They were hindered from doing much harm, and Sir Edward Michelborne reached England safely in the summer of 1606; but no wealth that he brought home could atone for the loss of Captain John Davis, the boldest and the manliest of the Arctic explorers under Queen Elizabeth.

* PURCHAS, vol. i., pp. 132—139.

## CHAPTER XIV.

THE PRELUDE TO THE GREAT ARMADA FIGHT.

[1585—1587.]

ALMOST from the day when Queen Elizabeth ascended the throne it was clear to far-seeing men that fierce war must eventually arise between Spain and England. During the brief reign of Mary, her husband Philip II., virtually King, had only been able to stamp down, in no way to stamp out, the hearty Protestantism of England; and when, with Elizabeth's accession, that hearty Protestantism was again able openly to become a guiding principle of English politics, prompted by a new hatred of Catholic intolerance and Catholic interference as represented especially by Spain, the antagonism was too great to issue in anything less than deadly fighting. But for a long time the old feud between England and France, which was also in lesser sort a feud between Lutherans and Papists, delayed the struggle; and while it was the wise policy of Elizabeth and her statesmen, who saw that thus only they could save their country from overwhelming danger, to avert aggression by playing the two great Catholic nations against one another, prudent Philip also saw that, for the sake of keeping at bay his more dangerous Catholic neighbour, it was well to preserve a show of friendship for the more distant kingdom of heretics. Therefore Elizabeth bore even with Spanish fostering of insurrection in Ireland, and Philip bore even with English piracy in the Spanish Main; and the war of races and of creeds was carried on for nearly thirty years only by pirates and freebooters.

Yet, during every one of those years, the contest became more imminent, and, by so long restraining it, diplomatists only rendered it more vindictive when at last it was allowed to be changed from individual piracy into national warfare. This was in great part due to the heroic battle of the Netherlanders for civil and religious freedom, unsurpassed and hardly rivalled in the whole world's history. Bringing the conflict between Protestantism and Catholicism, tyranny and freedom, to the very walls of England, with no other barrier than the Narrow Sea afforded, they forced Englishmen to take part therein, unless they chose meanly to hold aloof altogether from the movement of European politics, and to avail themselves of an insularity which it had been the effort of five centuries to make only artificial. This was by no means their choice. From the first sounding of the trumpet in Holland, English statesmen entered zealously into the crooked courses of diplomacy, and English adventurers went in crowds to swell the ranks of straightforward soldiership. All, too, who stayed at home showed, in more or less open ways, their sympathy for the champions of independence.

The first important evidence of this appeared in December, 1568. Five Spanish ships, conveying money to the Netherlands, to be there employed by the Duke of Alva in paying his troops, were attacked in the English Channel by a little fleet of French pirates equipped by the Prince of Condé. They took refuge in the harbours of Falmouth, Plymouth, and Southampton, and, after vainly trying to evade their pursuers and proceed safely to Antwerp, appealed to Queen Elizabeth for assistance, begging that she would protect them with some of her ships during the remainder of the voyage. Instead of that the Queen took the money into her own keeping, informing the Spanish ambassador that, as she understood it really belonged to some Genoese merchants, and had been only borrowed by Philip, she would borrow it herself. To this she was in part induced by the arguments of William Hawkins, John Hawkins's brother, who, having just heard of the misfortunes experienced by him at San Juan de Ulloa, urged that "her Majesty might now make stay of King Philip's treasure till recompense was made"—a course by which he "looked also to please God, for the Spaniards were God's enemies."* Her bold conduct of course gave great offence to the Spanish Government. Alva immediately seized all the property of the English merchants in the Netherlands, most of whom, however, with Sir Thomas Gresham at their head, had already been driven out of it by the turmoils and harassments of the civil war. Thereupon Elizabeth authorized re-

* RECORD OFFICE MSS., *Domestic*, vol. xlviii., No. 50.

prisals with her own ships, and gave implied sanction to the much greater reprisals resorted to by private adventurers upon the Spanish shipping that was forced, in its passage to and from the Low Countries, to pass through the English Channel. In such ways the struggle was hastened on.

Philip II., from that time, was anxious to enter upon avowed war with England. He was only restrained by the more cautious Duke of Alva, who argued that, seeing how hard was the punishment of the small and unaided insurgent nation of the Low Countries, it would be madness to force upon it the open and complete alliance of the much larger nation of England. Therefore he confined himself to underhand warfare, and plotted and schemed his utmost in encouraging rebellion among the Catholic subjects of Elizabeth both in Ireland and in England. He so far succeeded as to be amused with the hope, through every one of more than a dozen years, that English Papists and Spanish money would procure him an easy victory over what he called "the lost and undone kingdom" of Elizabeth. But the hope was too weak to be held by many but himself, and even he was now and then compelled to admit its folly. .Yet he continued to scheme and plot, with much substantial injury to England, and with much loss of wealth and credit to himself, sometimes with failures that made him the laughing-stock of Europe.*

* It will be seen that I here only briefly allude, so far as seems necessary to my purpose, to topics which are amplified in all the histories, and most fully, as regards the earlier of them, in the excellent *History of*

One of these failures was the work of John Hawkins. How fierce was Hawkins's hatred of Spain, and how fearlessly he showed it, we have already seen. But Hawkins could use duplicity as well as Philip. From the time of his return to England, after his defeat at San Juan de Ulloa in 1568, he did all in his power, by threat, by argument, and by entreaty, to procure the release of his comrades taken prisoners at San Juan, or forced afterwards to throw themselves upon the flinty rock of Spanish mercy in Mexico. When entreaty, argument, and threat had failed, he tried deception, and this, though it wrought no good for the poor sufferers in Mexico, led to famous results in England. In April, 1571, he sent a message to King Philip at Madrid, pretending that he was weary of Elizabeth's fickle and tyrannical rule, and offering to break his allegiance, and to give the Spaniards all the advantages of his maritime skill and his intimate acquaintance with English statecraft, on condition that his old friends should be set free, and that he himself should be suitably rewarded. To this astonishing proposal Philip gladly listened, but he asked for proof that he was not being played upon.* Proof satisfactory to him was sent in the shape of a letter cunningly procured from Mary Queen of Scots;† and in the following August a large sum of money was

---

England which Mr. FROUDE is now producing; and as regards the later of them, in Mr. MOTLEY'S no less excellent *History of the United Netherlands*.

\* *Simancas MS.*, cited by FROUDE, vol. x., pp. 262, 263.

† RECORD OFFICE MSS., *Scottish Series, Mary Queen of Scots*, vol. vi., Nos. 61, 71, 73.

transmitted by Philip to Hawkins, to be used by him in making traitors of other Englishmen, and in preparing some English ships for Spanish service. Even the details of the service on which they were to be employed were confided to him.* Seldom before had Philip been so duped. Hawkins straightway informed Queen Elizabeth, who was not ignorant of the preliminaries, of the state of affairs, and, while he kept Philip's money himself, enabled her to use Philip's secrets to his serious damage. "I have sent your Lordship the copy of my pardon from the King of Spain, in the very order and manner I have it," he said in a letter on the subject to Lord Burghley, dated the 4th of September. "The Duke of Medina and the Duke of Alva hath every of them one of the same pardons, more amplified to present unto me, though this be large enough, with my great titles and honours from the King—from which God deliver me! Their practices be very mischievous, and they be never idle. But God, I hope, will confound them, and turn their devices upon their own necks. I will put my business in some order, and give my attendance upon her Majesty, to do her that service that by your Lordship shall be thought most convenient in this case."† Hawkins soon showed himself to Philip as a true, though not a very truthful, Englishman.

In the meanwhile England's quarrel with Spain progressed. Personal jealousy of the great Prince of Orange, and resentment of his advocacy of popular

* FROUDE, vol. x., pp. 267, 268.
† RECORD OFFICE MSS., *Domestic*, vol. lxxxi., No. 7.

rights opposed to all theories of royal prerogative, caused Elizabeth somewhat to restrain it. Sympathising on some points with Spain, and on some others with the Low Countries, she watched the struggle with conflicting feelings through nearly twenty years, and according to her various inclinations to join issue with the Netherlanders or to leave Philip to crush them were her varying approval and condemnation not only of smaller piracies near home but also of such larger enterprises as those of Hawkins and Drake. She always showed more friendship for the Netherlanders than Philip approved; but, by reason of her efforts to conciliate him, as well as of her personal prejudices to the republicans, the friendship was often less hearty and less effective than the worthiest of her subjects desired. Tortuous diplomacy was never so tortuous as during these twenty years. But the end of it was forced to be straightforward and decisive. In the treaty which on the 16th of August, 1585, Elizabeth concluded with the United States of the Netherlands, asserting their independence, and pledging herself to its maintenance, she took a step which could not possibly be retraced without national disgrace, and entered irrevocably upon open war with Spain. Her reasons thereto were promptly announced to all the world in a noble and eloquent "Declaration of the causes moving the Queen of England to give aid to the defence of the people afflicted and oppressed in the Low Countries," which was published at the same time in English, Dutch, Italian, and French.*

* HOLLINSHED, vol. iii., pp. 1411-1419. See a whole chapter on this treaty and its antecedents in MOTLEY, vol. i., pp. 285-304.

By that treaty Queen Elizabeth undertook to assist the Netherlanders with five thousand foot soldiers and a thousand horsemen under the Earl of Leicester as Commander-in-Chief, and with Sir Philip Sidney as General of the Horse and Governor of Flushing; and, in conjunction with her allies, to organize a formidable fleet for further prosecution of the war under the direction of Lord High Admiral Howard. The land-forces set out at once to do memorable work, in which the brightest incident was the fatal prowess shown by Sidney at the battle of Zutphen. The movements of the fleet were perforce somewhat slower, but the work done by it was far more memorable.

Of the antecedents of Lord Charles Howard of Effingham we have already seen something. His first twelve years' service under Queen Elizabeth had little to do with seamanship. In July, 1559, before she had been a year on the throne, and when he was only twenty-two years old, he was sent by her with a message of sympathy to Henry II. on his illness, which message was turned into a mission of condolence and congratulation to Francis II. in consequence of Henry's death.\* He returned to England to shine in the Court and to win especial liking, by reason of "his most proper person," from the Queen. In 1562 he entered Parliament as knight of his native shire of Surrey; and in 1569 he served as General of the Horse in the army with which the Earl of Warwick suppressed the re-

\* STEVENSON, *Calendar of State Papers, Foreign Series, of the Reign of Elizabeth*, vol. i., Nos. 967, 985.

bellion of the Earls of Northumberland and Westmoreland.*

In 1570 began his naval career. On the 29th of August in that year he was made an Admiral, and appointed, along with Admiral William Winter, to the charge of ten ships sent by the Queen to escort Anne of Austria, the intended bride of Philip II., from Holland to Spain. If this work was intended merely as a compliment to the Spanish monarch, Howard, following the example of his father who, in 1554, had been sent in kindred manner to escort Philip to England for marriage with Queen Mary, managed to turn it into a defiance of the pride of Spain. His ten ships were in consort with a hundred and thirty Spanish sail, which on entering the English Channel still flaunted the Spanish flag. Thereupon Lord Charles Howard "environed their fleet in most strange and warlike sort, and enforced them to stoop-gallant and to vail their bonnets for the Queen of England." This done, "he performed all good offices of honour and humanity to that foreign princess."†

Other courtly work fell to him in the ensuing years. In February, 1582, he was employed in taking home the Duke of Anjou, after his visit to England in hope and expectation of being made the husband of Queen Elizabeth; on which occasion he wrote to Sir Francis Walsingham to advise that the Queen should part from

* COLLINS, *Peerage*, vol. iv., p. 269; RECORD OFFICE MSS., *Domestic*, vol. lx., No. 65; vol. lxiv., No. 22.
† RECORD OFFICE MSS., *Domestic*, vol. lxxiii., No. 36; HAKLUYT, *Dedication*.

the Duke at Canterbury instead of seeing him all the way to Dover, as Dover was not large enough to entertain them both.* Tougher work also came to him in looking after the welfare of the fleet, seeing that it was in good order for resisting invasion, and occasionally exercising some part of it in the pursuit of pirates. In these ways he so acted as to justify his appointment as Lord High Admiral, in succession to the Earl of Lincoln, who died in January, 1585. "The Queen," we are told, "had a great persuasion of his fortunate conduct, and knew him to be of a moderate and noble courage, skilful in sea matters, wary and provident, valiant and courageous, industrious and active, and of great authority and esteem among sailors."† That last was his best recommendation. "True it is," says another of his old panegyrists, "he was no deep seaman; but he had skill enough to know those who had more skill than himself and to follow their instructions, and would not starve the Queen's service by feeding his own sturdy wilfulness, but was ruled by the experienced in sea matters; the Queen having a navy of oak and an admiral of ozier."‡

The ozier and the oak fitted well together. Howard did his best to strengthen the English navy, and to prepare for the greater use of it that was to result from the treaty made with the Netherlands a few months after his appointment as High Admiral; and he had

* RECORD OFFICE MSS., *Domestic*, vol. clii., No. 34; NICHOLS, *Progresses of Queen Elizabeth*, vol. ii., p. 347.
† CAMDEN, *Annals*, p. 325.
‡ FULLER, *Worthies*.

excellent advisers and assistants in such men as Drake and Hawkins.

Hawkins, having retired from the personal contest with Spain in distant waters, which he had been the first to encourage, settled down to the hearty performance of his multifarious duties as Treasurer or Comptroller of the Navy, begun on the last day of 1578. Drake, being younger, and having been wonderfully successful in all his projects against Spain, continued to take the lead in actual seamanship.

So great was the fear already excited in Spain and its possessions by Drake's prowess, that, in 1582, King Philip offered a reward of 20,000 ducats to any one who would bring him his head or proof that it had been hindered from producing any more of his terrible handiwork.\* He seems to have been in England or near it, however, for nearly five years after returning from his famous voyage round the world. Dreading Spain too much to sanction just then any further voyaging of that sort, Queen Elizabeth kept him generally at Court, allowed him occasionally to reside in Plymouth, and sometimes employed him in catching pirates—if Spanish pirates, it would be all the better—in the Narrow Seas. He was thus employed in the autumn of 1583 and in the summer of 1584;† while in

---

\* RECORD OFFICE MSS., *Domestic*, vol. cliii., No. 49. This offer was made in the first instance to John Doughty, brother of the Thomas Doughty who was executed by Drake at Port Saint Julian. Doughty, however, seems to have done nothing more than slander Drake. (*Ibid.*, vol. cliii., No. 50.) That he took no legal steps to avenge his brother's death is some evidence in favour of Drake's innocence in the matter.

† RECORD OFFICE MSS., *Domestic*, vol.clxii., No. 33; vol.clxxxii., No. 38.

the following autumn we find him organizing volunteers in South Devon for the defence of the country against invaders and insurgents,* and, in company with a multitude of others, pledging himself by the most solemn oaths, "faithfully to serve and obey the Queen, to defend her against all estates, dignities, and earthly powers whatsoever, and to pursue to utter extermination all that shall attempt by any act, counsel, or consent to anything that shall tend to the harm of her Majesty's royal person."†

As soon as it was clear that England would go to war with Spain on behalf of the Netherlanders, and long before the signing of the treaty by which war was virtually declared, Drake was ready with a bold scheme for sharing in it. It was not his scheme alone. Sir Philip Sidney—whose desire to exchange courtly indolence for some worthy action, had led him, in 1576, to purpose going with Frobisher in search of a passage to Cathay, and, in 1583, to obtain from Queen Elizabeth authority to plant a colony in America—had, in 1584, begun to think of following Drake's example in attacking the West Indian colonies of Spain. He had discussed the project, among others, with Ralph Lane, the Governor of Raleigh's first unfortunate settlement in Virginia, and Lane, writing to him from Virginia in August, 1585, had urged him to take the work in hand, adducing arguments in its favour from his own experiences and observations. "I could not but write these

\* Record Office MSS., *Domestic*. vol. clxxiii., No. 33.
† *Ibid.*, vol. clxxxiv., No. 6.

ill-fashioned lines unto you," he said, "to exhort you, my noble general, by occasion, not to refuse the good opportunity of such a service to the Church of Christ, of great relief from many calamities that this treasure in the Spaniards' hands doth inflict upon the members thereof—very honourable and profitable for her Majesty and our country, and most commendable and fit for yourself to be the enterpriser of."*

Long before that letter arrived Sidney had started the enterprise and had withdrawn from actual part in it. During the summer of 1585 he was busily planning with Drake an expedition to the West Indies and the Spanish Main; and Sidney appears to have done his full share of the work. Besides giving all the money that he could save from his own scanty resources, we are told that he induced thirty gentlemen of good birth and estate to provide 100*l*. apiece for fitting out a fleet strong enough to act worthily in opposition to Spain; also that he used his influence in bringing together a body of volunteers " chosen out of the ablest governors of those martial times." The enterprise was to consist of a strong body of ships and of soldiers for service on land. Drake was to be commander of the fleet, Sidney to be general of the little army; and this arrangement seems to have been agreeable to both partners. But while the preparations were being made, Elizabeth's treaty with the Low Countries was completed, and it was the particular request of William of Orange, who had long before discerned his worth, that Sidney should

* RECORD OFFICE MSS., *Colonial*, vol. i., No. 5.

be English governor of Flushing, and hold an important place in the army sent to aid him from England. Sidney preferred this to sharing in Drake's expedition, and therefore the fitting out of the fleet was completed without him. Elizabeth, however, who looked upon Sidney as the special ornament of her Court, and who was ignorant of his plot for going so far away as Drake's fleet would take him, demurred even to his employment in the Netherlands. Upon that he recurred to the West Indian project, now aiming still more to keep his purpose a secret from the Queen. Just as Drake was ready for starting he stealthily went down to Plymouth and claimed the resumption of his bargain. But Drake, who had calculated upon having more complete authority than that bargain left him, while receiving Sidney "with a great deal of outward pomp and compliment," was by no means willing to have him for a partner; and thereupon ensued a curious little course of scheming. Drake caused a message to be sent to the Queen, informing her of Sidney's intended departure. In return a prompt order was despatched by her Majesty, to the effect that he was to be stayed: if he refused, the whole fleet was to be kept back: on no account was Drake to sail with him on board. That order, however, was preceded by news to Sidney that it was on its way, and he had time to dress up as sailors two soldiers whom he could trust, who hurried off to meet the courier, got into conversation with him, purloined the letter, and so prevented it from reaching its destination. Yet that was not successful. Drake lingered, and intelligence of the plot reached Elizabeth before he had set out. A more imperious mandate was at once prepared, and this time care was taken to have it properly conveyed. It was delivered into Sidney's own hands, we are told, by a peer of the realm. It carried with it "in the one hand grace, in the other thunder." The thunder was a threat that, if he quitted the Queen and her Court in this way, he should never return. The grace was a pledge that he should have employment under his uncle the Earl of Leicester, now going into the Low Countries. Sidney accepted the grace. He was sent to be governor of Flushing, and to die of his wound at Zutphen; and Drake went alone to the West Indies.*

Drake's fleet consisted of twenty-five vessels, large and small. In the largest of them, the *Elizabeth Bonaventure*, Drake went as Admiral, with Thomas Fenner for Captain. Under him, in charge of the *Primrose*, was Martin Frobisher, as Vice-Admiral, allowed, after seven years spent in idleness or piracy,† to share once more in memorable work. To Francis Knollys, as Rear-Admiral, was entrusted the *Leicester Galleon*; and in the *Tiger* went, as Lieutenant-General in command of the soldiers, Christopher Carlisle, Sidney's old friend, lately further connected with him through their marriage to two daughters of Sir Francis

* See my *Memoir of Sir Philip Sidney*, pp. 459–469.

† The Netherlanders, even after their formal alliance with Elizabeth, had to complain of the depredations committed upon their merchant ships by Frobisher and other Englishmen.—MOTLEY, *The United Netherlands*, vol. iii., pp. 173, 174.

Walsingham. Officers, soldiers, and seamen numbered in all 2,300 persons. The *Elizabeth Bonaventure* and the *Tiger*, if none of the others, were ships of the Queen's navy, and Drake and Carlisle bore commissions from the Queen. This expedition differed from all its predecessors, not only in size, but also in being distinctly authorized by the Crown to make war upon the King of Spain and his dominions. Drake, no longer a pirate, was now an acknowledged privateer. His enterprise was regarded by English Protestants and their allies as a direct piece of public warfare on their behalf, of extreme importance and wholly to be commended. "Upon Drake's voyage, in very truth," wrote Walsingham to the Earl of Leicester, " dependeth the life and death of the cause, according to man's judgment."*

The delays consequent upon Sidney's proposal to accompany it having come to an end, Drake left Plymouth on the 14th of September, 1585.† Proposing chiefly to attack Spain through her colonies, he was ready also, if possible, to strike some blows nearer home. Therefore, after capturing a Spanish fishing vessel on its way back from Newfoundland, and putting into Vigo, through stress of weather, on the 4th of October, he turned into the Road of Bayona, on the 10th, intending, " with the favour of the Almighty," to attack it. But the governor offered prompt submission, pro-

---

* *Leicester Correspondence*, edited by Mr. Bruce for the Camden Society (1844), p. 311.

† The following details, where no other authority is cited, are drawn from a narrative by Biggs, Cripps, and Cates, in HAKLUYT, vol. iii., pp. 534-548.

mising to liberate the persons and goods of English merchants that had been placed under arrest; and, while Drake was considering how to act, a true Biscayan storm arose, which partly dispersed his ships and forced him to lay out to sea. The storm lasted three days, and then Drake sent Carlisle to pay a second visit to Vigo.* Carlisle did damage to the inhabitants which it was thought 8,000*l*. would not recompense, but captured nothing of much value, his chief prize being "a cross of silver doubly gilt," belonging to the cathedral. Off the coast of Galicia the fleet appears to have stayed some little time, thereby enabling the Spanish authorities to send information concerning it to the West Indies, and so cause some trouble in the ensuing months.

The first trouble thus caused was at Palma, one of the Canaries, where, "by the naughtiness of the landing-place, well furnished with great ordnance," Drake was prevented from halting, and even driven off with some injury. Off Cape de Verde, also, he was able to procure very little of the booty which he sought. He stayed there, however, from the 14th to the 30th of November, and there the murder of one of his people was visited with terrible retribution. "We consumed with fire," it is said, "all the houses as well in the country as in the town of Santiago, the hospital excepted, which we left unconsumed." Perhaps the hospital was spared because the sickness that then began to show itself among the English inclined them to some little

* RECORD OFFICE MSS., *Domestic*, vol. clxxxiii., No. 10.

mercy towards sick Portuguese and Spaniards even. This sickness—consisting of " extreme hot burning and continual agues, whereof very few escaped with life, and those for the most part not without great alteration and decay of their wits and strength for a long time after "—lessened the force by more than two hundred men in the course of the passage which, after two months of loitering, was at length made to the West Indies.

There Dominica and Saint Kitts were first visited, not for war with Spaniards, but for refreshment obtained from the Indians, who were still their only inhabitants. Thence Drake sailed to Hispaniola, and on the 1st of January, 1586, twelve hundred men, apparently all that were left of the land force, were put on shore about a dozen miles from San Domingo, " being the ancientest and chief inhabited place in all the tract of country thereabouts," founded just ninety years before by the brother and deputy of Christopher Columbus. " Our General," says the chronicler, " after seeing all landed in safety, returned to the fleet, bequeathing us to God and the good conduct of Master Carlisle, our Lieutenant-General."

Between eight o'clock and noon, on this New-Year's Day, Carlisle's little army was marching up to San Domingo. When the city was in sight a hundred and fifty Spanish horse came out to meet the invaders, and after some brave fighting were driven within the walls. There were two seaward gates at which Carlisle resolved to enter. He planted half of his ordnance and a small force in front of each of them, and then, dividing the rest of his men into two parties, he intrusted one to Captain Powell, with orders to pass through one gate, while with the other, after vowing that, if God would help them, they would meet in the market-place, he forced his way through the other gate. The enemy, though not unprepared, were soon driven back. The English broke their ranks and "marched, or rather ran, so roundly into them, that pell-mell they entered the gates, and gave the Spaniards more care every man to save himself by flight than reason to stand any longer to their broken defence." Carlisle was the first to reach the market-place, "a place of very fair, spacious, square ground," and thence before nightfall they scoured the town sufficiently to find comfortable quarters for themselves. Next day Drake brought his vessels into the harbour, and landed most of his men to share in the spoil.

San Domingo was held for a month and leisurely ransacked, though Drake was disappointed at the small booty to be obtained in what had hitherto been supposed to be the richest storehouse of the exaggerated riches of the Spanish Indies. "We found here," it is said, " great store of strong wine, sweet oil, vinegar, olives, and such-like provisions, excellent white meal, woollen and linen cloth, and some silks, all which served us for great relief. Good store of brave apparel our soldiers also found for their relief. There was but little plate, or vessel of silver, in comparison of the great pride of other things in this town: yet some plate we found, and many other things very gallant and rich, which had cost them dear, although unto us they were of small importance."

The Spanish governor and most of the inhabitants, with all the troops, had taken refuge in a stronghold some three miles out of the town. Finding so little treasure in it, Drake was anxious to treat for a ransom, but the governor, hoping for the arrival of a fleet that had been promised him from Spain, was loth to treat. Then Drake sent a Negro boy, with a flag of truce to propose negotiations; but the messenger was met half way and so beaten that he could only crawl back to tell Drake how he had been handled, and then die at his feet. Thereat, we are told, "the General, being greatly passioned, commanded the provost marshal to cause a couple of friars, who were among his prisoners, to be carried to the same place where the boy was stricken, accompanied with a sufficient guard of soldiers, there presently to be both hanged; despatching at the instant another Spanish prisoner with the reason whereof this execution was done, and with this message further, that until the party who had thus murdered the general's messenger were delivered into our hands, to receive condign punishment, there should no day pass wherein there should not two prisoners be hanged until they were all consumed which were in our hands." The murderer was given up, and Drake caused him to be hanged by some of his own countrymen; but the governor refused to make any other concession. Drake accordingly ordered the destruction of the town, which was found to be " no small travail, being very magnificently built of stone, with high lofts." Every morning two hundred men were sent out to do this ugly work. " Yet," says the chronicler, " did we not, and could not, consume so much as one-third part of the town; and so, in the end—what wearied with firing, and what hastened by some other respects—we were contented to accept, and they at length to pay, 25,000 ducats"—about 7,000*l.*—" for the ransom of the rest."

Then Drake put to sea again and proceeded to Cartagena, the best fortified place on the Spanish Main. There the same course was pursued as at San Domingo, though with somewhat tougher fighting and with somewhat greater gain in money. Drake boldly entered the harbour which he had not been afraid to skirt, when a mere pirate, twelve years before. Carlisle and the troops being landed at midnight, three miles away from the town, pressed up to its walls, to find that Drake and the fleet, approaching by sea, had already done half of the fighting. Great wine butts, filled with earth, had been used for a barricade. " Notwithstanding it was well furnished with pikes and shot," says one of the soldiers, " the assault was, without staying, attempted by us. Down went the butts of earth, and pell-mell came our swords and pikes together after our shot had first given their volley, even at the enemy's nose. Our pikes were somewhat longer than theirs, and our bodies better armed, with which advantage our swords and pikes grew too hard for them, and they were driven to give place. In this furious entry the

Lieutenant-General slew with his own hands the chief
ensign-bearer of the Spaniards, who fought very manfully to his life's end." That was at the gates; and
the fighting was stoutly maintained at every street
corner and up to the market-place. The Spaniards,
braver than at San Domingo, were also much helped by
some Indian archers, " with their arrows most villainously empoisoned, so that, if they did but break the
skin, the party touched, unless it were by great marvel,
died." Many Englishmen, too, " were mischieved to
death by small sticks, sharply pointed, of a foot and a
half long, fixed in the ground, with the points poisoned,
right in the way from the place where they landed to
the town," which produced all the more harm because
the attack was made in the dark.

Cartagena was in the hands of the English at daybreak, and they held it for six weeks. Much pillage
ensued; but Drake, respecting the bravery of his
enemies, treated them honourably. " There passed
divers courtesies between us and the Spaniards," it is
said, " as feasting and using them with all kindness and
favour." The feasting, of course, was with Spanish
dainties. In the end, on receipt of about 28,000*l.* as
ransom, less than a third of the sum he had originally
asked for, Drake restored the shattered town to its
inhabitants.

To that moderation he was chiefly induced by the
illness that had afflicted his people ever since their
departure from Cape de Verde. The crews were much
reduced, and of the fighting men only eight hundred

and fifty remained, a hundred and fifty of those being too weak for any active service. Drake and his officers, after much consultation and with many regrets, resolved that it would be best not only to leave Cartagena with smaller ransom than they expected, but also to give up their plan of despoiling Nombre de Dios, and if possible, even crossing the Isthmus of Darien and attacking Panama.

Leaving Cartagena on the 31st of March, and blowing up its fort as a farewell show of power, Drake returned to it for a few days on finding that a great Spanish vessel which he had seized at San Domingo had sprung a leak and was in danger of foundering. He rearranged his stores and then set sail, intending to return to England with as little delay as possible. In that, however, there was some difficulty. The fleet was in need of fresh water, and for that it had to wander from one point to another in the neighbourhood of Cuba. A scanty supply was at length procured at San Antonio, the western cape of that island. "Here," says the chronicler, "I do wrong if I should forget the good example of the General, who, to encourage others and to hasten the getting water aboard, took no less pains himself than the meanest. Throughout the expedition, indeed, he had everywhere shown so vigilant a care and foresight in the good ordering of his fleet, accompanied with such wonderful travail of body, that, doubtless, had he been the meanest person, as he was the chiefest, he had deserved the first place of honour. And no less happy do we account him for being associated with Master Carlisle, his Lieutenant-General, by whose experience, prudent counsel, and gallant performance, he achieved so many and happy enterprises, and by whom also he was very greatly assisted in setting down the needful orders, law and course of justice, and the due administration of the same upon all occasions."

From Cuba Drake sailed up to Florida and coasted it to the northward, sacking and burning the new Spanish settlements of San Juan de Pinos and St. Augustine on his way, until he arrived at the island of Roanoke, containing Sir Walter Raleigh's luckless Virginian colonists. Them, as we have seen, he saved from the starvation that was imminent. After that a month's easy sailing brought him back to Portsmouth, which he reached on the 28th of July, after an absence of nine and a half months from England.

The expedition was much less successful than Drake and his friends had desired. Seven hundred and fifty of his twenty-three hundred followers had died on the way, chiefly of disease; and some of the principal places marked out for attack had been undisturbed. The gains, however, including two hundred and forty pieces of artillery, amounted in all to 60,000*l*., of which a third was given as prize-money to the soldiers and sailors, and the other two-thirds yielded a rich return to the fitters out of the fleet. Very great also was the English gain in injury to Spain. So great was Philip's alarm, when he heard of Drake's first coming to the coast of Galicia, that he forbade the sailing of the annual fleet for India or of any other trading ships from Spanish or Portuguese ports.* " Drake has played the dragon," was the cry of the frightened Spaniards; and the fright was steadily increased when the fleet of sixteen stout ships sent out by Philip in pursuit of Drake had to put back much damaged by a storm, and when every week brought some fresh report of his fierce doings in the Portuguese districts of Africa, in the Spanish Indies, and in the Spanish Main of America.† "Sir Francis Drake is a fearful man to the King of Spain," wrote Lord Burghley in a letter to the Earl of Leicester.‡

England just then had many fearful men to the King of Spain. On returning from his nine months' absence, Drake found that in the meanwhile great progress had been made in the quarrel between the two countries. Nearly every stay-at-home gentleman who had means enough fitted out a ship or two for employment in piracy or privateering against Spain. The European seas were crowded with them; and distant enterprises without number were projected, the most successful outcome of which was in the voyage of Thomas Cavendish, which has already been described. This was warfare by which Englishmen derived little but profit, and which brought upon Spaniards hardly anything but trouble. Philip and all good Catholics were resolved

* RECORD OFFICE MSS., *Domestic*, vol. clxxxiii., No. 28; vol. clxxxvi., No. 11.
† *Ibid.*, vol. clxxxvi., No. 19; vol. clxxxviii., Nos. 1, 8, 17, 53; vol. clxxxix., Nos. 4, 23, 24, 26, 42; vol. cxci., No. 35.
‡ *Leicester Correspondence*, p. 199.

that the insolent Protestant islanders must be punished in their own home; and to that end, even in the early part of 1586, preparations had begun to be made for the invasion of England. Drake found that counter-preparations were busily being made by Hawkins and Winter, and a hundred zealous subordinates in the oversight of shipbuilding and ship fitting, making of weapons, training of soldiers and sailors, and the like. He took his share in this work,* but he lost no time in planning other work in which he was likely to be of greater service to England and to Protestantism,—likely also to win for himself a larger share of wealth and fame.

He had only been in England a few months when he had perfected a plan for following up his raid upon the Spanish colonies by a raid upon the richest parts of Spain itself. English statesmen, gentlemen, and merchants were ready enough to help him in putting it in force. But Drake wished that his next enterprise should be much more than a privateering exploit. He desired "to singe King Philip's beard" with a formidable fleet of fighting ships, and was anxious, if possible, that his fleet should be recruited from the Netherlands as well as from England. With that object he proceeded to the Hague in November, and used the best arguments he could with the States-General, the burghers, and the seamen. The arguments had not much effect. "He found no disposition in the States and people," said one of Sir Francis Walsingham's correspondents, "at all to assent of his motions. They

* RECORD OFFICE MSS., *Domestic*, vol. cxciii., No. 49.

cannot yield to assist his voyage with any general contribution, but are content to deal with the inhabitants of the principal maritime towns, to furnish in every of them a ship or two."* But the maritime towns were as backward as the States-General, and Drake went disappointed back to England.

And in England he had not as much immediate support as he hoped for from Queen Elizabeth. This support was at last only given when the Queen had been convinced that instant action on her part was necessary. "Upon sundry advertisements and intelligences, very provably reported as well out of Spain as from other countries, of great provisions for the sea, prepared by the King of Spain with intent to employ the same in some attempt either against this realm of England or the realm of Ireland," it was said in the instructions given to Drake, " Her Majesty did think it very convenient, both for her honour and necessary defence, to have some strength and shipping at sea; to prevent or withstand such enterprises as might be attempted against her realms or dominions."† Accordingly, on the 16th of March, 1587, the Queen formally assigned to Drake, "by commission, covenant, promise and grant," four ships and two pinnaces, and allowed him to collect other vessels in any way that he could. On the 16th of March he signed a closing contract with some merchants of London, William Garway being one of the number, who agreed to provide him with

\* MOTLEY, vol. ii., p. 103.
† RECORD OFFICE MSS., *Domestic*, vol. cc., No. 17.

ten armed trading ships and pinnaces.* Nine or ten more appear to have been furnished by other adventurers. At any rate, by the end of March Sir Francis Drake was in command of about twenty-five vessels of all sizes, which he had used all the means in his power to make ready for immediate and efficient service at sea. " His commission," said Walsingham in a letter to Sir Edward Stafford, " is to impeach the joining together of the King of Spain's fleet out of their several ports, to keep victuals from them, to follow them in case they should be come forward towards England or Ireland, as also to set upon such as should either come out of the West or East Indies into Spain, or go out of Spain thither."†

Drake entered heartily into his work. On the 2nd of April he wrote from Plymouth to Sir Francis Walsingham, to say that the Queen's ships had just joined the private vessels that had been waiting for a week,‡ and that all was now ready for starting. " We have agreed upon all conditions between us and them, and have found them all so well affected and so willing in all our good proceedings, as we all persuade ourselves there was never more likely in any fleet, or a more loving agreement than we hope one of the other. I thank God I find no man but as all members of one

---

\* British Museum MSS., *Lansdowne*, lvi., No. 175, c.

† Record Office MSS., *Foreign*, cited by Mr. Hopper, in the Appendix to his edition of Robert Leng's *True Description of the Last Voyage of Sir Francis Drake, with his Service done against the Spaniards* (in vol. v. of the *Camden Miscellany*), p. 29.

‡ Record Office MSS., *Domestic*, vol. cc., No. 1.

body, to stand for our gracious Queen and country against Anti-Christ and his members. I assure your Honour there hath been no time lost, neither, with the grace of God, shall be in any other place. I have upon mine own credit supplied such victual as we have spent, and augmented as much as I could get, for that we are very unwilling to return errandless. If your Honour did now see the fleet under sail, and know with what resolution men's minds do enter into this action, as your Honour would rejoice to see them, so you would judge a small force would not divide them. Let me beseech your Honour to hold a good opinion, not of myself only, but of all the rest servitors in this action, as we stand nothing doubtful of your Honour; but if there be any ill affected, as there hath not wanted in other actions, and it is likely this will not go free, we hope that the parties may be known. If we deserve ill, let us be punished. If we discharge our duties in doing our best it is hard measure to be reported ill by those which will either keep their finger out of the fire, or too well affect to the alteration "—that is, overthrow—" of our Government, which I hope in God they shall never live to see." Herein Drake alluded to some of his followers who had run away: " we all think by some practice of some adversaries to the action, by letters written." These defections were easily supplied. Drake closed his letter in " haste, from aboard her Majesty's good ship, the *Elizabeth Bonaventure*." " The wind commands me away. Our ship is under sail. God grant we may so live in his fear, as the enemy may have cause to say that God doth fight for her Majesty as well abroad as at home, and give her long and happy life, and ever victory against God's enemies and her Majesty's. Let me beseech your Honour to pray unto God for us, that he will direct us the right way. Then shall we not doubt our enemies; for they are the sons of men."*

The Queen's ships which Drake thus led out so devoutly for spoliation of the Spanish Anti-Christ were, besides the *Elizabeth Bonaventure*, which he himself commanded, as he had done in the expedition of 1585, the *Golden Lion*, entrusted to Captain William Burrows as Vice-Admiral; the *Dreadnought*, under Captain Thomas Fenner; and the *Rainbow*, under Captain Bellingham. The *Merchant Royal*, as its name implies, was the leading contribution of the London citizens. The names of the other vessels are not recorded. The four largest were of about 500 tons apiece: one was of 400 tons; two were of 200 tons each; seven of 150 tons, and the rest were barks, pinnaces, and frigates of 50 tons and under. The total burthen amounted to 4,975 tons, and the sailors and soldiers employed numbered in all 2,648.†

Drake had hardly passed out of Plymouth Harbour on a Sunday which was to have all the fancied luck of a sailor's Sunday, when Elizabeth began to fear that she had been overbold in sending him to make war with King Philip in his own waters. Therefore, on the following Sunday, the 9th of April, a fresh set of in-

* RECORD OFFICE MSS., *Domestic*, vol. cc., No. 2.
† HOPPER, pp. 38, 53.

structions was drawn up by her Council. "Since your departure," it was said in these instructions, "her Majesty being advertised that the preparations of the King of Spain were not so great as was reported, and further, that they are of late dissolved"—certainly a false advertisement,—"and perceiving also by some other matter that hath proceeded from the said King of Spain and his ministers that he is desirous that the unkindness and jars happened of late years between her Majesty and him might be in some honourable sort compounded, her Majesty being, for her part, loth to exasperate matters further than they are, or to give cause to the world to conceive, by anything that may proceed from her or any of her ministers or subjects, that the present altercation between the said King and her is maintained or nourished by her, otherwise than forced thereunto for her own defence, hath commanded us to signify unto you, in her name, that her express will and pleasure is, you shall forbear to enter forcibly into any of the said King's ports or havens, or to offer violence to any of his towns or shipping within harbour, or to do any act of hostility upon the land. And yet, notwithstanding this direction, her pleasure is that you should do your best endeavour"—the words "as well by force as otherwise" were inserted and afterwards struck out—"to get into your possession, avoiding as much as may lie in you the effusion of Christian blood, such shipping of the said King's or his subjects as you shall find at seas."*

* RECORD OFFICE MSS., *Domestic*, vol. cc., No. 17.

These instructions, however, seem not to have reached Drake until his return to England. Before they could possibly have reached him he had done the work which he was ordered not to do. Having started with a fair wind on the morning of the 2nd of April, he fell in, on the afternoon of the 3rd, with two pirate-vessels from the Isle of Wight, which he attached to his fleet; and a few other stray ships appear, by design or accident, to have joined his force in the English Channel. Three days of quick sailing brought him within sight of Cape Finisterre; but then a violent storm arose which did some damage and wasted some time. The ships were driven out to sea and there dispersed during seven days. When they met on the 16th of April, it was found that the *Dreadnought* had been nearly wrecked and that a pinnace had been lost. Then Drake shaped his course to Cape Saint Vincent, which he passed on the 17th, " divers of his small barks and pinnaces shoring in and chasing within their bays their small barks and caravels, whereof they took one."*

It was Drake's plan to go at once to Cadiz, the greatest port of Spain, and there do as much mischief as he could. He reached its harbour on the 19th. " There we found," Drake said in a letter to Walsingham, " sundry great ships, some laden, some half laden, and some ready to be laden with the King's provisions for England. I assure your Honour the like preparation was never heard of, nor known, as the King of Spain hath and daily maketh to invade Eng-

* LENG, in HOPPER, p. 14.

land. His provisions of bread and wines are so great as will suffice forty thousand men a whole year, which, if they be not impeached before they join, will be very perilous. Our interest therefore is, by God's help, to intercept their meetings by all possible means we may, which I hope shall have such good success as shall tend to the advancement of God's glory, the safety of her Highness's royal person, the quiet of her country, and the annoyance of the enemy."*

A good deal of annoyance was done to the enemy during the two days which Drake spent in the Road of Cadiz. In a sentence he himself described the most daring exploit of English sea-fighting that had ever yet been done. " We sank a Biscayan of 1200 tons, burnt a ship of the Marquis of Santa Cruz of 1500 tons, and thirty-one ships more of 1000, 800, 600, 400, and 200 tons apiece, and carried away four with us laden with provisions, and departed thence at our pleasure with as much honour as we could wish, notwithstanding that during the time of our abode there we were both oftentimes fought withal by twelve of the King's galleys, of whom we sank two and always repulsed the rest, and were, without ceasing, vehemently shot at from the shore; but to our little hurt, God be thanked."† Some of his comrades sent home fuller reports, differing slightly as regards figures, which have come down to us.‡

* RECORD OFFICE MSS., *Domestic*, vol. cc., No. 46. No. 47 is a similar letter written by Drake, on the same day, April 27, to Secretary Wolley.

† RECORD OFFICE MSS., *Domestic*, vol. cc., No. 46.

‡ LENG, pp. 14-16; HAKLUYT, vol. ii., part ii., pp. 121-123; *Newes out of the Coastes of Spain*, attributed to Captain Fenner, and published

From them we learn that it was on the afternoon of Wednesday that the fleet came within sight of Cadiz. "So soon as we were descried," says one, "two of their galleys made towards us, and, judging what we were, made haste into shore again, not offering to shoot one shot at us. Yet before they could return, our admiral, with others of our fleet, shot them through and slew ten of their men. Presently there came forth from the town ten other galleys and fought with us; but we applied them so well with our great ordnance that two of them were fain to be hauled up that night." Very great was the consternation in the town at the report of this English arrival. All the women and children were hurried for safety into the fortress, twenty-seven of them being crushed to death in the turmoil. Every man who could and would handle a weapon made ready to use it. A flying messenger was despatched to the Duke of Medina Sidonia, in charge of the army at San Lucar, for succour. Soldiers and volunteers crowded the quay and all the seaward streets, and the large guns of the fortress were prepared for service. But the great galleys, some of them twice or thrice as large as the largest of the English ships, and, with the smaller fighting craft, making a force twice as great as Drake's in number of vessels, four or five times as great in number of men and guns, offered no resistance for that night

---

in 1587; BRITISH MUSEUM MSS., *Harleian*, clxvii., fols. 104, 105; *Ibid.*, *Lansdowne*, xc., No. 21; and a French account by a resident in the town, copied from the RECORD OFFICE MSS., *Foreign*, in the Appendix to LENG, pp. 35-38,—from which the above extracts have been made.

after the first defeat of the two scouts and the ten galleys that followed them. In the dusk Drake quietly sailed into the harbour with his four Queen's ships and some of the lesser vessels, while the *Merchant Royal* and several of the other merchants' ships, spreading themselves from end to end of the little bay, forced back a number of Spanish, French, Italian, and other sail, mostly trading vessels, that attempted to escape at the first brunt of danger. Many of these were boarded and despoiled, with no loss of life to either side, save in the drowning of a few of the sailors who swam towards the shore in hope of saving themselves.

Almost as easy was Drake's greater victory. The Spanish galleys were valiant only in show. They retreated under shelter of the fortress and left Drake to do as much mischief as he could while in pursuit of them and in his subsequent seizure of the trading ships that were in port. "The same night," says one of the company, pious and patriotic as ever, " our General, having, by God's favour and sufferance, good opportunity to punish the enemy of God's true gospel and our daily adversary, and further willing to discharge his expected duty towards God, his prince, and country, began to sink and fire divers of their ships." The chief of these was the private property of the Marquis of Santa Cruz, Philip II.'s High Admiral,—" a princely bark," said an English Papist, who sympathized with Spain, " esteemed at the value of 18,000 ducats; which warmeth him, who, for fear of losing his honour before, was always hanging back from meddling or matching with English pirates."

We can well believe that it was burnt with special pleasure by the prince of English pirates. A great Genoese argosy, of 1,000 tons, was sunk. "sore against all their wills," because in it, besides rich stuffs of all sorts, were thirty-six pieces of brass ordnance. Four other ships almost as large were sunk, one from Venice, one from Lucca, one from Florence, and one of French ownership, though all chartered by Philip for service in his invasion of England. Five great Spanish carracks, richly laden for the East Indian trade, and about twenty other vessels of various size and value, were also sunk, after being despoiled of the choicest portions of their cargoes. All the injury done to Drake's fleet, in return for this damage, was in the loss of a little Spanish caravel, captured the day before, with five Englishmen on board. "This caravel," it is said, "being far astern, came in very late, so as the galleys intercepted her with much shot and many muskets, but they would never strike and so were taken." Forty galleys from neighbouring ports were sent to attack Drake, and some of them followed him into the harbour; "but in vain, for their chiefest gain was expense of powder and shot."

Drake herein certainly did work enough for one afternoon and evening. Had he been able to land on the same night he might have made terrible havoc of Cadiz, and even, perhaps, have seized its fortress; but he and his brave comrades were tired out for the time. Therefore they kept on shipboard; "in which," says a Frenchman resident in the town, "God showed great favour to the people, for fear and confusion caused them marvellous trouble." In the morning arrived the reinforcements that had been sent for, and then it was too late for the little body of Englishmen to land with any chance of success. In the harbour, however, they continued their work of destruction all through Thursday and for a great part of the following night. The spoiling, sinking, and burning of the enemy's shipping was carried on with terrible effect.* " The galleys made divers bravadoes upon us," we are told. " The town and their forts also played upon us all day long. But they did us little hurt, saving that the master gunner of the *Golden Lion* had his leg broke with a shot from the town." " During our abode," says another of the party, "they gave us small rest, by reason of their shot from the galleys, fortresses, and shore, where continually they placed new ordnance at places convenient to offend; which notwithstanding, we continually fired their ships as the flood came in, to the end to be cleared of them; the sight of which terrible fires were to us very pleasant, and mitigated the burthen of our continual travail; wherein we were busied for two nights and one day, in discharging, firing, and lading of provisions, with reservation for good, laudable, and guardable defence of the enemy. It may seem strange, or rather miraculous, that so great an exploit should be performed with so small loss; the place to endamage

* It is most likely that much of the spoliation attributed to the first evening belonged to the following day and evening; but I have followed the accounts, in which there is some discrepancy, natural where each authority saw the occurrences from a different point of observation.

us being so convenient, and their force so great, as appeared, from whom were shot at us at the least two hundred culverin and cannon shot. But in this, as in all others our actions heretofore, though dangerously attempted, yet happily performed, our good God hath and daily doth make His infinite power manifest to all Papists; and His name by us His servants continually honoured!"

The total amount of damage done by Drake is variously reported. By an average of the conflicting statements it would appear that he destroyed some forty or fifty vessels, large and small, of about 9,000 or 10,000 tons in the aggregate. The loss of stores alone, to King Philip and his subjects, was estimated at half a million ducats, not far short of 150,000*l.* Among the goods burnt and sunk were 4,000 pipes of wine, 20,000 quintals of biscuits, and 30,000 hundredweight of wheat and other provisions.* Out of the destruction was saved as much food as the English ships had room for. "We rest victualled," it was said, "with bread and drink for six months in our ships, and have besides two fly-boats full laden with bread sufficient for a good army for three months."

Having done as much mischief as he could in Cadiz Harbour, Drake sailed out of it at two o'clock in the morning of Friday, the 21st of April. "When we were a little out," adds the chronicler, "we fell becalmed, and ten galleys followed us and fought with us all that forenoon. But, whether for lack of powder and shot,

* LANSDOWNE MS. in HOPPER, p. 41.

or by reason of the heat of the day, I know not, or some of them shot through, which was most likeliest as we judged, they lay aloof for the space of three hours, and never after durst come within our shot. Which our General seeing, that afternoon he sent to the captain of those galleys to know if he had any Englishmen in the galleys as slaves there, as also to will him to deliver unto him the five Englishmen whom they had taken at our coming into Cadiz; and he would deliver so many Spaniards or Portuguese for them. At which time he sent his boat unto our General, presenting him with sucket "—or sweetmeats—" and such other novelties as they had, certifying him that they had none, but only those whom they had taken with the caravel, who were living and in the town at Cadiz: to satisfy which, if it pleased him to stay until the next day, they would make his request known unto the governor of the town, and would return to him again with answer." But, as Drake had reason for supposing that by another day's waiting off Cadiz he would expose himself to a formidable attack from a great fleet which was being collected, he refused to assent to "their devilish practice," and, "finding the wind for his purpose," put out to sea before night.

For ten days he loitered at sea, in the neighbourhood of Cape Saint Vincent. On the 27th of April he sent home a concise report of his achievements which has been quoted from, and with his despatch went some of the other letters which have supplied us with the details of the raid on Cadiz. "We all remain in great love with our general and in unity throughout the whole fleet," it was said in one of them. That statement was not correct. Drake deserved the love of his comrades, and he generally obtained it. But, like other brave and daring men, he was sometimes imperious and always resolute in carrying out the plans that commended themselves to his own judgment, without much regard for the opinions of others. Thereby offence was given to some, and especially to William Burrows, the Captain of the *Golden Lion* and Vice-Admiral of the whole fleet. On the 30th of April he wrote a foolish letter to Drake, pouring out the grievances which seem to have been troubling him all through the four weeks they had been at sea, and which had become important during the attack on Cadiz. " I have found you always so wedded to your own opinion and will," he said, " that you rather disliked and showed as though it were offensive unto you that any should give you advice in anything,—at least I speak it of myself. For which cause I have refrained often to speak that which otherwise I would and in reason, in discharge of the duty I owe to her Majesty and the place I serve in, I ought to have done; which place you make no account of, nay, you deal not so with me as you do to others." Burrows represented that he had all the more ground of complaint because his slighted advice accorded more than Drake's practice, as he supposed, with the instructions issued by the Queen. Drake ought, he said, merely to have watched the Spanish coast and attacked any hostile fleet that might have come out to meet him, instead of going, in excess of boldness, to attack the shipping in the Spanish forts, as had been done at Cadiz. Much more of that timid, grumbling sort wrote Burrows.* Drake's answer to the letter was, immediately upon receiving it, to place the discontented Vice-Admiral under arrest. Burrows was confined to his cabin for two days, and only reinstated after he had written a penitent letter, promising obedience in the future.† The breach was not healed, but any serious hindrance of Drake's projects was averted.

Burrows' special ground of complaint had been a plan propounded by Drake on the 29th of April, for employing a thousand men upon a land attack on Lagos. This plan he put in force, with nearly enough failure to justify Burrows' objections, on the 4th of May. The thousand men were disembarked five miles from the town, and marched boldly up through cornfields and vineyards. Four hundred horsemen, " bravely horsed, but very ill manned," came out to meet them, but ran away before they were within reach of shot. The town, however, was too well guarded for its capture to be possible, and the invaders had to retire after sustaining considerable injury, which was feebly atoned for by the distant bombardment of the fleet. The English waited on the shore for two hours, hoping that the Spaniards would come out and fight. The challenge being refused, they went back to their ships.

* RECORD OFFICE MSS., *Domestic*, vol. cc., No. 57.
† *Ibid.*, vol. ccii., No. 14.

Better success attended an attack which was made next day upon Sagres, half way between Lagos and Cape Saint Vincent. " We landed about eight hundred men, all musket, small shot, and pikemen," says the chronicler of the expedition, "our General meaning to satisfy his valiant mind in doing some worthy exploits upon our enemy's land. When we had landed our men, we marched towards a fort called Avalera, upon which was a flag; from which fort, when they saw us so boldly to approach them, they fled unto their great fort or castle Cape Sagres. The fort called Avalera, with certain brass pieces we took; which with certain of our men was kept. All the rest marched towards the castle, the walls whereof were esteemed thirty foot high and ten foot broad, and on the east, south, and west it is all a main rock, without passage, at least thirty fathoms high, and fifteen brass pieces were therein planted. As we marched along by them they shot at us, but did us no hurt. And then and there, by the commandment of our General, thirty musket shot went and skirmished with them in the castle; and, when they had continued some time in skirmishing with them, and spent most of their powder and shot, they all returned to our main battle again, having no man slain, but some a little hurt. Upon which our General summoned the captain of the castle to a parley, commanding him to yield it up, which he then utterly denied. Whereupon our General sent for wood from our ships to set on fire the uttermost gate; and he himself, to see the same act performed, with great industry carried of the said wood and other provision in person, and did help to set it on fire, whilst the vanguard of our main battle skirmished with them in their faces on the walls; during which time of fight with them we had two of our men slain outright, and divers sore hurt. In which time, the captain of the castle being sore wounded, and they all within, to the number of two hundred and forty, wonderfully daunted with our bold enterprises, they put out their flag of truce, and yielded; when we entered, and finding within the said castle the foresaid number of two hundred and forty persons, our General most favourably licensed them to depart." From that fortress Drake sent to the captains of the castle at Cape Saint Vincent, quite as large as the one he had conquered, and another fort in the neighbourhood, such messages as led to the peaceable surrender of their keys and the hasty retreat of the soldiers in charge of them. He stayed on shore for the night, and next morning, having taken from them as many of their guns as he could carry away, he set both castles and both forts on fire, and brought his fleet into the harbour of Cape Saint Vincent.*

There he halted for four days, destroying all the war shipping that he could find. He had done the same on his way from Cadiz, and he continued to do it for the rest of his stay in Spanish waters. During the ten days preceding, and the ten days following his arrival at Cape Saint Vincent, as he said in a letter to Walsingham, "we have taken forty ships, barks, and caravels,

* LENG, pp. 17, 18.

and divers other vessels more than a hundred, most laden, some with oars for galleys, plank and timber for ships and pinnaces, hoops and pipe-staves for casks, with many other provisions for this great army," which was to invade England. " I assure your Honour the hoops and pipe-staves were above 16,000 or 17,000 tons in weight; all which I commanded to be consumed into smoke and ashes by fire, which will be unto the King no small waste unto his provisions, besides the want of his barks."*

Part of this mischief was done after Drake had quitted Cape Saint Vincent. Setting sail again on the 10th of May he went towards Lisbon, which by Philip's seizure of Portugal in 1580 had become the greatest of Spanish ports, intending to treat its shipping as he had treated that of Cadiz. There and on the way thither, however, the enemy's force was so great that even he, with all his boldness, was deterred from causing very much destruction. In one long day a favourable wind took him up to Cascaes, at the mouth of the Tagus ; and there he lay at anchor, caring little for the shot that was aimed at him from the castle and from eight galleys in the harbour, and being little hurt by it. Thence he sent a message to the Marquis of Santa Cruz, proposing to give up his Spanish captives for English prisoners, man for man.† " The Marquis sent me word," he says, " that, as he was a gentleman, he had none, and that I should assure myself that, if he had any, he

* RECORD OFFICE MSS., *Domestic*, vol. cci., No. 33.
† LENG, pp. 18, 19.

would surely have sent them me; which I knew was not so, for I had true intelligence by Englishmen and Portuguese that the Marquis had divers Englishmen both in his galleys and prisons. Whereupon it is agreed by us all, her Majesty's captains and masters, that all such Spaniards as it shall please God to send under our hands, shall be sold unto the Moors, and the money reserved for the redeeming of such of our countrymen as may be redeemed therewith."* Many fresh captures of Spaniards he made with this handling of them in view, and a great deal of further mischief he effected among the smaller shipping that was to be found between Cascaes and Lisbon and along the opposite shore. He was anxious that the Marquis of Santa Cruz should bring out his galleys, of which as many as twenty-four were assembled near Lisbon, for open fight. But this the Spaniards dared not do, and Drake durst not attack them in harbour, where they were under cover of the great artillery on land. So he returned to Cape Saint Vincent on the 12th of May.†

There he waited for six days, intending to wait much longer. He had done his utmost in fulfilment of his purpose "to singe King Philip's beard," and now he paused in hopes that Philip would send a fleet to resist him, and be defeated by him, in open sea. He waited also for instructions from home. "For the revenge of these things," he said in a letter to Walsingham, dated the 17th of May, "what forces the country is able to

* RECORD OFFICE MSS., *Domestic*, vol. cci., No. 33.
† *Ibid.*; LENG, pp. 19, 20; Appendix to the same, p. 46.

make, we shall be sure to have brought upon us, as far as they may, with all the devices and traps they can devise. When they come, they shall be but the sons of mortal men, and, for the most part, enemies to the truth, and upholders of balls to Dagon's image, which hath already fallen before the ark of our God, with his hands, arms, and head stricken off. As long as it shall please God to give us provisions to eat and drink, and that our ships and wind and weather will permit us, you shall surely hear of us near this Cape of Saint Vincent; where we do and will expect daily what her Majesty and your Honours will farther command. God make us all thankful that her Majesty sent out these few ships in time. If there were here six more of her Majesty's good ships of the second sort, we should be the better able to keep their forces from joining, and haply take or impeach their fleets from all places in the next month, and so after, which is the chiefest time of their return home,—which I judge, in my poor opinion, will bring this great monarchy to those conditions which are meet. God make us all thankful, again and again, that we have, although it be little, made a beginning upon the coast of Spain. If we can thoroughly believe that this which we do is in the defence of our religion and country, no doubt but our merciful God, for His Christ our Saviour's sake, is able, and will give us victory. There must be a beginning of any great matter, but the continuing unto the end, until it be thoroughly finished, is the true glory.*

* RECORD OFFICE MSS., *Domestic*, vol. cci., No. 33.

Drake waited in vain for instructions. Along with his reports of his achievements, and his opinions thereupon, Queen Elizabeth received letters from Spain and from the Spanish authorities in the Netherlands, complaining bitterly of the mischief that was being done in her name, and demanding Drake's immediate recall and punishment, unless she was prepared to receive in her own seas and realm the direst vengeance that Spain could bring upon her. To these her Council replied that she had sent special orders to Drake forbidding uch conduct as he was reported to have been guilty of, but that the ship entrusted with these orders had been driven back by contrary winds, so that they had never reached him. "And for the better manifesting of her Majesty's disposition therein," it was added, "we can assure you that her Highness, understanding of some attempts of the said Drake's by land, is greatly offended with him for the same, and meaneth at his return to carry him to his answer; which showeth most apparently the continuance of her Majesty's good disposition."* It is clear that Queen Elizabeth in her heart approved of Drake's proceedings; but she still wished to maintain a show of friendliness towards King Philip; therefore, having equally good reasons for neither recalling nor reinforcing him, she prudently abstained from sending him any communication at all.

Nor did Drake wait long for a communication from England. On the 17th of May he heard that ten

* RECORD OFFICE MSS., *Flanders Correspondence*, in HOPPER, pp. 43, 44.

Spanish galleys, probably the ten that he had left at
Cadiz, had come to Lagos, intending, if possible, to join
the force of twenty-four ships at Lisbon. Next morning he went in pursuit of them, and with a few vigorous
broadsides drove them close into the harbour, where he
did not find it expedient to follow them. He therefore
returned to his halting-place, finding a little amuse-
ment on his way in driving three small vessels aground.
On the following day, for another small diversion, he
put four hundred men on land near Sagres, who despoiled
and set fire to a fishermen's village.*

That was ignoble work, and Drake seems to have
grown tired of it. It was wearisome also to the captains
of the merchant ships who, being sent out with the
special object of acquiring rich booty, had not much
satisfaction in the destruction of property which, though
very ruinous to the Spaniards, yielded no direct profit
to the English. Therefore, a new series of exploits was
resolved upon, to be begun by an expedition to the
Azores, the usual halting-place of the richly-laden
carracks of Spain and Portugal coming from the East
and West Indies. With this object, Drake spent two
days in transferring most of the captured stores and all
his sick and wounded men to five vessels which he had
taken from the Spaniards at Cadiz and elsewhere. That
was done, and the detachment started for England to
have a short and easy passage on the 22nd of May.†

Drake's new project, however, was in great part
frustrated. Directing his course on the same day for

* LENG, p. 20.   † Ibid.

the Azores, a terrible storm befell his fleet before midnight. It lasted for three days, during which the vessels were dispersed. The *Elizabeth Bonaventure* was in sore danger of being wrecked, and all the other ships were more or less damaged. When, on the 25th, Drake proceeded to collect them, he found that all his merchant auxiliaries had taken fright and made for England.\* Nor was that his only trouble. The old discontent of William Burrows had never been really overcome. "Burrows hath not carried himself in this action so well as I wish he had done for his own sake," Drake said in a letter to Burghley on the 21st of May; "and his persisting hath committed a double offence, not only against me, but it toucheth further."† Then, or before, he had been again superseded, and Captain Marchant had been put in charge of the *Golden Lion*; but this change wrought no good. A mutiny broke out in the ship on the 26th or 27th of May, and, deserting Drake in his time of trouble, it followed the merchant ships to England; whence, on the 5th of June, Burrows wrote to Lord Admiral Howard, detailing his account of the affair.‡ This was followed, a month or two afterwards, by a long and lame contradiction of the charges brought against him by Sir Francis Drake,§ which so far succeeded as to save him from a severe punishment.

\* LENG, p. 21.
† BRITISH MUSEUM MSS., *Cotton*, cited by BARROW, *Life of Drake*, p. 229.
‡ RECORD OFFICE MSS., *Domestic*, vol. ccii., No. 14.
§ BRITISH MUSEUM MSS., *Lansdowne*, cited by BARROW, pp. 249-255. See also RECORD OFFICE MSS., *Domestic*, vol. ccii., Nos. 66. 67; vol. cciii., No. 1; vol. ccviii., No. 77.

In 1588 he did some useful service in the Armada Fight.

After the defection of the *Golden Lion* and the merchant ships, Drake's fleet was reduced to nine vessels, the three ships and two pinnaces furnished by the Queen, and four others, which probably belonged to himself and his friends. With this force he judged it impossible to do more in attacking Spain in its own waters, defended by galleys and other fighting craft which, though individually no match for his vessels, were numerous enough to overwhelm him with ease. Therefore he determined to return promptly to England. First, however, in accordance with his previous plan, he proceeded, in search of booty, to the Azores. There, with very little difficulty, he had as much success as he could have hoped for. On the 8th of June, after sixteen days' sailing, he came within sight of Saint Michael's Island. "In the morning of the 9th," says the chronicler of the voyage, "we descried a great sail, who, by our judgment, made towards us, and we, having a pretty gale of wind, with all speed made towards her; but by the time we had sailed towards her about one league, we might perceive her to be a mighty ship, which was then called a carrack, having out a Portugal flag and red cross. But we, knowing what she was, would put out no flag until we were within shot of her, when we hanged out flags, streamers, and pendants, that she might be out of doubt to know who we were; which done, we hailed her with cannon-shot, and having shot her through divers times, she shot at us, sometimes at one, sometimes at another. Then we began to apply her hotly, our flyboat and one of our pinnaces lying thwart her hawse, at whom she shot and threw fireworks, but did them no hurt, for that her ordnance lay so high over them. Then, she seeing us ready to lay her on board, all of our ships applying her so hotly and resolutely, determined to make short with her, six of her men being slain, and divers sore hurt, they yielded unto us; whom, when we boarded, we found to be the King of Spain's own ship come from the East Indies, called by his name, Philip, and the greatest ship in all Portugal, richly laden, to our happy joy and great gladness. There were also in her four hundred Niggers, whom they had taken to make slaves in Spain and Portugal, whom our General, with the captain and his company, to the number of two hundred and forty, put into our flyboat to go whither they list, and further dealt most favourably with them."*

Drake might well afford to deal favourably with the crews and captives of the *San Filipe*, as the great carrack was called. Guarding her with his little fleet, he set sail at once for England, and reached Plymouth on the 26th of June, just twelve weeks after his departure.† His great achievements won for him the enthusiastic admiration of all honest patriots, and, if Queen Elizabeth ever meant to punish him for going beyond his instructions in the daring work that had done so much harm and caused so much annoyance to the Spaniards, she now no longer thought of it.

* LENG, pp. 21, 22. † *Ibid.*, p. 22.

Even greater, however, than the joy that arose from his great destruction of Spanish shipping, and his notable wasting of the Spanish preparations for invading England, seems to have been the joy with which the great prize that he brought home was regarded by both Queen and people. No merchant ship so large or so richly laden had ever before been seen in England. The spices and drugs, silks and taffetas, calicoes and carpets, that it contained were valued at 108,049*l.* 13*s.* 11*d.*, and by it alone were defrayed all the expenses of the expedition, with surplus enough to give ample profit both to Queen Elizabeth and to the other adventurers who had embarked their ships and money in the work.*

But the gain in money to England and the loss in money to Spain was as nothing in comparison with England's gain and Spain's loss in credit. Sir Francis Drake's great exploits probably did not delay the invasion of England, which Philip was reported to be preparing for 1587, as the preparations were not completed in time for that year; and they certainly gave an immense stimulus to the further preparations which issued in the despatching of the Invincible Armada in 1588. But they showed to English Protestants and their friends upon the continent, that the reputation acquired by Spain for superiority over all other nations was only a pretence, and cleared the way for the much

* RECORD OFFICE MSS., *Domestic*, vol. cciv., Nos. 2, 8, 9, 27, 28, 30, 31, 33, 39, 40, 52; vol. ccv, Nos. 2, 12, 54, 55; vol. ccvi., No. 4. See also an estimate of the value of the *San Filipe* and its cargo, differing from the amount stated above, in the BRITISH MUSEUM MSS., *Lansdowne*, cxv., No 89.

completer spoiling of the delusion that was presently to take place. Drake had succeeded very well in the intention with which he had quitted England, "to singe King Philip's beard." King Philip, irritated beyond endurance by that last and greatest of a series of indignities that he had been receiving from English seamen during thirty years, put out all his strength to resent it; but only to receive a yet greater indignity, which was the turning-point in the crooked course of his tyrannical rule, and also the beginning of the decadence of Spain.

## CHAPTER XV.

THE GREAT ARMADA FIGHT.

[1588.]

IF Sir Francis Drake's great exploits on the coast of Spain and Portugal prevented Philip II. from invading England in 1587, they were certainly a great incentive to the invasion that was attempted in 1588. The preparations thereto which had been in process for some years, and which Drake had so seriously retarded, were continued with redoubled energy as soon as it was known that he was once more in England. Philip's eagerness to be revenged for that injury was further quickened by the disgrace which it had brought upon him and his forces among both enemies and friends. Even Pope Sixtus V. is reported, when he heard of Drake's successes, to have exclaimed "that the Queen of England's distaff was worth more than Philip's sword."\* That taunt, and the hundreds like it that

---

\* MOTLEY, vol. ii., p. 461. Mr. Motley having said so much about the history of the Armada Fight, and the theme having been so often handled by others, I have here made my account as brief as possible, limiting myself almost entirely to such illustrations of English seamanship as seemed absolutely necessary to my subject, and drawing these, as far as possible, from new or little-used material.

were muttered or said openly in and out of Philip's hearing, determined him to do his utmost towards retrieving his disgrace, and resenting the indignities that had been accumulating for nearly thirty years, by one decisive and overwhelming movement.

The movement was to be made by as formidable and well-manned a fleet as Philip could put upon the sea, under the command of the Chief Admiral, the Marquis of Santa Cruz, and send to the neighbourhood of Calais for further augmentation by Alexander Farnese, Prince of Parma, the Viceroy in the Netherlands in succession to the Duke of Alva, who was to take command of the whole expedition. Fortunately for England and the world, Santa Cruz was over-timid. The public indignities and the private losses that Drake had put upon him in 1587 had only served to dishearten the Chief Admiral, never very bold. He feared to place himself in any fresh contact with Drake and Drake's countrymen, and, after repeated orders to complete his arrangements and set sail, which he met with elaborate excuses and elaborate delays, he died of worry and vexation. Thereby the invasion, which had been planned for January, was not entered upon until the middle of June, and England had time to prepare for resisting it.

That resistance was made difficult through the dilatoriness of Queen Elizabeth and Lord Burghley. Remembering how easily Drake had damaged the Spaniards off Cadiz, and hoping to the very last that their diplomacy would prevent Philip from putting his threats in force, they showed a lack of foresight, and a blindness even to the plain tokens of the present, that were a marvel to all but themselves and the few who thought with them, and a source of honest annoyance, honestly expressed, to every ardent patriot. "Since England was England," wrote Lord Admiral Howard to Walsingham on the 27th of January, with reference to efforts on behalf of peace that were being made in the Netherlands and ostensibly favoured by the Prince of Parma, "there never was such a stratagem and mask to deceive her Majesty as this treaty of peace. I pray God that we do not curse for this a long grey beard with a white head witless"—the head and beard being Burghley's—"that will make all the world think us heartless. For my part, I have made of the French King, the Scottish King, and the King of Spain, a Trinity that I mean never to trust to be saved by, and I would that others were of my opinion."\*

Many others were of that opinion, and Elizabeth and her temporising counsellors were forced to yield to it, in part at any rate. Howard showed his wisdom in adopting and promoting the views of men more experienced than himself. As heretofore Drake was most zealous in argument, Hawkins in such modes of action as appertained to his multifarious duties as Comptroller of the Navy. Throughout the later months of 1587 and the early part of 1588 Hawkins was doing his utmost to see that all the Queen's ships were duly fitted out for service, well victualled and properly manned.†

\* RECORD OFFICE MSS., *Domestic*, vol. ccviii., No. 30.
† *Ibid.*, vol. ccvi., Nos. 30, 42, and other papers.

On the 21st of December, 1587, Howard, newly commissioned as "Lieutenant-General and Commander-in-Chief of the Navy and Army prepared to the seas against Spain," went to Chatham to take charge of the *White Bear*, a ship of 1,000 tons burthen, and next day he reported that in it and in the other ships there stationed were "as sufficient and able a company of sailors as ever was seen."* This squadron was afterwards entrusted to Sir Henry Palmer, soon to be superseded by Lord Henry Seymour, and appointed to watch the Narrow Seas.† Another squadron was being prepared by Sir Francis Drake at Plymouth, for the protection of the west coast.‡ Lord Howard, in the meanwhile, went to superintend the further preparations that were being made at Dover, Harwich, Portsmouth, and other sea-towns.§ He found that there were twenty ships in all, manned by two thousand and ninety-four sailors.||

This was certainly no great armament. On the 1st of February Howard wrote to Walsingham begging for further strengthening of the fleet instead of the weakening of the force which was contemplated. "The enemy now make but little reckoning of us," he said, "and know that we are but like bears tied to stakes, and that they may come like dogs to offend us."¶

On the same day Hawkins wrote to urge that the only way to gain solid peace was to enter upon a determined

---

* RECORD OFFICE MSS., *Domestic*, vol. ccvi., Nos. 41, 42, 43, 46.
† *Ibid.*, vol. ccviii., Nos. 6, 7.  ‡ *Ibid.*, vol. ccviii., Nos. 6, 8.
§ *Ibid.*, vol. ccviii., No. 14.   || *Ibid.*, vol. ccviii., No. 27.
¶ *Ibid.*, vol. ccviii., No. 46.

and resolute war. "We might have peace," he said, "but not with God. Rather than serve Baal, let us die a thousand deaths. Let us have open war with these Jesuits, and every man will contribute, fight, devise, or do, for the liberty of our country." He begged to be allowed the use of six large and six small ships for four months, with eighteen hundred mariners and soldiers, to be employed in another raid upon the Spanish coast and in all sorts of hindering of the Armada, whether in port or on its way. He promised that he would "distress anything that went through the seas," and besides the injury to Philip, that he would acquire booty enough to pay four times over the cost of the expedition.*

That offer was rejected, as also was a more modest and less useful one of Lord Howard's, to use the Narrow Seas squadron in an attack upon Scotland, then in feeble league with Spain.† But the sea force was steadily augmented. By the middle of February the crews had risen in number to three thousand and fifteen.‡ "Our ships do show like gallants here," wrote Sir William Winter to Hawkins, on the 28th of the month. "It would do a man's heart good to behold them. Would to God the Prince of Parma were on the seas with all his forces, and we in sight of them. You should hear that we would make his enterprise very unpleasant to him."§

Next day, in a letter to Burghley, Lord Howard, still begging for reinforcements, expressed similar con-

* RECORD OFFICE MSS., *Domestic*, vol. ccviii., No. 47.
† *Ibid.*, vol. ccviii., No. 67.    ‡ *Ibid.*, vol. ccviii., Nos. 65, 70.
§ *Ibid.*, vol. ccviii., No. 85.

fidence. "Let me have the four great ships and twenty hoys, with but twenty men apiece, and each with but two iron pieces, and her Majesty shall have a good account of the Spanish forces, and I will make the King wish his galleys home again. Few as we are, if his forces be not hundreds, we will make good sport with them when they come."* The four ships asked for were the *White Bear*, the *Triumph*, the *Elizabeth Jonas*, and the *Victory*,† which, as Howard bitterly complained in a letter to Walsingham on the 9th of March, her Majesty was keeping "to protect Chatham Church withal, when they should be serving their turn abroad." He complained also of the Queen's conduct to Drake, by which he had been prevented from not getting his Plymouth squadron in complete order for sea-service.‡ "The fault is not in him," he added, two days later, "but I pray God her Majesty do not repent her slack dealing. All who come out of Spain must concur in one to lie, or else we shall be stirred very shortly with a 'heave ho!' I fear ere long her Majesty will be sorry she hath believed some so much as she hath done."§

Her Majesty and her more cautious advisers, however, persisted in believing, their belief being much aided by a desire to spend as little money as possible in the work of defending England from the threatened invasion. Amid a heap of documents showing how the whole country was astir with eager preparation—how

* RECORD OFFICE MSS., *Domestic*, vol. ccviii., No. 87.
† *Ibid.*, vol. ccix., No. 27.   ‡ *Ibid.*, vol. ccix., No. 12.
§ *Ibid.*, vol. ccix., No. 15.

every gentleman who had a bark or boat in any way
adapted for fighting was furnishing it anew, and how
rude fishermen all along the coast crowded up to offer
their services as sailors; how the merchants of London
and their apprentices met every Tuesday to exercise
themselves and the great body of the citizens in warlike practices, and how honest shopkeepers and shop-
boys, from Exeter up to Hull, and from Dover up to
Chester, were following their example—it is curious to
find, with others of the same sort, calculations in Lord
Burghley's handwriting as to the economy of feeding
the sailors in the Queen's ships with fish on three days
and bacon once a week, instead of the usual ration of
fourpennyworth of beef each day.* And Queen Elizabeth herself was of the same mind. The four ships
which Howard had asked for were ordered to be furnished for active service; but the Queen was loth to
use any of them, and especially the *Elizabeth Jonas*,
a stout vessel of 900 tons burthen, which carried more
guns and not fewer seamen than any of the other ships.
" Lord! when should she serve if not at such a time as
this?" wrote Howard to Walsingham on the 7th of
April. "Either she is fit now to serve or fit for the fire.
I hope never in my time to see so great a cause for her
to be used. The King of Spain doth not keep any
ship at home, either of his own or any other that he
can get for money. I am sorry that her Majesty is so
careless of this most dangerous time. I fear me much,
and with grief I think it, that she relieth on a hope that

* RECORD OFFICE MSS., *Domestic*, vol. ccix., Nos. 16, 17.

will deceive her and greatly endanger her, and then it will not be her money nor her jewels that will help. Well, well, I must pray heartily for peace, for I see the support of an honourable war will never appear. Sparing and war have no affinity together."[*] And next day we find Howard writing even more boldly to Lord Burghley, to complain of the way in which the ships were only supplied with rations for a month at a time. "King Harry, her Majesty's father, never made a lesser proportion of supply than six weeks."[†]

Yet Elizabeth was a true daughter of the great King Harry, and she spoke no more than truth in the famous words with which, before the fate of the Invincible Armada, already vanquished, was known on land, she encouraged the soldiers who, after three more months of waiting and preparation, had little need of encouragement, in Tilbury camp. Some of her counsellors, dreading Catholic treachery, had begged her not to show herself just then in public. "Let tyrants fear," she said; "I have always so behaved myself that, under God, I have placed my chiefest strength and safeguard in the loyal hearts and goodwill of my subjects; and therefore I am come amongst you, as you see, at this time, resolved, in the midst and heat of the battle, to live or die amongst you all; to lay down for my God, for my kingdom, and for my people, my honour and my blood even in the dust. I know I have the body but of a weak and feeble woman; but I have the heart of a

[*] RECORD OFFICE MSS., *Domestic*, vol. ccix., No. 74.
[†] *Ibid.*, vol. ccix., No. 78.

king, and of a King of England too, and think it foul scorn that Parma, or Spain, or any prince of Europe, should dare to invade the borders of my realm, to which, rather than any dishonour shall grow by me, I myself will take up arms, I myself will be your general, judge, and rewarder of every one of your virtues in the field."\*

There would have been no need for Elizabeth to head her land-forces, few and feebly armed as they were, in resisting the Spanish invaders on their first landing upon English ground. There was no need even for those forces to waste any of their scanty store of ammunition in anything but peals of rejoicing at the victory won by their comrades on the sea.

The strongest body of those comrades, after the squadron of the Queen's own ships, was the irregular squadron prepared at Plymouth by Sir Francis Drake. Drake, like Hawkins, had been anxious during all the waiting time to go out and meet the Armada in Spanish waters, or even hinder it from ever passing out of Spanish harbours. "It will put great and good hearts," he said, writing from Plymouth to the Lords of the Council, on the 30th of March, "into her Majesty's loving subjects both abroad and at home, for that they will be persuaded in conscience that the Lord of all strengths will put into her Majesty and her people courage and boldness not to fear any invasion in her own country, but to seek God's enemies and her Majesty's where they may be found; for the Lord is on our

\* *Somers Tracts*, vol. i., p. 429.

side, whereby we may assure ourselves our numbers are greater than theirs. My very good lords, next under God's protection the advantage and gain of time and place will be the only and chief mean for our good. With fifty sail of shipping we shall do more good upon their own coast than a great many more will do here at home, and the sooner we are gone the better we shall be able to impeach them. As God in His goodness hath put my hand to the plough, so, in His mercy, He will never suffer me to turn back from the truth." *

Queen Elizabeth so far heeded Drake's project as to write and ask him how he proposed to deal with Philip's forces. "If your Majesty," he answered, on the 13th of April, " will give present order for our proceeding to the sea and send to the strengthening of this fleet here four more of your Majesty's good ships and those sixteen sail of ships with their pinnaces which are preparing in London, then shall your Majesty stand assured, with God's assistance, that, if the fleet come out of Lisbon, as long as we have victual to live withal upon that coast, they shall be fought with, and I hope, through the goodness of our merciful God, in such sort as shall hinder their quiet passage into England; for, I assure your Majesty, I have not in my lifetime known better men and possessed with gallanter minds than your Majesty's people are for the most part, which are here gathered together voluntarily to put their hands and hearts to the finishing of this great piece of work." But Drake reminded the Queen that even God could

* RECORD OFFICE MSS., *Domestic*, vol. cix., No. 40.

not be expected to supply the mariners with victuals, unless her Majesty consented to be His instrument, and that, unless better care was taken of them than had hitherto been done, everything might be lost "for the sparing of a few crowns." "Whereof," he added, "I most humbly beseech your most excellent Majesty to have such consideration as the weightiness of the cause requireth."*

Drake's arguments, as regards the expedition against Spain, though not as regards the increased issue of victuals, prevailed with the Queen, but not soon enough to be of any use. On the 21st of May, leaving with Lord Henry Seymour a sufficient fleet to protect the Narrow Seas from any invasion that might be attempted by the Prince of Parma with the small naval force at his command, Lord Howard left Dover with the greater number of the Queen's ships and a great many private vessels furnished by London and other ports in the eastern counties, forty or fifty sail in all. On the morning of the 23rd he entered Plymouth Road, and there was met by Sir Francis Drake and a goodly fleet of sixty vessels, a few of them Queen's ships and the rest stout barks and pinnaces fitted out by the towns and private adventurers in the west country.†
There he intended to stay only two days, but he was detained a week or more by contrary winds. On the 28th he wrote two letters to Burghley, saying that his

* RECORD OFFICE MSS., *Domestic*, vol. ccix., No. 89. No. 112 is a similar letter from Drake to the Queen, dated the 28th of April.
† *Ibid*, vol. ccx., No. 28.

fleet of about a hundred sail had only victuals for eighteen days;—" with the gallantest company of captains, soldiers, and sailors ever seen in England it were pity they should lack meat!"—but that at the first suitable moment he should sail towards Spain to meet the Armada, which was supposed to be on its way. Go out they must, though they should starve—" the fault lay not with him"—as it seemed to him far better to conquer the Spaniards away from England than off the coast, where, even if they were beaten, they would be likely to do much damage in their desperate struggle for life.*

He did go out a day or two after thus writing, intending to take up his station off Bayona, and there wait for the Spanish fleet, unless he met it on the way. But before he had gone so far, a violent gale from the south disarranged his plans. His ships were driven out to sea, partly dispersed, and, through a three days' storm, as he said, " danced as lustily as the gallantest dancers in the Court." Fearing that thus the Armada might pass him unobserved and reach England before him, he went back with the wind, and returned to Plymouth on the 13th of June.† There he found a letter from Walsingham, reproving him in the Queen's name for having gone so far away, and leaving England almost unprotected.‡ In his answer he justified his conduct. " It was deeply debated," he said, " by those whom the world doth judge to be men of the greatest experience

---

\* RECORD OFFICE MSS., *Domestic*, vol. ccx., Nos. 35, 36.
† *Ibid.*, vol. ccxi., Nos. 17, 18.   ‡ *Ibid.*, vol. ccxi., No. 8.

that this realm hath, which are these:—Sir Francis
Drake, Master Hawkins, Master Frobisher, and Master
Thomas Fenner; and I hope her Majesty will not think
we went so rashly to work, or without a principal or
choice care and respect of the safety of this realm. If
we found they did but linger on their own coast, or put
into the isles of Bayona or the Groyne, then we thought,
in all men's judgments that be of experience here, it
had been most fit to have sought some good way, and
the surest we could devise, by the good protection of
God to have defeated them." He added that he was
more likely to miss the enemy near home than off the
coast of Spain, seeing that they must necessarily pass
Bayona and Cape Finisterre on their way from Lisbon,
but that after that it was uncertain whether they
would go eastward towards the Netherlands, coast the
west of Ireland, and land somewhere to the south of
Scotland, or try to secretly get possession of the Isle of
Wight, there to fortify themselves, and proceed to
invade England at leisure. "But," he said, "I must
and will obey."*

That move of Howard's was as bold as anything in
the history of sailor boldness under the Tudors. With
the scanty information that has come down to us,
we can neither condemn nor justify it. It had this
advantage, at any rate, that it gave to Howard, Drake,
and the other leaders of the fleet an opportunity of
testing their powers in managing a force far greater
than had ever yet been under their command, its first

* RECORD OFFICE MSS., *Domestic*, vol. ccxi., No. 26.

trial of strength being in contest with nothing but a boisterous storm.

Only a narrow chance prevented the small battle with wind and sea from being simultaneous with a great battle with the Spanish fleet. The storm that gave annoyance to the English ships somewhere to the north of the Spanish coast was causing serious damage to the Armada off Cape Finisterre, and a few hours' delay of the gale would probably have brought them within sight of one another.

The Most Fortunate and Invincible Armada, after waiting a month at Lisbon for fair weather, had passed out of the Tagus on the 20th of May.* It comprised a hundred and thirty-two ships of various sizes, entrusted, after the death of the Marquis of Santa Cruz, to the Duke of Medina Sidonia as Captain-General or Lord Admiral. Its total tonnage was about 60,000. Its cannon and demi-cannon, culverins and demi-culverins, and other kinds of great guns, numbered 3,165 in all. Besides 8,766 sailors it gave employment to 2,088 galley-slaves, and it conveyed 21,855 soldiers, officers, and volunteers for the invasion of England, besides about 300 monks, priests, and functionaries of the Inquisition, who were to take spiritual charge of the heretic island as soon as it was conquered. There was room also for some 17,000 soldiers to be taken on board with the Prince of Parma, as Commander-in-Chief, somewhere near to Calais. The entire fighting force at sea was

* The 30th of May is the date usually given from Spanish authorities. Spain then used the new style; England adhered to the old. I have therefore followed throughout the English mode of reckoning.

thus about 50,000 strong; though only half that number could leave the ships, and march up to London.*

To withstand this great armament, Queen Elizabeth had only thirty-four of her own ships, with an aggregate tonnage of 11,850, containing in all 837 guns, and 6,279 sailors and soldiers, less in numerical strength than a fourth of the Spanish force. But London and all the seaports from Bristol round the coast to Hull, wealthy noblemen and patriots of all grades, as we

* These are the official statistics of its size and composition:—

| No. of Ships. | — | Tons. | Guns. | Sailors. | Soldiers. |
|---|---|---|---|---|---|
| 12 | The Squadron of Portuguese Galleons, under the Duke of Medina Sidonia . . . . . . . | 7,739 | 389 | 1,242 | 3,080 |
| 16 | The Fleet of Castile, under Don Diego de Valdez . . . . . | 8,054 | 474 | 1,793 | 2,924 |
| 11 | The Fleet of Andalusia, under Don Pedro de Valdez . . . . . | 8,692 | 315 | 776 | 2,359 |
| 14 | The Fleet of Biscay, under Don Juan Martinez de Ricaldé . . | 5,861 | 302 | 906 | 2,117 |
| 14 | The Fleet of Guipuzcoa, under Don Miguel de Oquendo . . . . . | 7,192 | 296 | 608 | 2,120 |
| 10 | The Eastern or Italian Fleet, under Don Martin de Bartendona . | 8,632 | 319 | 844 | 2,792 |
| 23 | A Squadron of Hulks or Store Ships, under Don Juan Gomez de Medina . . . . . . | 10,860 | 466 | 950 | 4,170 |
| 24 | A Squadron of Tenders and Caravels, under Don Antonio Hurtado de Mendoza . . . . . | 2,090 | 204 | 746 | 1,103 |
| 4 | A Squadron of Neapolitan Galeasses, under Don Hugo de Moncada . . . . . . . | ? | 200 | 477 | 744 |
| 4 | A Squadron of Portuguese Galleys, under Don Diego de Medrado . | ? | 200 | 424 | 410 |
| 132 | | 59,120 | 3,165 | 8,766 | 21,855 |

have seen, helped to swell the force.* Twenty barks, the largest of 85 tons burthen, were contributed by the Netherlanders, who had only just begun to build war-

* Some scores of more or less conflicting statements are among the RECORD OFFICE MSS. and elsewhere. The numbers given in MURDIN's *State Papers* give about the average of them, and are, therefore, probably tolerably correct :—

| No. of Ships. | | Tons. | Men. |
|---|---|---|---|
| 34 | Her Majesty's Ships, under the Lord High Admiral . . . . . . . . . . . . | 12,250 | 6,279 |
| 10 | Chartered Ships under the Lord High Admiral. | 750 | 239 |
| 32 | Volunteers serving with Sir Francis Drake . . | 5,120 | 2,348 |
| 38 | Ships fitted out by the City and Merchants of London . . . . . . . . . . . | 6,130 | 2,710 |
| 20 | Coasters with the Lord High Admiral . . . | 1,930 | 993 |
| 23 | Coasters with Lord Henry Seymour . . . . | 2,248 | 1,073 |
| 18 | Volunteers with the Lord High Admiral . . | 1,716 | 859 |
| 15 | Victuallers . . . . . . . . . . . . | ? | 810 |
| 7 | Other Vessels not described . . . . . . | ? | 474 |
| 197 | | 30,144 | 15,785 |

The details of the Queen's own Navy are as follows :—

| Names of the Ships. | Names of the Captains. | Tons. | Men. | Guns. |
|---|---|---|---|---|
| *Ark Royal* . . . | Lord Charles Howard, Lord High Admiral . | 800 | 425 | 55 |
| *Revenge* . . . . | Sir Francis Drake, Vice-Admiral . . . . | 500 | 250 | 40 |
| *Victory* . . . . | Sir John Hawkins, Rear-Admiral . . . . | 800 | 400 | 42 |
| *Elizabeth Bonaventure* | Earl of Cumberland . . | 600 | 250 | 34 |
| *Rainbow* . . . . | Lord Henry Seymour . | 500 | 250 | 38 |
| *Golden Lion* . . . | Lord Thomas Howard . | 500 | 250 | 38 |
| *White Bear* . . . | Lord Edmund Sheffield . | 1,000 | 500 | 40 |
| *Vanguard* . . . . | Sir William Winter . . | 500 | 250 | 40 |
| *Elizabeth Jonas* . . | Sir Robert Southwell . | 900 | 500 | 56 |
| *Antelope* . . . . | Sir Henry Palmer . . | 400 | 160 | 30 |
| *Triumph* . . . . | Sir Martin Frobisher . | 1,100 | 500 | 42 |
| *Dreadnought* . . . | Sir George Berton . . | 400 | 200 | 32 |
| *Mary Rose* . . . | Edward Fenton . . . | 600 | 250 | 36 |
| *Nonpareil* . . . . | Thomas Fenner . . . | 500 | 250 | 38 |

ships for themselves; and the whole fleet commanded by Lord Howard comprised about two hundred vessels, large and small, more in mere numbers than the Spanish fleet, with an aggregate of about 30,000 tons burthen, and containing some 16,000 mariners and fighting men, each about half as numerous as those of the Spaniards. Under Howard, Sir Francis Drake served as Vice-Admiral, and Hawkins as Rear-Admiral. Lord Henry Seymour was still employed, with three or four of the Queen's ships, and most of the Dutch reinforcements, in watching the Narrow Seas, and seeing that Parma made no attempt to cross them with any part of his army. The rest of the ships had Plymouth for their head-quarters.

| Names of the Ships. | Names of the Captains. | Tons. | Men. | Guns. |
|---|---|---|---|---|
| Hope | Robert Cross | 600 | 250 | 48 |
| Bonavolia | William Burrows | ? | 250 | ? |
| Swiftsure | Edward Fenner | 400 | 200 | 42 |
| Swallow | Richard Hawkins | 360 | 160 | 8 |
| Foresight | Christopher Baker | 300 | 160 | 37 |
| Aid | William Fenner | 250 | 120 | 18 |
| Bull | Jeremy Turner | 200 | 100 | ? |
| Tiger | John Bostock | 200 | 100 | 22 |
| Tramontana | Luke Ward | 120 | 70 | 21 |
| Scout | Henry Ashley | 120 | 70 | 10 |
| Achates | Henry Rigges | 100 | 60 | 13 |
| Charles | John Roberts | 70 | 40 | 16 |
| Moon | Alexander Clifford | 60 | 40 | 9 |
| Advice | John Harris | 50 | 40 | 9 |
| Spy | Ambrose Ward | 50 | 40 | 9 |
| Martin | Walter Gower | 50 | 35 | 7 |
| Sun | Richard Buckley | 40 | 30 | 5 |
| Cygnet | John Shrive | 30 | 20 | ? |
| Brigantine | Thomas Scott | ? | 35 | ? |
| George-a-Hoy | Richard Hodges | 120 | 24 | ? |
| | | 12,220 | 6,279 | 835 |

There Howard, with Drake, Hawkins, Frobisher, and Fenner for his chief advisers, watched eagerly for the coming of the Armada, and, during five weeks of further waiting, did his utmost to prepare for the struggle that was impending. Hardly a day passed without his sending to the Queen or her ministers some fresh letter of entreaty and persuasion for support in his work. "For the love of God," he wrote to Walsingham on the 19th of June, "let her Majesty care not now for charges."* "For the love of Jesus Christ," he wrote to the Queen on the 23rd, "I implore your Majesty to awake thoroughly and see the villainous treasons round about you."† "Let her Majesty trust no more to Judases' kisses," he wrote to Walsingham on the same day. "Let her defend herself like a noble and mighty prince, and trust to her sword and not to their word, and then she need not to fear, for her good God will defend her."‡ In the same strain he wrote over and over again during the ensuing weeks.

In the meanwhile the Armada was slowly working its way to England. Bad weather, the clumsiness of the great galleons and galeasses, and the incompetence of the Duke of Medina Sidonia, made the voyage a very long one. Three weeks were spent in passing from Lisbon to Cape Finisterre, and there the fleet, being overtaken by the storm that drove Howard back to England, was seriously damaged. One of the largest

* Record Office MSS., *Domestic*, vol. ccxi., No. 37.
† *Ibid.*, vol. ccxi., No. 50.
‡ *Ibid.*, vol. ccxi., No. 51.

of the galleys was wrecked. Two others, in the confusion, were carried out of reach by their galley-slaves, some of them being Englishmen and all haters of Spain, headed by David Gwynn, a Welshman, who slew the Spaniards and took the vessels and their cargoes to France. Many others were so much disabled by the storm that they had to put in for safety at various ports of Galicia, and finally to assemble and spend a month in repairing their injuries at Corunna, then generally known to Englishmen as the Groyne. On the 12th of July, reinforced with men and stores from Lisbon, they again set sail. Towards evening on Friday, the 19th, they had sight of Lizard Point. Thence they lay out to sea for the night, intending to surprise the English fleet at Plymouth, and begin their possession of England on the following morning.*

But they had been descried early on that Friday, somewhere between Scilly Islands and the Lizard, by a Cornish pirate named Fleming. Putting out all sail, he hurried off to Plymouth, and reported the enemy's approach. There is a tradition that Howard, Drake, and several other officers were on shore just then, playing at bowls on the Hoe. When Fleming's news arrived most of the players were for returning to their ships at once, but Drake objected. "Nay," he said, "let us play out our match. There will be plenty of time to win the game and beat the Spaniards too."†

We can well believe, however, that the game was

* MOTLEY, vol. ii., pp. 470-473; SOUTHEY, vol. ii., p. 349.
† TYTLER, Life of Raleigh.

quickly ended. Howard and his chief advisers lost no time in getting the ships ready for the work that was before them. All hands were brought on board, and set to work in overhauling the sails and rigging, seeing that guns, ammunition, and war-gear of all sorts were in good condition, and ranging the vessels in order for passing out of the harbour in the morning. Everything was ready for this soon after daybreak, when sixty-seven vessels, a third of the whole available shipping of England—the rest being either with Lord Henry Seymour off Dover, or keeping watch and ward at various points along the south coast—entered Plymouth Road. By nine o'clock they were in the open channel, and there Howard judged it best to wait, feeling sure that the Armada would make its way direct to Plymouth, or that, if a landing at any intermediate place was attempted, his scouts would bring the news soon enough for him to go to the rescue.*

He had to wait all day. The Spanish fleet did not come in sight till three o'clock in the afternoon. It showed itself to the English on-lookers like a vast array of floating castles, arranged in the shape of a half-moon, with a space of seven miles between the extremities of the crescent. Its ships, we are told, approached "very slowly, though with full sails, the winds being, as it were, weary with wafting them, and the ocean groaning under their weight."† Its lazy pomp Howard did not attempt to disturb during the short

* RECORD OFFICE MSS., *Domestic*, vol. ccxii., No. 80.
† CAMDEN, vol. iii., p. 411.

remainder of that day, especially as the wind was against him. And the Spaniards, seeing to their great regret that their hope of surprising Plymouth had been vain, were glad enough to anchor for the night in the little bay off Looe.

Next morning, being Sunday, the 21st of July, they weighed anchor betimes. Having failed in his plan of seizing Plymouth at once, and so entering England, the Duke of Medina Sidonia and the more experienced Admirals who did their best to make up for his incompetence, he being a skilful soldier upon land but quite unpractised in seamanship, seem to have resolved to fight their way to the Isle of Wight, there, if possible, to find a harbour and effect a landing, or, failing in that, to go on to the Hague, and take on board their appointed chief, the Prince of Parma. Howard so far acceded to this plan as to let the Armada get ahead of him, determining, without coming to a full engagement, to harass it in the rear, until, having collected his dispersed ships, and come within reach of Seymour's squadron, he could be strong enough to attack the enemy in both front and rear, and win a thorough victory. Therefore, keeping his sixty or seventy ships in the haven, he allowed the Spanish armament to come within sight of Plymouth.*

That was done by nine o'clock on the Sunday morning. Then Howard weighed anchor and hoisted sail. "We durst not adventure to put in amongst them, their fleet being so strong," he said in his brief report of the first

* RECORD OFFICE MSS., *Domestic*, vol. ccxii., No. 80.

day's work.* But he managed to do them considerable injury. A swift pinnace, fitly named the *Defiance*, fired the first shot. "Fire, smoke, and echoing cannon begun the parley," says the old historian; "and bullets, most freely interchanged between them, were messengers of each other's mind."† The rest of the English fleet carried on the fierce dispute. Howard, in the *Ark Royal*, singled out a great galley which he supposed to be the Admiral's flag-ship, but which proved to belong to the Vice-Admiral in charge of the northern wing, and forced her to retreat. Drake, Hawkins, and Frobisher beat the Admiral of the rear squadron. Then, with threescore other brave sea-captains, they sailed round and round the unwieldy mass of Spanish shipping, like bees around a furious bull, pausing often to inflict their sting, and then darting off before they could be punished for their boldness. The huge galleons and galeasses poured out their artillery, only to pass over the low barks and pinnaces, and sink into the sea. This unequal struggle lasted for six hours. "We had some small fight with them that Sunday afternoon," said Hawkins.‡ By three o'clock the great Spanish fleet was in utter confusion, and the Englishmen, tired of fighting for the present, paused to eat their suppers, say their prayers, and write their letters. "I will not trouble you with any long letter," said Howard in his

---

\* RECORD OFFICE MSS., *Domestic*, vol. ccxii., No. 80.

† SPEED (ed. 1632), p. 1181. Some authorities call this pinnace *Disdain*; an apt name, too.

‡ RECORD OFFICE MSS., *Domestic*, vol. ccxiii., No. 71.

report to Walsingham. "We are at this present otherwise occupied than with writing. Sir, the captains in her Majesty's ships have behaved themselves most bravely and like men hitherto, and I doubt not will continue to their great commendation. There shall nothing be either neglected or unhazarded that may work the Spaniards' overthrow. And so, commending our good success to your godly prayers, I bid you hearty farewell." "Sir," he added in a postscript, "for the love of God and our country, let us have, with some speed, some great shot sent us of all bigness, for this service will continue long, and some powder in it."* Drake's letter was to Lord Henry Seymour, informing him of the Armada's arrival. "We had them in chase, and so, coming up unto them, there hath passed some common shot between our fleet and theirs, and, as far as we perceive, they are determined to sell their lives with blows." Drake never doubted that the Spaniards' lives would be sold, and he urged Seymour to prepare his squadron without delay for taking part in the purchase. The superscription of his letter was "To the Lord Henry Seymour or, in absence, to Sir William Winter, give these with speed—haste, haste, haste!"†

The spoiling of the Armada did not pause while the English rested. As soon as he had brought his fleet into some sort of order, the Duke of Medina Sidonia proceeded to scold his gunners for having spent their powder and shot in vain. Thereat the master gunner

---

* RECORD OFFICE MSS., *Domestic*, vol. ccxii., No. 80.
† *Ibid.*, vol. ccxii., No. 82.

of the flag-ship of the Guipuzcoan squadron, a Dutchman, whose wife had been abused by a Spanish officer on board, determined that some powder, at any rate, should not be spent in vain. Laying a train to the ship's magazine, he fired it and then jumped overboard. In the explosion two hundred men were blown into the air and lost; fifty, who remained in the shattered hull, and some treasure, which was thought more valuable than the men, were with difficulty saved. Many of the "scorched Spaniards" were afterwards brought into Weymouth, "to the great joy of the beholders," and a quantity of gunpowder which, by a lucky accident, had not shared in the general explosion, rescued from the wreck, was employed with much satisfaction by Howard against its former possessors.*

The Spanish fleet was in fresh confusion consequent on that occurrence when the English returned to the pursuit. The flag-ship of the Andalusian squadron, under Don Pedro de Valdez, who had been a chief adviser in the expedition, came in collision first with one and then with another of the Spanish vessels that were hurrying hither and thither. Thereby her foremast was carried away and her mainmast was crippled. She could not keep up with the rest, and was therefore quietly abandoned by the Duke of Medina Sidonia. "He left me comfortless in sight of the whole fleet," said Don Pedro in his letter of complaint to Philip II.; "and greater inhumanity and unthankfulness was never

* CAMDEN, vol. iii., p. 412; SPEED, p. 1182; RECORD OFFICE MSS., Domestic, vol. ccxiii., Nos. 42, 43.

heard of among men."* The Duke's apology for this conduct was that by halting for Don Pedro's assistance, instead of making good use of the night-time in escaping from the English fleet, the whole Armada would in all likelihood have been sacrificed.† Therefore Don Pedro was left to be attacked by Frobisher in the *Triumph* and Hawkins in the *Victory*. He defended himself bravely and successfully through the night; but in the morning Drake came up in the *Revenge*. "Espying this lagging galleon," says the quaint chronicler, "Sir Francis sent forth a pinnace to command them to yield, otherwise his bullets should force them without further favour. Valdez, to seem valorous, answered that they were four hundred and fifty strong, that himself was Don Pedro, and stood on his honour, and thereupon propounded certain conditions. The knight sent his reply that he had not leisure to parley; if he would yield, presently do it; if not, he should well prove that Drake was no dastard. Thereupon Pedro, hearing that it was the Fiery Drake, ever terrible to Spaniards, who had him in chase, came on board Sir Francis's ship with forty of his followers; where, first giving him the *congé*, he protested that he and all his were resolved to die in defence had they not fallen under his power, whose valour and felicity was so great that Mars and Neptune seemed to attend him in his attempts, and whose gene-

* RECORD OFFICE MSS., *Domestic*, vol. ccxv., No. 26.
† BARROW, *Naval Worthies of Queen Elizabeth's Reign*, p. 263, citing an interesting Spanish narrative by an officer in the Duke's flag-ship, which passed from the Simancas Collection into private hands in England during the Revolutionary War.

rous mind towards the vanquished had often been experienced even of his greatest foes. Sir Francis, requiting his Spanish compliments with honourable English courtesies, placed him at his own table and lodged him in his own cabin. The residue of that company were sent unto Plymouth, where they remained eighteen months until their ransoms were paid; but Sir Francis's soldiers had well paid themselves with the spoil of the ship, wherein were 15,000 ducats in gold, which they shared merrily among them."* After keeping Don Pedro and the other chief prisoners on board the *Revenge* for ten days, Drake sent them up to London, begging Queen Elizabeth to accept the ransom they were willing to pay as a present from himself.†

By taking this galleon Drake gave great offence to Frobisher, who had hoped to make the capture and seize the spoil himself. Of Frobisher's hot temper we have already had some proof. "He thinketh to cozen us of our shares of the 15,000 ducats," he is reported to have said of Drake on the 10th of August, when all the Spanish fighting was over, and Englishmen had time to quarrel with one another; "but we will have our share, or I will make him spend the best blood in his belly, for he hath done enough of those cozening cheats already." But the quarrel ended in words.‡

Drake's capture had been made on the Monday morning. He and the two or three ships that were with

---

\* SPEED, pp. 1181, 1182.
† RECORD OFFICE MSS., *Domestic*, vol. ccxiii., No. 73.
‡ *Ibid.*, vol. ccxiv., Nos. 63, 64.

him soon overtook the fleet with which through the
night Lord Howard had been dogging the path of the
Armada. But nothing of importance was done through
that day, save that the Duke of Medina came to a
standstill on part of it, not, as Howard supposed, to
offer battle, but to rearrange his ships and try to lessen
their unfitness, already becoming apparent to him, for
the work before them. Three galeasses, four galleons,
and three dozen smaller vessels, were entrusted to Don
Alonzo de Leyva for the special task of resisting the
flying attacks of the English barks and pinnaces, while
the main body of the Armada crawled superbly along
the Channel. At the same time, in consequence of
mutinous threatenings that had already reached him,
the Duke appointed a serjeant-major to each ship, with
instructions to hang at once any captain or subordinate
who made the least objection to the orders transmitted to
him.* In the evening he despatched a sloop with letters to the Prince of Parma, asking when and where he
was to take on board the forces waiting for him in the
Netherlands; begging also for some pilots acquainted
with the British waters. "In case of the slightest gale,"
he said, "I know not how or where to shelter such large
ships as ours."†

On Tuesday, the 23rd of July, at five o'clock in the
morning, great ships and small were a little past Port-
land, stretching out in the direction of St. Alban's Head,
the English fleet being close behind them, when the

---

\* *Spanish Narrative* in BARROW, p. 264
† *Ibid.*; MOTLEY, vol. ii., p. 478.

wind changed from north-west to north-east. This caused some confusion, in the course of which a group of London volunteers was surrounded by Don Alonzo de Leyva's squadron. Thereupon ensued a long day of vigorous fighting. "This was the most furious and bloody skirmish of all," said the Dutch chronicler, "in which the Lord Admiral of England continued fighting amidst his enemy's fleet."* "We had a sharp and long fighting," said Hawkins.† Yet it was only skirmishing. Neither party wished for a regular battle. The Duke of Medina Sidonia desired to press on till he could effect a junction with Parma's forces. Howard thought it best to wait for Seymour's squadron and other reinforcements.

Many reinforcements he received during this Tuesday's fighting. A famous crowd of courtiers, hearing of the arrival of the Armada, had hurried from London down to the various ports at which they had appointed their little pinnaces and frigates to be in waiting. Sir Walter Raleigh, and the Earls of Cumberland, Northumberland, and Oxford were among the number. "Out of all havens of the realm resorted ships and men," it is said; "for they all with one accord came flocking thither as unto a set field, where immortal fame and glory was to be attained and faithful service to be performed unto their prince and country."‡ The English force, which had numbered sixty sail on Saturday, had been in-

---

* METEREN, in HAKLUYT, vol. i., p. 599.
† RECORD OFFICE MSS., *Domestic*, vol. ccxiii., No. 71.
‡ HAKLUYT, vol. i., p. 599.

creased to a hundred by Tuesday afternoon, when the fighting was abandoned, with the sullen consent of both sides.

It was only resumed on Wednesday by a few ships of either fleet, which, coming within gun-shot of one another, expended a few rounds of artillery apiece. Howard's ships had none to spare. Towards afternoon they were obliged to hang back and send to every town and fishing village that they passed, begging for every ounce, and every pound, and every hundredweight of powder that could be procured from cottage, hunting-box, or castle. Howard employed the waiting-time also in holding a more deliberate council of war than there had lately been leisure for. The result was the redistribution of the English fleet into five squadrons. The first was to be under the Lord Admiral himself, the second under Drake, the third under Hawkins, and the fourth under Frobisher: the fifth was to be formed of Seymour's little fleet when it arrived. "Out of every squadron small vessels were appointed to give the onset and attack the enemy on all sides simultaneously in the dead of night."\*

On Thursday, the 25th of July, there was some sharp fighting off the Isle of Wight. The *Santa Anna*, a great Spanish hulk, and a Portuguese galleon, being somewhat apart from the rest, were singled out by Frobisher for attack by his little squadron. Don Alonzo de Leyva, with a large force, hurried out to relieve them, and Frobisher found it hard work to defend himself, until

\* HAKLUYT, vol. i., p. 599.

Lord Admiral Howard, in his *Ark Royal*, with the *Golden Lion*, under Lord Thomas Howard, and four other large ships, came to the rescue. They opened out upon the Spanish flag-ship, and in a short time so cut up her rigging and her crew that she was forced to retire. Howard thus diverted from Frobisher more force of opposition than he could withstand. Then he gave the order for retreat, and his ships were out of reach of the Spaniards before they had time to retaliate. " These two ships, the *Ark* and the *Golden Lion*," we are told, " declared this day to each fleet that they had most diligent and faithful gunners. The galeasses, in whose puissance the greatest hope of the Spanish fleet was founded, were never seen to fight any more: such was their entertainment that day." In the evening the Duke of Medina wrote to the Prince of Parma, begging him to send him thirty or forty small fighting ships, if such could be procured in the Low Countries—" the heaviness of our ships," as he said, " compared with the lightness of theirs, rendering it impossible in any manner to bring them to close action."\*

On Friday Lord Admiral Howard knighted Frobisher, Hawkins, and some others for their valiant conduct in the previous day's engagement.† Unless compelled thereto by some unlooked-for occurrence, he resolved to have no more fighting until he was joined by the squadron of the Narrow Seas, and, as the Spaniards

\* PETRUCCIO UBALDINO, *A Discourse concerning the Spanish Invasion* in the *Harleian Miscellany*, vol. i., pp. 127, 128; *Spanish Narrative* in BARROW, p. 267.
† HAKLUYT, vol. i., p. 599.

also wished to pass on without delay, the two fleets proceeded quietly along the coast of Sussex as far as Dungeness, and thence across the Straits of Dover towards Calais. There the Spaniards anchored on Saturday evening, and the English stationed themselves within gunshot.

Not far from Calais, Howard was overtaken by Seymour's force of about twenty ships, which, sorely to the regret of Seymour and Sir William Winter, who was second in command, had been prevented from earlier joining in the struggle by the need of a force in the Downs to avert any invading movement that might be made separately by the Prince of Parma.* There, with some private reinforcements, he raised the entire number of the fleet to about a hundred and forty sail, and made it as strong as Howard could hope to have it, the fifty or sixty other vessels completing the naval force of England being only small craft required for the defence of special points. This statement of the number of Howard's fleet, however, is somewhat deceptive. Every man on board was a brave and honest patriot, eager to work miracles in defence of his country and his creed. But many of them were landsmen, who could do no work at all on shipboard, unless by a miracle; and many of the vessels were as useless as their masters. "If you had seen the simple service done by the merchants' and coast ships," wrote Winter to Walsingham, "you would have said we had

---

* RECORD OFFICE MSS., *Domestic*, vol. ccxiii., Nos. 30, 49, 50, 53 ; vol. ccxiv., Nos. 2, 5, 6, 7.

been little holpen by them, otherwise than that they did make a show."*

Yet the show was worth making, and worth seeing. A rare spectacle was offered to the throng of Frenchmen who looked out to sea from Calais, and the dozen miles of shore on either side of Calais, through the moonlit night of Saturday, and the brilliant Sunday morning. To the left lay the greatest fleet that England—already, though unknown, the strongest maritime nation in Europe—had ever launched. To the right lay the greatest fleet ever constructed by the proud Spaniards who openly aspired to the empire of the world. And, stupendous as was the English armament, the Spanish armament far outshone it in splendour. "Flemings, Walloons, and French," we are told, "came thick and threefold to behold it, admiring the exceeding greatness of the ships and their warlike order."† They did well to look without delay and wonder without restraint. It was a sight to be seen only for a day.

Through that bright Sunday, the 28th of July, both fleets remained in eager suspense. On his arrival off Calais, the Spanish Admiral was met by messengers who informed him that the Prince of Parma was making all possible preparations for debarkation at Dunkirk, but that he could not be ready for a dozen hours or two, and that, until further orders were given, the Armada was to remain at Calais, that being a safer halting-

* RECORD OFFICE MSS., *Domestic*, vol. ccxiv., No. 7.
† STOW, p. 748.

place. Howard knew of this, and knew that the great battle which had been delayed for a week must not be delayed for an hour after the Spaniards had weighed anchor. They must be beaten before reaching Dunkirk if they were to be beaten at all.

He had little doubt of success; but his week's experience had taught him that, though it was easy to annoy the great galleys, galeasses, and galleons of Spain, it was not easy to demolish them with the smaller ships which formed the great body of his fleet. At nine o'clock on Saturday evening, in the midst of his uncertainty as to the best way of proceeding, he was visited on board the *Ark Royal* by Sir William Winter, who had only joined the fleet some two hours before. "Considering their hugeness," Winter said in answer to Howard's request, "'twill not be possible to remove them but by a device." The device was not wanting. Winter communicated it that night to Howard, and next morning it was decided in a council of war that Sir Henry Palmer should hasten across to Dover, and there procure thirty boat-loads of faggots, pitch, sulphur, and other combustibles. Sir Henry Palmer did his errand; but he had not long been gone when the English leaders judged that it would be better not to wait for his return, which, the wind being southerly and therefore against him in each passage, could not be counted upon before Monday. Therefore they determined to make shift with such materials as they had among them. Six of the oldest vessels were emptied of all that was valuable in them, replaced by the worst guns that the fleet contained, all loaded to the mouth with bullets, old iron, and every sort of destructive implement that could be collected. The hulls also were laden with combustibles of all sorts, and smeared with pitch. Twelve hours were thus employed with as much secrecy as possible, and at midnight the fire-ships were conducted within bow-shot of the Invincible Armada. Then a carefully-laid train was fired and the bold convoys rowed quickly back to the English fleet.

Fortune favoured the rough expedient, which Winter had borrowed from an Italian named Gianibelli, who had practised it with great success in aid of the Netherlanders' defence of Antwerp from Parma's siege three years before. In the evening a storm had succeeded the calm of the three previous days. The full moon was eclipsed, and amid pelting rain, and in utter darkness, a fierce south-west wind bore the rude fire-ships into the centre of the crescent-grouped fleet of Spain. A sudden blaze, a series of explosions, and an outpouring of the stuffing of the cannons threw it into instant and hopeless consternation. "The fire of Antwerp!" exclaimed the Spanish sailors and soldiers. "Cut your cables! get up your anchors!" shouted the captains of the six-score vessels. The direct injury done by the fire-ships was slight. But a panic ran through all the fleet. In their efforts to get out of danger the Spaniards beat against one another, and, hurrying out into the open channel, with sails ill set and crews unnerved, they were driven by wind and tide into the more angry sea of Ostend, and up to the mouth of the Scheldt.*

Pharaoh's chariots and horsemen, according to the tradition cherished by the hearty Protestants of Tudor times, were engulphed in a moment by the waters of the Red Sea. The angel of death passed over the hosts of Sennacherib, and in an hour they were all dead men. The God of the Calvinists dealt more slowly, but hardly less surely with the Invincible Armada of Philip II. "God hath given us so good a day in forcing the enemy so far to leeward," said Drake, in a hurried letter to Walsingham, "as, I hope in God, the Prince of Parma and the Duke of Sidonia will not shake hands these few days; and, whensoever they shall meet, I believe neither of them will greatly rejoice of this day's service. God bless her Majesty, our Gracious Sovereign, and give us all grace to live in His fear. I assure your Honour, this day's service hath much appalled the enemy."†

Sunday night's rough work was followed by rough work on Monday and for many days to come. The English fleet entered on speedy pursuit of the frightened Spaniards. Most of them had fled, but a great Neapolitan galeass, the *Capitana*, " the very glory and stay of the Spanish navy," having lost her rudder, and being otherwise much damaged, was still beating about in Calais harbour. Howard sent his long-boat and a small pinnace

---

\* RECORD OFFICE MSS., *Domestic*, vol. ccxiii., No. 32; vol. cxiv., No. 7; HAKLUYT, vol. i., p. 601; CAMDEN, vol. iii., p. 415.

† RECORD OFFICE MSS., *Domestic*, vol. ccxiii., No. 65.

belonging to the merchants of London, to seize her. "We had a pretty skirmish for half an hour," says one of the hundred Englishmen, armed slightly with muskets and swords, who bravely attacked the huge craft of 1,200 tons burthen, possessed of forty guns and with nearly seven hundred men on board: "they seemed safe in their ship, while we in our open pinnaces, and far under them, had nothing to shroud and cover us." The captain, Don Hugo de Moncada, smiled when called upon to surrender. The smile had hardly passed away when a bullet struck him in the forehead and he fell dead upon the deck. Thereupon his crew and soldiers, all but about twenty, threw themselves into the sea, to sink at once, or to sink when they were too tired to swim, and the English captors, scaling the high bulwarks with difficulty, had an hour and a half of welcome plunder. They took 50,000 ducats, more than 10,000*l.*, "a booty well fitting the English soldiers' affections." The great ship was claimed by the Governor of Calais; but the English were content, seeing that she was lost to Spain.*

In the meanwhile, on Monday, the 29th of July, there was yet more memorable fighting off Gravelines, fighting which decided the fate of the Armada. While Howard waited to watch the capture of the *Capitana*, the main force of the English sped on in pursuit of the main force of the Spaniards. A battle, which men who had served in both declared to be far more fierce and

* RECORD OFFICE MSS., *Domestic*, vol. ccxiii., No. 67; *Harleian Miscellany*, vol. i., p. 141; MOTLEY, vol. ii., pp. 493-498.

energetic than that of Lepanto, was fought between ten in the morning and four in the afternoon. At about nine o'clock the fleetest of the English ships, with Drake's *Revenge*, Frobisher's *Triumph*, and Hawkins's *Victory*, representatives of the revenge, the triumph, and the victory of all England, in the van, came within sight of the enemy, whom they found painfully struggling, against the fears of the men and a strong north-west wind and heavy tide, which threatened to strand them all on the Flemish shoals, to recover their customary arrangement in the shape of a half-moon. Without loss of time, and taking upon himself the responsibility of beginning the fight before the Lord Admiral's arrival, Drake, followed by Hawkins, Frobisher, Thomas Fenner, and many others, bore down upon the middle of the crescent, there to work terrible mischief among the Spanish flag-ships and to cause hopeless confusion through the whole fleet. Many ships were disabled by dashing against one another in their efforts to escape, where there was small chance of escape. Some pressed out to sea, to be further harassed by the angry waves. Some sought the protection of the shore, to run imminent peril of wreck upon the sands. And in either direction there was peril also from the English. Lord Henry Seymour in his light *Rainbow*, Sir Henry Palmer in his swift *Antelope*, and some others, took charge of the larboard wing and the coast line, first spoiling three great galleons and then attacking other ships that came in their way. Sir William Winter in the *Vanguard*, and a great number of barks and merchant ships, kept out to sea and did most injury of all. "I tell you on the credit of a gentleman," he wrote to Walsingham, "that there were five hundred discharges of demi-cannon, culverin and demi-culverin from the *Vanguard;* and when I was farthest off in firing my pieces, I was not out of shot of their harquebus, and most time within speech one of another."*

Throughout six hours the English carried on their work of havoc. "And albeit there were many excellent and warlike ships in the English fleet," it was said and must be remembered, "yet scarce there were two or three and twenty among them all which matched ninety of the Spanish ships in bigness, or could conveniently assault them. Wherefore, using their prerogative of nimble steerage, whereby they could turn and wield themselves with the wind which way they listed, they came oftentimes very near upon the Spaniards, and charged them so sore that now and then they were but a pike's length asunder; and so, continually giving them one broadside after another, they discharged all their shot, both great and small, upon them, spending a whole day in that violent kind of conflict."† Every ship in the Spanish fleet received its share of injury. A great Biscayan galley and a great galleon went down during the fight. Another great galleon, after desperate fighting, was captured

---

\* *Spanish Narrative* in BARROW; RECORD OFFICE MSS., *Domestic,* vol. ccxiii., No. 71; vol. ccxiv., Nos. 2, 3, 7, 27.

† HAKLUYT, vol. i., p. 601.

and taken into Flushing. A third great galleon, dismasted and riddled, was borne along by the wind and sea and wrecked near Ostend.* A score of others were made ready for shipwreck during the next few days. Drake estimated their deaths by gunshot and by drowning at five thousand.† No English ship was lost or seriously damaged, and certainly not more than a hundred men were killed and wounded. "God hath mightily preserved her Majesty's forces with the least losses that hath ever been heard of, being within the compass of so great volleys of shot, both small and great," wrote Fenner to Walsingham. "I verily believe there is not threescore men lost of her Majesty's forces."‡

"Their force is wonderful great and strong," wrote Lord Admiral Howard, who, hurrying up from Calais, joined in the battle when it was nearly over; "but we pluck their feathers by little and little."§ There had been very considerable plucking of the Armada's peacock feathers during those six hours of fighting. But, as it seems, nothing save Queen Elizabeth's and Lord Burghley's parsimony hindered the victory from being complete. The Duke of Medina Sidonia, it was reported, was so disheartened with the day's work that such further havoc as Howard, Drake, and all the brave sea-captains were eager to make would have forced him to capitulate or even to make unlimited submission.‖

* *Harleian Miscellany*, vol. i., p. 141.
† RECORD OFFICE MSS., *Domestic*, vol. ccxiv., No. 65.
‡ *Ibid.*, vol. ccxiv., No. 27.
§ *Ibid.*, vol. ccxiii., No. 64.
‖ MONSON in CHURCHILL's *Collection of Travels*, vol. iii., p. 159.

But the scant supplies of ammunition which, with daily entreaties, Howard had been able to procure from home, were nearly exhausted by four o'clock, and the English had to stay their hands for the present. Their firing abated, and the Spaniards taking advantage of this, gathered together their shattered forces and, favoured by a change of wind towards the south, sped northward in full sail. "Notwithstanding that our powder and shot was well near all spent," said Howard, "we set on a brag countenance and gave them chase."*

The chase lasted through Monday night and Tuesday and Wednesday and Thursday and part of Friday. "We have the army of Spain before us," wrote Drake to Walsingham, on Wednesday, "and mind, with the grace of God, to wrestle a pull with him. There was never anything pleased me better than seeing the enemy flying with a southerly wind to the northwards. God grant you have a good eye to the Duke of Parma, for, with the grace of God, if we live, I doubt it not but ere long we shall so handle the matter with the Duke of Sidonia as he shall wish himself at St. Mary's Port among his orange trees. God give us grace to depend upon Him, so shall we not doubt victory, for our cause is good."†

The rest of the victory, however, was not of Drake's or Howard's winning. On Tuesday afternoon the Lord Admiral, being off the coast of Holland, sent Seymour

* Record Office MSS., *Domestic*, vol. ccxiv., No. 42.
† *Ibid.*, vol. ccxiii., No. 73.

and Winter back to England with the Narrow Seas squadron, there to be prepared for any further attempt at invasion that might be made by the Prince of Parma, and many of the smaller adventurers' ships returned with them. The rest of the fleet followed the flying Spaniards, driven by a strong wind and their own fears, through nearly the whole length of the North Sea.

On the morning of Friday, the 2nd of August, when midway between the Frith of Forth and the Skager Rack, Howard was forced to abandon the pursuit. "As well to refresh our ships with victuals, whereof most stood in wonderful need, and as also in respect of our want of powder and shot," he said, "we made for the Frith and sent certain pinnaces to dog the fleet until they should be past the Isles of Scotland."* That move was fortunate. After a day's waiting in the Forth, the English fleet sailed southwards, and on Sunday was overtaken, as Howard averred, by "a more violent storm than was ever seen before at that time of the year."† By it the ships were dispersed and, though very little injured, prevented from appearing in warlike trim again until Friday, the 9th of August, by which time they had all or nearly all assembled in Margate Road. Howard then found himself in command of a hundred and nineteen ships, including Seymour's squadron, with 11,120 sailors and fighting men on board.‡ This force, in spite of Lord Burghley's

---

* RECORD OFFICE MSS., *Domestic*, vol. ccxiv., No. 42.
† *Ibid.*, vol. ccxiv., No. 50.  ‡ *Ibid.*, vol. ccxiv., No. 60.

proposal that, now that the great danger was over, the ships should be at once discharged,* he maintained for a little time, to be in readiness for any return of the Armada, or any separate attempt of the Prince of Parma's.

The very parsimony which caused Burghley to wish for the immediate discharging of the men caused their retention in service longer than was necessary, and throws some ugly shadows over the last page of the story of England's victory over the Great Armada. During the months of preparation for that victory, Sir John Hawkins, as Treasurer of the Navy, by the Queen's directions, had induced sailors and fighting men to do their work to a great extent on credit. When the time came for their discharge he had to make urgent demands for money with which to pay them. At the end of August, writing to Burghley for advances, he reported that a sum of 19,000*l.* was due for the time previous to the great fight off Gravelines, besides all the claims for the subsequent period. "Mr. Hawkins cannot make a better return," added Howard in a postscript; "God knows how the lieutenants and corporals will be paid."† Instead of being paid off, they were kept hanging on, with such scanty allowance of food, such miserable supplies of clothing, and such unhealthy housing, that they died by hundreds. The men who had saved England in its time of greatest peril were left to perish like vagabonds and outlaws. "'Tis a most

* RECORD OFFICE MSS., *Domestic*, vol. ccxiv., No. 54.
† *Ibid.*, vol. ccxv., No. 56.

pitiful sight," wrote Howard to Burghley on the 10th of August, "to see how the men here at Margate, having no place where they can be received, die in the streets. The best lodging I can get is barns and such outhouses, and the relief is small that I can provide for them here. It would grieve any man's heart to see men that have served so valiantly die so miserably."* While on shipboard, pursuing the Armada with "a brag countenance," they had been reduced by want of food and other necessaries to such extremities as it is not possible to describe in decent English, and had suffered terribly in consequence.† Their sufferings continued, with only partial abatement, when they were again in port. "They sicken one day and die the next," said Howard in a letter to the Queen, on the 22nd of August.‡ Receiving no money from London for the assistance of these poor fellows, Howard was obliged to appropriate some that was on its way thither as a contribution to the Queen's Exchequer. "By the Lord of Heaven," he said, writing to Walsingham on the subject, on the 27th of August, "had it not been mere necessity I would not have touched one crown; but if I had not some to have bestowed upon some poor and miserable men I should have wished myself out of the world."§ On the following day Hawkins wrote in a similar strain to Burghley, who had just written down to reprove him for having asked for money when the

---

* RECORD OFFICE MSS., *Domestic*, vol. ccxiv., No. 66.
† *Ibid.*, vol. ccxiv., Nos. 50, 53.   ‡ *Ibid.*, vol. ccxv., No. 40.
§ *Ibid.*, vol. ccxv., No. 59.

Exchequer was so empty.* Slowly and with difficulty, however, the sick were healed, and both sick and well were paid their due and put in readiness for other patriotic work.

In the meanwhile the Invincible Armada was being finally vanquished. The storm of the 4th of August that had harassed the English ships on their return to the Downs brought terrible misfortune on the Spanish ships in the North Sea. Some were wrecked on the shores of Norway; some on the shores of Scotland; some on the shores of Ireland. The story of all the grievous troubles and dismal adventures of the Spaniards who came out to conquer England would fill a volume. Early in October a shattered remnant of the famous fleet found its way back to Spain,—fifty-three ships out of the hundred and thirty-two that had at first composed it; ten thousand spiritless men out of the thirty thousand who had embarked.

Hardly even then could Philip II. believe that his Armada had been defeated. For many weeks Catholic Europe had been cheating itself with the belief that already England was being restored to the true faith and had been brought under subjection to the Cæsar of the sixteenth century by Spanish soldiers and by the agents of the Holy Inquisition. "They were not ashamed," as Sir Francis Drake said in a very memorable letter, which sums up the whole story in one long sentence, "to publish in sundry languages great victories in words, which they pretended to have obtained against this

* RECORD OFFICE MSS., *Domestic*, vol. ccxv., No. 63.

realm, when, shortly after, it was happily manifested in very deed to all nations how their Navy, which they termed Invincible, consisting of one hundred and forty sail of ships were, by thirty of her Majesty's own ships of war and a few of our merchants, by the wise, valiant, and advantageous conduct of the Lord Charles Howard, High Admiral of England, beaten and shuffled together even from the Lizard to Calais, and from Calais, driven with squibs from their anchors, were chased out of the sight of England round about Scotland and Ireland; where, for the sympathy of their religion hoping to find succour and assistance, a great part of them were crushed against the rocks, and those other that landed, being very many in number, were notwithstanding broken, slain and taken, and so sent from village to village, coupled in halters, to be shipped into England; where, her Majesty disdaining to put them to death and scorning either to retain or entertain them, they were all sent back again to their countries to witness the worthy achievement of their Invincible Navy. With all their great terrible ostentation, they did not, in all their sailing round about England, so much as sink or take one ship, bark, pinnace or cockboat of ours, or even burn so much as one sheep-cot on this land."*

* Stow, p. 750.

## CHAPTER XVI.

THE SEQUEL TO THE GREAT ARMADA FIGHT.

[1588—1603.]

"GREAT thanks," Philip II. is reported to have said, when intelligence of the entire overthrow of his Invincible Armada was brought to him—"great thanks do I render to Almighty God, by whose generous hand I am gifted with such power that I could easily, if I chose, place another fleet upon the seas. Nor is it of very great importance that a running stream should be sometimes intercepted, so long as the fountain from which it flows remains inexhaustible."\* But Philip overrated his own power. The fountain from which, through thirty years, had flowed the poisonous stream of Spanish aggrandizement and tyranny was beginning to fail. Tokens of failure had appeared even before the time of the Great Armada Fight, and during every one of the next twelve years, until haughty Philip was forced to seek relief from the injuries brought upon him by the open warfare and the privateering enterprises of England by virtually giving up the contest, it was made more and more apparent. Throughout those twelve years Spain and her possessions were the sport and

\* MOTLEY, vol. ii., p. 535.

the prey not only of hardy English seamen and singlehearted English patriots, but even of inexperienced adventurers highly born or highly placed, who set themselves herein to relieve the monotony of courtly avocations and to acquire wealth that should help them to shine with freshened splendour in the showy Court of Queen Elizabeth.

While the defeated Armada was being wrecked upon the shores of Scotland and Ireland, Englishmen were planning further retribution upon Spain for her insolent attempt to conquer England. Uncertainty as to the whereabouts of the Armada and the expedience of maintaining a strong force in the Narrow Seas to be on the watch for any invasion that might be attempted by the Prince of Parma, prevented Lord Admiral Howard from giving it any further chase. He also prudently discountenanced a project which seems to have been advanced by Queen Elizabeth herself or by some of her courtiers, more zealous than wise, for utilizing a part of the naval force then stationed off Dover in an expedition to the Azores, there to wait for the passing of a fleet of Spanish and Portuguese trading ships on their way back from the Indies. "Upon your letter," he wrote to Walsingham on the 27th of August, "I presently sent for Sir Francis Drake, and showed him the desire that her Majesty had for intercepting of the King's treasure from the Indies; and so we considered it, and neither of us find any ships here in the fleet anyways able to go such a voyage before they have been aground, which cannot be done in any place but at Chatham, and it will be fourteen days before they can be grounded. Belike it is thought the islands be but hereby," he added, with a touch of scorn: "it is not thought how the year is spent. I thought it good, therefore, to send with all speed Sir Francis Drake, although he be not very well, to inform you rightly of all. He is a man of judgment and acquainted with it, and will tell you what must be done for such a journey."*

The result of Drake's visit to Court was the partial abandonment of the intended expedition to the Azores and the planning of a much more formidable expedition against Spain to be sent out next spring, with Drake himself for leader. The other project issued only in the lending of two ships to George Clifford, Earl of Cumberland, for such work as he could manage to do with it. This nobleman, born in 1558, had won fame for himself in earlier years as the best tilter in England, and in all courtly tournaments he appeared as the Queen's champion. Following the tide of seafaring zeal, he had in 1586 sent out two barks, Sir Walter Raleigh contributing a third, under Robert Withrington, for voyaging in the South Sea. Withrington reached Brazil and then, proving coward, returned to England, when all men grieved " to see my Lord's hopes thus deceived and his great expenses cast away."† In 1587 the Earl of Cumberland took a small part in the war in the Netherlands, and during the Armada Fight he

* RECORD OFFICE MSS., *Domestic*, vol. ccxv., No. 59.
† HAKLUYT, vol. iii., pp. 769-778.

distinguished himself as captain of the *Elizabeth Bonaventure*. Anxious to do further service, he obtained from Queen Elizabeth in the following October permission to fit out at his own expense the *Golden Horn* and the *Scout*, and employ them in fighting against Philip.* He captured a Spanish vessel in the English Channel or near it, but, before he could reach Spain, a storm split the larger ship's mainmast and he had to abandon his intended work.† A contemporary project of Sir Walter Raleigh's for leading a few of the Queen's ships to the coast of Ireland and there adding to the troubles of the Armada and its shipwrecked crews, troubled enough in other ways, was also entered upon and abandoned without any noteworthy result.‡ The next great work was that undertaken by Sir Francis Drake and Sir John Norris.

The work was first discussed in the middle of September, 1588;§ and on the 11th of October a commission was issued by the Queen to Drake and Norris, entrusting them with "the whole charge and direction of an enterprise to invade and destroy the powers and forces of all such persons as had in that past summer, with their hostile armadas, sought and attempted the invasion of the realm of England and the dominions of the same." They were also instructed, if possible, to place Don Antonio, the claimant of the crown of Portugal,

* RECORD OFFICE MSS., *Domestic*, vol. ccxvii., No. 32; vol. ccxxxvii., No. 34.   † PURCHAS, vol. ii., p. 1142.

‡ RECORD OFFICE MSS., *Domestic*, vol. ccxv., No. 64; vol. ccxvi., Nos. 2, 24, 28; vol. ccxviii., No. 3.

§ *Ibid.*, vol. ccxvi., Nos. 32, 33, 59.

which had been seized by Philip II., in the way of making good his claim.* Drake was to organize an efficient fleet, composed of Queen's ships and private ships, and to see that they were well officered, well manned, and well furnished: Norris was to make proper arrangements for the organizing of a little army to be conveyed and landed by Drake in any parts that might be fixed upon. This was in fact, with far greater force than Drake had had at his disposal in 1587, and with far less pomp than had been shown in the preparation of the Armada, to be a vigorous piece of retaliation upon Spain.

All through the autumn and winter the joint commanders were busy with their work, and prompt and hearty assistance was afforded to them by Queen and statesmen, courtiers and commoners, parsons and seamen.† Queen Elizabeth contributed ships worth 16,000*l*.; and the requisite funds for fitting them out were furnished by private adventurers, 2,000*l*. by Drake; 6,000*l*. by Drake's friends; 20,000*l*. by Norris and his friends; 15,000*l*. by the City of London and its leading merchants.‡ Each party was to look for payment of these outlays, and as much profit as could be acquired, from an equitable division of the rich prizes that were to be taken in Spain and in Spanish waters. Vague promises of recompense were made by Don Antonio, and much actual assistance was rendered by the people of the Netherlands.§ On the

* RECORD OFFICE MSS., *Domestic*, vol. ccxvii., No. 15.
† *Ibid.*, vol. ccxvii., Nos. 23, 25.
‡ *Ibid.*, vol. ccvii., Nos. 56, 57; vol. ccxviii., No. 56; vol. ccxix., No. 45; vol. ccxxiii., No. 56. § CAMDEN, vol. iii., p. 428.

23rd of February, 1589, when the arrangements were nearly completed, a fresh commission was issued to Drake and Norris, with detailed instructions appointing them in the first place to attack the shipping of the King of Spain on his own coasts, and afterwards to seize some of the Azores and there lie in wait for the trading fleets coming from both the East and the West Indies.*

Drake and Norris were at Plymouth with their ships and men, ready for departure, early in March. But they were detained for nearly a month by bad weather, and during that time was consumed a great part of the scanty supply of provisions that was to last out during the voyage. The money which Lord Burghley should have sent down by the end of March for the purchase of a further store did not arrive until the 26th of April;† and in consequence there ensued many desertions, and much trouble to the whole company. "I did never write to your Lordship with so discontented a mind as I do now," said Drake in a letter to Burghley on the 8th of April. "We have used our best means as long as we could to uphold the service, as far as our own abilities and the credit of our friends could any way be stretched to serve our turns; but, for that the numbers of our men are so many and our daily charge so great by reason of our stay, we are no further able to continue the same as we have done. If this action should now be dissolved by any particular wants, the

* RECORD OFFICE MSS., *Domestic*, vol. ccxxiii., Nos. 88, 89.
† *Ibid.*, vol. ccxxiii., Nos. 101, 102.

dishonour must needs be great to her Majesty, the loss not a little to us and such as are adventurers, and the clamour of the numbers which must be discharged most intolerable."* " What misery the detracting of the time of our setting out did lay upon us," says one of the adventurers, "too many can witness, and what extremity the want of that month's victuals, which we did eat during the month we lay at Plymouth, might have driven us unto, no man can doubt of that knoweth what men do live by, had not God in the end given us a more prosperous wind and shorter passage unto Galicia than hath been often seen, where our own force and fortune revictualled us largely."†

Drake and Norris did not wait for the provisions that Burghley and his agents were so tardy in procuring. Judging that they could not possibly have greater troubles than befell them while they were waiting at Plymouth, and leaving directions that the food should be sent after them, they set sail on Friday, the 18th of April.‡ Contrary winds, however, detained them at the entrance to the harbour for a day and a half longer, and, during that fresh waiting time, several of the volunteer-ships, containing three thousand men, turned deserters, and had made good their escape before their absence was discovered. What was the precise force of the fleet that actually proceeded to Spain is not clear.

* RECORD OFFICE MSS., *Domestic*, vol. ccxxiii., No. 70.

† WINGFIELD, *A True Discourse of the Voyage to Spain and Portugal*, 1589, in HAKLUYT, vol. ii., part ii., pp. 134-155, which is the authority for the ensuing details when no other is given.

‡ RECORD OFFICE MSS., *Domestic*, vol. ccxiii., No. 95.

It included six of the Queen's ships; the *Revenge*, with Drake and Norris on board; the *Nonpareil*; the *Dreadnought* under Thomas Fenner; the *Swiftsure*, the *Foresight*, under Sir William Winter; and the *Aid*, under William Fenner. These ships had an aggregate burthen of 2,350 tons, and contained 1,500 seamen. There were also said to be 11,000 soldiers, and a large number of sailors, on board private barks and pinnaces, variously estimated at eighty and a hundred and forty sail, though after all the desertions the number was probably much less than the smaller estimate. The entire company was reported to consist of 23,000 persons, from which number also must be made a large deduction for the deserters. Fifty or sixty vessels of all sorts and about 15,000 men of all ranks probably formed the ultimate strength of the expedition.*

All its early troubles being overpassed, it sailed out of Plymouth waters at eight o'clock on Sunday morning, the 20th of April, and, favoured at last by a brisk and steady north wind, sighted Cape Ortegal at four o'clock on Wednesday afternoon. On Thursday it passed into the haven of Corunna, then, as now, commonly called the Groyne. Four great Spanish ships were burnt before dark, after the taking of sixty-eight brass pieces of cannon from one of them, and under cover of the night all the soldiers were landed about a mile from the town.

Upon that followed a fortnight's siege of Corunna,

---

* RECORD OFFICE MSS., *Domestic*, vol. ccxxiii., No. 102; HAKLUYT, vol. ii., part ii., p. 133; BARROW, *Life of Drake*, p. 338.

then one of the strongest cities in Spain. Sir John Norris put to good use all the fighting experience that he had acquired in France under Coligni, in Ireland under Walter, Earl of Essex, and in the Netherlands under William of Orange, and Drake was land-soldier enough to render him efficient service. On Friday, the 25th of April, three parties made a simultaneous attack upon different sides of the lower town, and it was soon captured with a loss of twenty Englishmen against five hundred Spaniards.* There all the men who could be spared from the ships took up their quarters, feasting upon the food that they found in it, and turning it and all the towns and villages round about into ruins. To the upper town of Corunna, very well fortified, they laid siege, but without any real success. The gates were once entered, but the assailants were driven back. A breach was made in the wall, but the mine laid by the English effected more than was intended: just as they were entering a tower fell and crushed nearly three hundred of them, leaving time to the Spaniards to construct fresh fortifications out of the fragments before another onset was attempted. A second breach was made; but the besieged, led by a brave woman named Maria Pita, precursor in very similar circumstances of the Maid of Saragoza, offered a resistance too fierce to be overcome.† After that the siege was abandoned.

It was followed by a battle in open field, consequent on the arrival of 15,000 fresh Spanish troops for the

\* RECORD OFFICE MSS., *Domestic*, vol. ccxxiv., No. 24.
† SOUTHEY. vol. iii., p. 212.

relief of the town. Intelligence was brought of their being encamped at Puente de Burgo, five miles from Corunna. "Whereupon, on Tuesday the 6th of May," wrote Drake and Norris in their report to the Queen's Council, "we marched towards them with 7,000 soldiers, leaving the rest for the guard and siege of the town. Encountering them, they continued fight the space of three-quarters of an hour; and then we forced them to retire to the foot of a bridge, whereon not above three could march in rank, and from whence, although they were there defended by some fortifications, and had the benefit and succour of certain houses and other places adjoining, they were followed with our shot and pikes, with such courage and fierceness as, after some few volleys on both sides, they entered the bridge, whence, with the push of the pike, they were forced to make retreat into their trenches to the further foot of the bridge, which also, being pursued, they forsook and betook themselves to flight, abandoning their weapons, bag and baggage, and lost about 1,000 in skirmish and pursuit."* "How many 2,000 men, for of so many consisted our vanguard, might kill in pursuit of four sundry parties, so many, you may imagine, fell before us that day," says one sharer in this cruel butchery; "and to make the number more great, our men, having given over the execution and returning to their stands, found many hidden in the vineyards and hedges, whom they despatched."† Of the English, it

* RECORD OFFICE MSS., *Domestic*, vol. ccxxiv., No. 15.
† HAKLUYT, vol. ii., part ii., p. 112.

is said, only two common soldiers and one corporal were killed, and four officers were wounded.*

For their stay at Corunna Drake and Norris were greatly blamed by Queen Elizabeth. Writing to them on the 20th of May, she charged them with allowing " a haviour of vain-glory to obfuscate the eyes of their judgment," and bade them lose no further time in complying with her former instructions to them to spoil the King of Spain's navy, and then seize his Indian treasure-ships off the Azores.† Their excuse was that, having left Plymouth with hardly a week's store of provisions, it was absolutely necessary they should pillage the first port they could arrive at, and that this they had done with all possible prudence and despatch.

They left Corunna on the 8th of May, and proceeded to the neighbourhood of Lisbon. Adverse winds and an angry sea, however, made the voyage a very long one. They were troubled also by much sickness, induced by over-eating and over-drinking at Corunna. On the 13th they fell in with the promised transports, bringing wholesomer food from Plymouth, with which came as a convoy the *Swiftsure*, which, by accident or plan, had failed to accompany them at starting. In the *Swiftsure* was an unwelcome volunteer, Robert, Earl of Essex. The young Earl—Sidney's successor, and with far less merit, in Queen Elizabeth's especial favour—had attempted to join the fleet in England. Not yet two-

* RECORD OFFICE MSS., *Domestic*, vol. ccxxiv., No. 15.
† *Ibid.*, vol. ccxxiv., No. 53.

and-twenty, being born in 1567, he had spent all his slight patrimony, and 23,000*l.* lent him by his royal mistress, in dalliance at Court. "Her Majesty's goodness hath been so great," he now said, "as I could not ask more of her. No way left but to repair myself by mine own adventure, which I had much rather undertake than to offend her Majesty with suits, as I have done heretofore."\* But the generally penurious Queen was more ready to lend money to the young spendthrift than to do without his gay society. Hearing that he desired to go with Drake and Norris, she had written to them, bidding them, at the risk of her eternal displeasure, prevent his project, and, if they found him, send him back to Court without an hour's delay.† Their vigilance had kept him back at Plymouth; and now that he joined them off the coast of Spain, they wrote specially to excuse themselves to the Queen. "As soon as we met with the Earl of Essex," they said, "we did our endeavours for his Lordship's present return; but we doubted whether we might spare out of the fleet a ship of so good service as the *Swiftsure*," which would have been needed to take him home.‡ Therefore they helped him to become a seaman as well as a courtier.

Halting at Peniche, some forty miles from Lisbon, on the 16th of April, Drake landed Sir John Norris and the soldiers. With most of the ships he proceeded to the mouth of the Tagus. Without difficulty he seized

---

\* Devereux, *Lives of the Earls of Essex*, vol. i., p. 206.
† *Ibid.*, p. 200.   ‡ *Ibid.*, p. 202.

the fort of Cascaes and sixty vessels, chiefly laden with
corn, that lay in its harbour, and there he waited for
Norris's army, which, after marching up to Lisbon, and
attempting to besiege it during three days, had abandoned the undertaking as impracticable with so small a
force. The details of its work,* being soldiers' and not
seamen's work, need not here be given.

Nor is there much more to be chronicled concerning
this expedition. Meeting at Cascaes on the 1st of June,
Drake and Norris found that there was so much sickness among their men, and so much defection among
their volunteer shipping, that it was impossible to make
any useful effort at further spoliation of the Spanish
coast. They returned to Galicia, and there divided
their fleet. Norris, with most of the merchant vessels,
went homewards as quickly as he could, though with
much hindrance on the way. Drake, with the Queen's
ships and some others, attempted to fulfil the instructions for proceeding to the Azores, there to lie in wait
for prizes. But a violent storm proved to him that his
worn-out crews were unfit for further service. He
therefore set sail for England, and reached Plymouth
about the 22nd of June, twelve days before Norris.

The undertaking had been to a great extent a failure.
By it had been done much less injury to Spain than
had been hoped for: very little booty had been taken;
and there had been terrible loss of life. But Philip II.
had been insulted in his own land: a Spanish army had
been defeated in Galicia: Cascaes had been forced to

* RECORD OFFICE MSS., *Domestic*, vol. ccxxiv., Nos. 77–79.

surrender; and the English, after showing their contempt for the power of Spain, had returned home conquered by nothing but sickness and incapacity in their own ranks. If, compared with previous exploits of Drake's, the expedition of 1589 had been unfortunate, it had been a brilliant success in comparison with the failure of the Great Armada of 1588. Sir John Norris, writing from Plymouth on the 4th of July, to deprecate the Queen's condemnation of his proceedings, said truly that "had the enemy done as much against the English, they would have made bonfires in most parts of Christendom."* Queen Elizabeth, in her reply, instead of scolding, acknowledged herself "infinitely bound to Almighty God for the success it had pleased Him to give to their attempts in Spain and Portugal," and hardly less indebted to Drake and Norris for their hearty and valiant services.†

Drake had not been in England a fortnight, and his mariners had not yet been paid off, when Sir John Hawkins, on the 6th of July, submitted to Lord Burghley a scheme for staying his fleet, and sending it back in September, with reinforcements in ships and men, and ample supplies of food and ammunition, to capture Cadiz and sink all the Spanish galleys to be found in its harbour and the neighbourhood. "It is not honourable," he said, "for her Majesty to seem to be in any fear of the King of Spain."‡ That project was not heeded, and no important work was given to Drake

* RECORD OFFICE MSS., *Domestic*, vol. ccxxv., No. 5.
† *Ibid.*, vol. ccxxv., No. 15. ‡ *Ibid.*, vol. ccxxv., No. 11.

for four years and more. He even fell so far, after his good friend Walsingham's death, into disgrace with Queen Elizabeth, that King Philip was foolish enough to make overtures to him, in the spring of 1590, for the transference of his services to Spain.* We can understand with what scorn those overtures were rejected.

In the meanwhile England's war with Spain was carried on without abatement. On the 18th of June, 1589, a few days before Drake's arrival at Plymouth, the Earl of Cumberland, unsuccessful in his earlier privateering projects, had started from it on a new enterprise, " his spirit remaining higher than the winds, and more resolutely, by storms, compact and united in itself."† At his own cost he had fitted out the *Victory*, one of the largest of the Queen's ships, which she had lent to him for this purpose, two barks, the *Meg* and the *Margaret*, and a small pinnace. The *Margaret* was found unfit for the hard work in store for her, and soon sent home. With the other vessels, committing some piracies on French and Dutch traders on the way, the Earl proceeded to the Azores. There four other barks and pinnaces joined his force. He was a few days too late for the East Indian fleet; and, though just in time for the West Indian fleet, consisting of fifteen richly-laden vessels, his pursuit of it was futile. But there were other treasure-ships to come. Meeting two great hulks from Brazil, he captured one of them, with

* RECORD OFFICE MSS., *Domestic*, vol. ccxxxi., No. 94.
† PURCHAS, vol. ii., p. 1142.

a loss of eighty men, and this he sent home at once with the *Meg*. Soon afterwards he fell in with another galley, coming from San Juan de Ulloa, and made an easy capture of it, and its stores of silver, cochineal, sugar, and hides, valued in all at 100,000*l*. According to one of his party, however, " these summer services and ships of sugar proved not so sweet and pleasant as the winter was sharp and painful."\* His great prize, with all its cargo, was wrecked off Cornwall, and he himself had difficulty in escaping from drowning and starvation on his way back to England, which he reached on the 20th of December. His other prizes yielded a hundred per cent. upon the outlay of the voyage, and with this he had to be content.†

In spite of their misfortunes the English found advantage enough, both in the value of their captures and in the patriotic satisfaction which they derived from the spoliation of Spanish and Catholic possessions, to continue their fierce warfare upon the seas. Half a dozen volumes would be needed for a full rehearsal of the work done by commissioned officers and by private adventurers, by Queen's ships, and pirate barks, and merchants' vessels, during these twelve busy years. King Philip's beard, according to Drake's favourite expression, having been singed and pulled, Englishmen of all ranks felt it their bounden duty to God, their country, and themselves, and certainly made it their great delight, to swarm around him, like an army

\* Monson, in Churchill's *Collection*, vol. iii., p. 181.
† *Ibid.*, p. 184.

of elves, and pluck it out, hair by hair, or in handfuls together, by the roots. The more he winced, the more he swore, the more he uttered vows of vengeance which he was unable to perform, the better they were pleased.

The most memorable of these exploits alone can here be recounted, and these but briefly. But some of the smallest enterprises, by reason of their wonderful daring and their wonderful success, are as memorable as the greatest. Of this sort was a fight between ten English merchant ships and twelve Spanish galleys that took place in the Straits of Gibraltar in 1590. These ten merchantmen had gone for trade to Venice, Constantinople, and other ports in the Mediterranean and the Levant, and in returning home had met for mutual protection near the coast of Barbary. Immediately after this meeting, on Easter Monday, the 23rd of April, they descried twelve great galleys, " bravely furnished and strongly provided with men and ammunition," lying in wait for any English ships that might pass Gibraltar. Let the story be told in the words of one of the party. "In the morning early," he says, " being the 24th of April, according to our usual customs we said service and made our prayers unto Almighty God, beseeching Him to save us from the hands of such tyrants as the Spaniards, whom we knew and had found to be our most mortal enemies upon the sea. And having finished our prayers, and set ourselves in readiness, we perceived them to come towards us, and that they were indeed the Spanish galleys that lay under the conduct of Andrew Doria, who is Viceroy for the King of Spain in the Straits of Gibraltar, and a notable enemy to all Englishmen. So when they came somewhat nearer to us, they waved us amain for the King of Spain, and we waved them amain for the Queen of England, at which time it pleased Almighty God greatly to encourage us all in such sort, as that the nearer they came the less we feared their great multitudes and huge number of men, which were planted in those galleys to the number of two or three hundred men in each galley. And it was thus concluded among us, that the four first and tallest ships should be placed hindmost, and the weaker and smallest ships foremost, and so it was performed, every man being ready to take part of such success as it should please God to send. At the first encounter the galleys came upon us very fiercely, yet God so strengthened us, that, if they had been ten times more, we had not feared them at all. Whereupon the *Solomon*, being a hot ship, and having sundry cast pieces in her, gave the first shot in such a sour sort as that it sheared away so many men as sat on the one side of a galley, and pierced her through in such manner as that she was ready to sink, which made them to assault us the more fiercely. Whereupon the rest of our ships, especially the *Margaret and John*, the *Minion*, and the *Ascension*, followed, and gave a hot charge upon them, and they at us, where began a hot and fierce battle with great valiancy the one against the other, and so continued for the space of six hours. About the beginning of this our fight there came two

Flemings to our fleet, who seeing the force of the galleys to be so great, the one of them presently yielded, struck his sails, and was taken by the galleys, whereas, if they would have offered themselves to have fought in our behalf and their own defence, they needed not to have been taken so cowardly as they were to their cost. The other Fleming, being also ready to perform the like piece of service, began to vail his sails, and intended to have yielded immediately. But the trumpeter in that ship plucked forth his falchion, and slipped to the pilot at the helm, and vowed that if he did not speedily put off to the English fleet, and so take part with them, he would presently kill him; which the pilot, for fear of death, did, and so by that means they were defended from present death, and from the tyranny of those Spaniards, which doubtless they should have found at their hands. Thus we continued in fight six hours and somewhat more, wherein God gave us the upper hand, and we escaped the hands of so many enemies, who were constrained to flee into harbour and shroud themselves from us, and with speed to seek for their own safety. This was the handiwork of God, who defended us from danger in such sort as that there was not one man of us slain. And, in all this fierce assault made upon us by the Spanish power, we sustained no hurt or damage at all more than this, that the shrouds and backstays of the *Solomon*, who gave the first and last shot, and galled the enemy shrewdly all the time of the battle, were clear stricken off. After the battle was ceased, which was on Easter Tuesday, we stayed for want of wind before Gibraltar until the next morning, where we were becalmed, and therefore looked every hour when they would have sent forth some fresh supply against us, but they were far unable to do it, for all their galleys were so sore battered that they durst not come forth of the harbour, by reason of our hot resistance, which they so lately before had received."*

Nearly every year there were fights as valiant as that. English merchant ships generally held their own, in Spanish waters, against the once formidable galleys of Spain, and Spanish merchant ships and galleys alike were over and over again beaten, burnt, or captured, and always held in awe, by privateering fleets sent out from England. Even failures, as they were esteemed by Queen Elizabeth and the private adventurers who hoped in these ways to make profits larger than the most prosperous trade could yield, were great successes as far as injury to Spain was concerned.

So it was with an expedition conducted by Sir John Hawkins in this same year. A scheme proposed by him to Lord Burghley in July, 1589, has been referred to. That scheme was rejected, but soon afterwards Hawkins produced another, which caused some stir, though its nature has not been recorded. It was talked of in February, 1590; and apparently had for its object an attack upon Spain, quite as formidable as that attempted by Drake and Norris in the previous year.† It also,

* HAKLUYT, vol. ii., part ii., pp. 167, 168.
† RECORD OFFICE MSS., Domestic, vol. ccxxx., Nos. 79, 80, 94, 99.

however, was abandoned. On the 1st of March, Hawkins wrote disconsolately to Burghley on the subject, saying that now he was out of hope that he should be allowed to perform "any royal thing."* He was so disheartened that on the 16th of April he wrote again, begging, since her Majesty was not satisfied with him, that he might be relieved from "the importable care and toil" of his duties as Treasurer of the Navy. "No man living," he said, "hath so careful, so miserable, so unfortunate, and so dangerous a life."†

He was not permitted to retire, and in May a modification of his project was adopted. He was sent, with Sir Martin Frobisher for his Vice-Admiral, at the head of either twelve or fourteen ships, with about fourteen hundred men on board, to do as much mischief as he could on the coast of Spain, and to try and intercept the fleet of Portuguese carracks coming from India.‡ For five months Hawkins and Frobisher applied themselves heartily to their work, but without much profit. They kept Spain in such awe that, we are told, every valuable that could be removed was taken from Corunna, Lisbon, Cadiz, and other ports to inland towns, and all the Spanish galleys were lodged in the safest corners that were open to them.§ But they had no orders, and were not in sufficient force, to attack Spain itself, and therefore there was nothing there for them to do. The trading fleets also had been warned

* RECORD OFFICE MSS., *Domestic*, vol. ccxxxi., No. 2.
† *Ibid.*, vol. ccxxxi., No. 83.
‡ *Ibid.*, vol. ccxxxii., Nos. 13–15, 18; vol. ccxxxiv., No. 9.
§ *Ibid.*, vol. ccxxxii., No. 17.

of their presence, and, by Philip II.'s directions, were kept back.* So, after cruising about for five months, the adventurers had to return at the end of October, empty handed or with so few prizes that they did not pay for the fitting out of the expedition.† Very great, we are told, was Queen Elizabeth's indignation at the result. Hawkins tendered an elaborate apology. "Paul might plant, and Apollos might water," he said in its conclusion, "but it was God only who gave the increase." The quotation was not soothing to the Queen. "God's death!" she exclaimed, "this fool went out a soldier and is come home a divine!"‡

Unprofitable, also, was a third privateering enterprise in which the Earl of Cumberland embarked in the spring of 1591. With one of the Queen's ships and four smaller vessels, he took many prizes, from hostile Spaniards and friendly Dutch alike, during a few months' cruise off the coast of Spain; but he was unable to hold the best of them. His chief adviser, the famous Sir William Monson of Stuart times, was taken prisoner, and after that, says Monson, "the Earl durst not abide the coast of Spain, and thought it more discretion to return to England, having taken nothing whatever toward defraying the charges of his outfit."§

Contemporary with that expedition of the Earl of Cumberland's to the neighbourhood of Spain, was one, yet more famous, led by Lord Thomas Howard and

* HAKLUYT, vol. ii., part ii., p. 183.
† RECORD OFFICE MSS., *Domestic*, vol. ccxxxiii., No. 118.
‡ SOUTHEY, vol. iii., p. 223.
§ *Ibid.*, vol iii., pp. 9-17.

Sir Richard Grenville against the Spanish ships coming from the West Indies. Lord Thomas Howard, born in 1561, and the eldest son of Thomas, fourth Duke of Norfolk, had only been released in 1585 from the attainder consequent on his father's conspiracy in favour of Mary Queen of Scots. Immediately after that he began to take a prominent share in public movements. In 1588 he had distinguished himself under his cousin, the Lord Admiral, in the Armada Fight; and in 1591 he determined to win further renown in an independent exploit. With him was associated Sir Richard Grenville, whom we have already seen in his connection with Raleigh's Virginian colony, and who had for many years worked heartily, and very much to his advantage, in the trade of piracy and privateering against Spain. Their especial object was to try and seize the West Indian fleet which had escaped the search of Hawkins and Frobisher in 1590 by lying in concealment at Havannah, where it waited all through the winter, " choosing rather to hazard the perishing of ships, men, and goods, than that they should become the prize of the English."

Seven of the Queen's ships, the *Defiance*, the *Revenge*, the *Nonpareil*, the *Elizabeth Bonaventure*, the *Lion*, the *Foresight*, and the *Chase*, six victualling ships, and the *Bark Raleigh*, which was Sir Walter Raleigh's contribution to the enterprise, with two or three pinnaces, made up the fleet.* It left Plymouth soon after the 10th of March, proceeded to the Azores, and there waited for

* RALEIGH in HAKLUYT, vol. ii., part ii., p. 170.

about five months, making a few small captures, but watching in vain for the expected West Indian treasure-ships. Philip, on hearing of Lord Thomas Howard's designs, had ordered the further detention of these ships at Havannah, and had also ordered the preparation of a formidable fleet to go out and to conduct them home, and, if possible, to defeat the English at the same time.

This was the greatest fleet sent out of Spain since the defeat of the Armada. It comprised over fifty sail;—thirty great Portuguese, Biscayan, and Andalusian galleys, ten Dutch fly-boats that had been seized near Lisbon, and a dozen or more of miscellaneous craft.* Howard was informed of its setting out, on the 30th of August, by a message from the Earl of Cumberland. His own ships, said Sir Walter Raleigh, were "all pestered and rummaging, everything out of order, very light for want of ballast, and, what was most to their disadvantage, half the men of every ship sick and utterly unserviceable." He had hardly had a day in which to try and put things in order, however, when, on the 31st of August, the Spanish fleet, coming towards him at once, either by accident or by a change in plan, appeared in sight. Taken by surprise, he put out to sea, designing thus to get more time in which to prepare for battle. But Grenville, in the *Revenge*, was unable to do this before the Spaniards came within gun-shot, and in consequence a battle was fought at once.†

* RALEIGH in HAKLUYT, p. 173; LINSCHOTEN in the same, p. 185.
† RALEIGH in HAKLUYT, vol. ii., part ii., p. 170.

It was a battle eminently characteristic of the daring seamanship of England under the Tudors. Sir Richard Grenville, finding himself, in a single vessel, face to face with fifty Spanish ships, nearly all of them twice or thrice the size of the *Revenge*, might easily have retreated, getting out of reach of the enemy's guns before they had done much harm. "But," says Sir Walter Raleigh in a vivid description of the fight, "Sir Richard utterly refused to turn from the enemy, alleging that he would rather choose to die than to dishonour himself, his country, and her Majesty's ship, persuading his company that he would pass through the two squadrons and enforce the Spaniards to give him way." Applying himself to that bold plan, he pressed into the crowd of Spanish galleys. The first four or five that gathered round him he bravely defied; but he was soon overwhelmed. "The great *San Felipe*," says Raleigh, "being in the wind of him, and coming towards him, becalmed his sails in such sort as the ship could neither make way nor feel the helm, so huge and high-charged was the Spanish ship, being of 1500 tons," just thrice as large as the *Revenge*. The *San Felipe* and the other great Spanish ships easily closed upon the *Revenge*; but they did not find it easy to board her.

From three o'clock in the afternoon till daybreak next morning, Grenville and his few followers fought as even Englishmen had rarely fought before. Troops after troops of Spaniards, attempting from their high bulwarks to make what seemed an easy descent upon the deck of the *Revenge*, were driven back. Galley after galley, riddled through and through by English cannon-balls, was forced to retire; some to founder, all the rest to need much tinkering before they were fit for further service. "The Spanish ships," says Raleigh, "were filled with companies of soldiers; in some two hundred, besides the mariners, in some five, in others eight hundred. In ours there were none at all beside the mariners, save the servants of the commanders, and some few voluntary gentlemen. But they were still repulsed again and again, and at all times beaten back into their own ships, or into the seas. As they were wounded and beaten off, so always others came in their place, the *Revenge* having never less than two mighty galleys by her side. Ere the morning, from three o'clock of the day before, there had fifteen several armadas assailed her; and all so ill approved their entertainment as they were, by the break of day, far more willing to hearken to a composition than hastily to make any more assaults. But as the day increased, so our men decreased, and as the light grew more and more, by so much more grew our discomforts. For none appeared in sight but enemies, save one small ship called the *Pilgrim*, who hovered all night to see the success; but in the morning, bearing with the *Revenge*, she was hunted like a hare amongst many ravenous hounds, but escaped."

The heroes of the *Revenge* were too proud to escape, as even now they might have done. They fought on to the last. "All the powder, to the last barrel," says Raleigh, "was now spent, all the pikes broken, forty of the best men slain, and most part of the rest hurt. In the beginning of the fight she had but one hundred free from sickness, and fourscore and ten sick, laid in hold upon the ballast. A small troop to man such a ship! a weak garrison to resist so mighty an army! By those hundred all was sustained, the volleys, boardings, and enterings of fifteen ships of war, besides those which beat her at large. The Spaniards were always supplied with soldiers brought from every squadron, all manner of arms, and powder at will: unto ours there remained no comfort at all, no hope, no supply either of ships, men, or weapons; the masts all beaten overboard, all her tackle cut asunder, her upper-work altogether rased, and she, in effect, evened with the water, nothing being left but the very foundation or bottom of a ship, not able to move one way or other, but as she was moved with the waves and billows of the sea."

Then, after fifteen hours' fight, and the spending of eight hundred charges of great artillery and rounds of small shot without number, Grenville resolved, not to surrender to the Spaniards, but to cease fighting with them. "He persuaded the company," says Raleigh, "or as many as he could induce, to yield themselves unto God, and to the mercy of none else; but, as they had, like valiant and resolute men, repulsed many enemies, they should not now shorten the honour of their nation by prolonging their own lives for a few hours, or a few days. The master gunner readily consented, and divers others; but the captain and the master were of another opinion, and besought Sir Richard to have care of them, alleging that the Spaniards would be as ready to entertain a composition as they were willing to offer the same, and that, there being divers sufficient and valiant men yet living whose wounds were not mortal, they might do their country and prince acceptable service hereafter. And, whereas Sir Richard had alleged that the Spaniards should never glory to have taken one ship of her Majesty's, seeing they had so long and so notably defended themselves, they answered that the ship had six foot of water in hold, and three shot under water, which were so weakly stopped as, with the first working of the sea, she must needs sink, and was besides so crushed and bruised, as she could never be removed out of the place. As the matter was thus in dispute, and Sir Richard refusing to hearken to any of those reasons, the master of the *Revenge,* while the captain won unto him the greater party, was conveyed aboard the General Don Alonzo Bazan"—who was a brother of the Marquis of Santa Cruz—"who, finding none overhasty to enter the *Revenge* again, doubting whether Sir Richard would have blown them up and himself, and perceiving by the report of the master of the *Revenge* his dangerous disposition, yielded that all their lives should be saved, the company sail for England, and the better sort to pay such reasonable ransom as their estate would bear, and in the mean season, to be free from galley or imprisonment. To this he so much the rather condescended, as well, as I have said, for fear of further loss and mischief to themselves, as well as for the desire he had to recover Sir Richard Grenville, whom for his notable valour he seemed greatly to honour and admire. When this answer was returned, and that safety of life was promised, the common sort being now at the end of their peril, the most drew back from Sir Richard and the master gunner, being no hard matter to dissuade men from death to life. The master gunner, finding himself and Sir Richard thus prevented and mastered by the greater number, would have slain himself with a sword, had he not been by force withheld and locked into his cabin. Then the General sent many boats aboard the *Revenge*, and divers of our men, fearing Sir Richard's disposition, stole away aboard the general and other ships. Sir Richard, thus overmatched, was sent unto by Alfonso Bazan to remove out of the *Revenge*, the ship being marvellous unsavoury, filled with blood and bodies of dead and wounded men, like a slaughter-house. Sir Richard answered that they might do with his body what they list, for he esteemed it not, and, as he was carried out of the ship, he swooned, and, reviving again, desired the company to pray for him. The General used Sir Richard with all humanity, and left nothing unattempted that tended to his recovery,"— he had been grievously wounded about twelve o'clock the night before,—"highly commending his valour and worthiness, and greatly bewailing the danger wherein he was; being unto him a rare spectacle and a resolution seldom approved, to see one ship turn toward so many enemies, to endure the charge and boarding of so many huge armadas, and to resist and repel the assaults and entries of so many soldiers."*

A rare spectacle indeed! "I account," said Sir Richard Hawkins, the only other Elizabethan Englishman who yielded to the Spaniards, and who did so almost as gloriously as Grenville, "that he and his country got much honour in that occasion; for one ship, and of the second sort of her Majesty's, sustained the force of all the fleet of Spain, and gave them to understand that they be impregnable; for, having bought dearly the boarding of her, divers and sundry times, and with many jointly, and with a continual fight of fourteen or sixteen hours, at length leaving her without any mast standing, like a log in the seas, she made notwithstanding a most honourable composition of life and liberty for above two hundred and sixty men, as by the pay book appeareth;† all which may worthily be written in our chronicles in letters of gold, in memory for all posterities, some to beware, and others, by their example in like occasions, to imitate, the true valour of our nation in these ages."‡

Sir Richard Grenville died of his wound two or three days after his surrendering. "Here die I," he is reported to have said to the Spanish hidalgos, who, forgetting every animosity in their honour of his

* HAKLUYT, vol. ii., part ii., pp. 171, 172.
† This is nearly double the number given by Raleigh. Hawkins adds, that "Her Majesty, of her free grace, commanded, in recompense of her service, to be given to every one his six months' wages."
‡ *The Observations of* SIR RICHARD HAWKINS *in his Voyage into the South Sea* (Hakluyt Society, 1847), pp. 20, 21.

excellent bravery, vied with one another in striving to comfort him in his hours of pain, and who treasured up his dying words with reverent admiration,—" Here die I, Richard Grenville, with a joyful and a quiet mind, for that I have ended my life as a good soldier ought to do, who has fought for his country and his Queen, for honour and religion. Wherefore my soul joyfully departeth out of this body, leaving behind it an everlasting fame, as a true soldier who hath done his duty as he was bound to do. But the others of my company have done as traitors and dogs, for which they shall be reproached all their lives, and have a shameful name for ever."*

That bitter condemnation was not quite undeserved. Had even two or three of his consorts who watched Grenville's desperate fight from a safe distance, shared his valour, though in humbler sort, they might have worsted the whole Spanish fleet. Lord Thomas Howard, it is said, desired to attempt this, or at any rate to rescue the *Revenge* from the fiftyfold force in number of ships, more than a hundredfold in number of men and guns, with which she was mated. But his crews refused : his own master gunner vowed to throw himself into the sea rather than do work which must certainly end in the ruin of the Queen's ships and his own punishment as a galley-slave under the Spaniards. Therefore, after two hours of desultory fighting on the outskirts of Grenville's battle scene, the main body of the English fleet disgracefully retired. Captain Thomas

\* Linschoten, cited by Southey, vol. iii., p. 337.

Vavasor, in the little *Foresight*, fought on and worked his way very near to the *Revenge*; but his bark was disabled before night time, and he barely managed to save himself from capture by the Spaniards. Yet bolder was the bearing of the little *Pilgrim*, as we have seen, and of a small merchant vessel, the *George Noble*, which pressed right up to the *Revenge*, and only retired when Sir Richard Grenville, thanking her captain for his bravery, told him that the vessel was too small and, with nothing but small guns, too poorly armed to be of service in such a contest, and begged him to save himself while he could.*

Lord Thomas Howard's fleet did nothing else of note. Lying in wait for the passing of the West Indian treasure-ships, which came up a few days afterwards, it allowed them to get under protection of the Spanish fleet, and then, capturing one or two of their outlying numbers, but not daring to engage in a general battle, it returned to England. The East and West Indian treasure, which Philip had been so anxious to keep out of English hands, however, was not saved thereby. The ships and their convoys, galleys and galleons, merchant vessels and sloops, when all had been collected at the Azores, numbered a hundred and forty sail. They had just started for the Tagus, when a hurricane drove them back among the rocks, and caused such fearful havoc that, out of the hundred and forty vessels only forty escaped wreck. The *Revenge*, which had been patched up for a trophy, with two hundred

* HAKLUYT, vol. ii., part ii., pp. 171, 173.

Spaniards on board, went down. It was reckoned that ten thousand men, in all, were lost, and the loss in treasure, of more value to Philip than men, could not be reckoned up.*

It is hardly to be wondered at that the English, seeing how strangely wind and water sided with them in their warfare with the Spaniards, should have fancied that they were the especial favourites of the Almighty, and that Jehovah was fighting as stoutly for them as in former times He had fought for the chosen race of Israel. And, seeing how much cruelty was supposed, in Jewish times and circumstances, to be of Divine appointment, it is not strange that Christian Englishmen should also hold themselves both authorized and bound to do many cruel and unworthy things in the name of God. The marvel is rather that, with so many precedents and opportunities for wrong-doing, so little of it was done. The English fought with Spain in order that they might have their share of the wealth of the Indies, arrogantly and covetously claimed by Spain as its peculiar property; but they fought much more against the tyrannical and bigoted principles which were the foundation and the superstructure of Spain's dominion, and they generally demeaned themselves as became the champions of a good and honest cause.

The man who in the later years of Elizabeth's reign held these views most persistently, and held them worthily in spite of some personal characteristics which were not altogether worthy, was Sir Walter Raleigh.

* HAKLUYT, vol. ii., part ii., p. 187.

Not himself much of a seaman, we have seen how much he did to foster seamanship by his experiment of the first English colony in America. Virginia failed through the vices of subordinates which he is to be blamed for not using more effort than he did use to correct. When Virginia was abandoned, he applied himself yet more earnestly to work which was quite as helpful to the progress of English seamanship and to the general well-being of England. He had no objection to the winning of Spanish treasure for its own sake; but he saw with regret that the energies of his countrymen were, in these later years, becoming too exclusively devoted to this object. He therefore, both in writing and in his speeches in Parliament, earnestly advocated the continuance of public war with Spain, having for its primary object the crippling of her forces instead of the seizing of her precious goods. Zeal in that object had taken him as a volunteer in the great expedition of 1589 under Norris and Drake. Zeal in that object caused him in Parliament to urge, with all the eloquence that he possessed, and urge successfully, the carrying of war into the enemy's new place of lodgment in Brittany, a lodgment which, Raleigh represented, made the attitude of Spain, in spite of all her naval reverses, more formidable than it had been even in 1588.

While that project was being slowly adopted, Raleigh applied himself to another bold enterprise against Spain. Procuring two ships from the Queen, and fitting out thirteen others, he planned an expedition to the Spanish Main, and especially to the Isthmus of

Darien, where there was good hope of securing the annual store of treasure coming home, through Panama and Nombre de Dios, from Chili and Peru.* With this fleet he put to sea on the 6th of May, 1592. On the following day he was overtaken by Sir Martin Frobisher coming in a swift pinnace with a letter from Queen Elizabeth, bidding him return at once to be punished for making love to her pretty maid-of-honour, Elizabeth Throgmorton. It is not clear that this recall had not been previously arranged with Raleigh, and it is even possible that he never intended to go with the fleet himself, seeing that there was talk of his being brought home and replaced by Frobisher two months before he started.† At any rate, he did return, after conducting the fleet only so far as Cape Finisterre.

There, on the 11th of May, he divided his ships into two squadrons, entrusting one to Frobisher, the other to Sir John Burroughs. Frobisher he directed to cruise about the coast of Spain, " thereby to amaze the Spanish fleet;" Burroughs was to go to the Azores, and thence to the West Indies, unless he met the Panama fleet on the way.‡

The squadrons had not fairly separated before a great Biscayan ship, with a valuable cargo, came in sight, to be easily captured and sent home. This was

* HAKLUYT, vol. ii., part ii., p. 194; MONSON, in CHURCHILL, vol. iii., p. 156.

† I shall not attempt to explain his famous letter to Sir Robert Cecil, for which every one of his biographers has a separate explanation.

‡ HAKLUYT, vol. ii., part ii., p. 195.

all the good fortune that fell to Frobisher. His small force, though it may have amazed the Spaniards, was not strong enough to frighten them, and, after sailing up and down for a little time, he found it expedient to go home. Sir John Burroughs was more successful. Sailing towards the Azores, he heard that Philip II. had, upon intelligence of Raleigh's project, ordered that no treasure should be sent home that year from Panama; but at the same time he heard that a fleet of East Indian carracks was on its way to Lisbon. On that account he partly altered his course, and in doing so he fell in with five other English ships, which proved to be a little fleet fitted out by the Earl of Cumberland on a fourth privateering expedition.*

Cumberland, like Raleigh, had conducted his ships into Spanish waters and then returned to England. Captain Norton, who was left in charge of them, being at the Azores, had also heard of the approach of the East Indian carracks. Meeting Burroughs, he placed his ships under his command, and the combined fleets, numbering ten or eleven vessels in all, lay in wait for the East Indiamen. They soon fell in with one, the *Santa Cruz*, and gave her chase till she ran against a rocky island among the Azores. Then, having saved as much of her cargo as they could, they watched for other carracks, spreading out in a line which extended over nearly a hundred miles from north to south. After four days of watching, a huge carrack, called the *Madre de Dios*, of about 1,600 tons burthen, came in sight.

* HAKLUYT, vol. ii., part ii., p. 195; PURCHAS, vol. ii., p. 1145.

Thereupon they soon closed round her. The only Queen's ship, the *Foresight*, pressing up to her side, was caught by her grappling-irons, and borne along, like a ship's boat, for a little distance, while she attempted, in full sail, to outstrip her other small pursuers. But they soon pressed up, and about midnight the *Tiger*, a merchantman of 600 tons, twice as large as any of the others, began to board her on one side, while the *Foresight* and another belaboured her on the other. A tough struggle ensued, "the forecastle being so high that, without any resistance, the getting up had been difficult; but here was strong resistance, some irrecoverably falling by the board, and the assault continued an hour and a half, so brave a booty making the men fight like dragons." The dragons won, although their work was nearly spoilt by a fire which broke out through the upsetting of some candles in the turmoil. Captain Norton put out the fire, and, before morning, so many as survived of the seven hundred sailors, soldiers, and officers of the huge *Madre de Dios* had been made prisoners, and the captors were able leisurely to inspect their prize, by far the largest that had ever fallen into English hands.*

"The true proportion of the vast body of this carrack," says the narrator of the exploit, " did then, and still may, justly provoke the admiration of all men not formerly acquainted with such a sight. But albeit this first appearance of the hugeness thereof yielded sights enough to entertain our men's eyes, yet the pitiful

* HAKLUYT, vol. ii., part ii., p. 197.

object of so many bodies slain and dismembered could not but draw each man's eye to see, and heart to lament, and hands to help, those miserable people, whose limbs were torn with the violence of shot. No man could almost step but upon a dead carcase or a bloody floor; for, the greatness of the steerage requiring the labour of twelve or fourteen men at once, and some of our ships beating her in at the stern with their ordnance, oftentimes with one shot slew four or five labouring on either side of the helm, whose room being still furnished with fresh supplies, and our artillery still playing upon them with continual volleys, it could not but be that much blood was shed in that place."*

With commendable humanity Sir John Burroughs caused the wounded Spaniards and Portuguese to be tended by his surgeons, and then, placing both whole and lamed in one of his smaller craft, he sent them back, with a fair allowance of their own provisions, to their native country. On the way, however, they fell among other English privateers, who despoiled them of " nine hundred diamonds, besides other odds and ends," which they had concealed about their persons. Burroughs also hurried home, anxious to have his rich prize safe in English waters. When its riches were distributed, soon after his arrival at Dartmouth, near the end of August, they were found to consist of spices, drugs and dyes, silks, calicoes and damasks, pearls, jewels, and the like, worth in all 150,000*l*., " which," it is said, " being divided among the adventurers, whereof

* HAKLUYT, vol. ii., part ii., p. 198.

her Majesty was the chief, was sufficient to yield contentment to all parties."* The Earl of Cumberland, who seems not to have been content, received as his share 36,000*l*.† Raleigh had certainly not less.

This capture of the *Madre de Dios* added greatly to the privateering enterprise that had already been entered upon so zealously as to need no further stimulus. From Plymouth, from Exeter, from Bristol, and from a dozen other trading towns expeditions were every year sent out which, being sometimes disastrous, were at other times successful enough to pay for the failures and yet leave large profits. And gentlemen and noblemen were as eager as the traders by profession. The Earl of Cumberland, lordliest of pirates and privateers, equipped nine ships, two of them borrowed from the Queen's navy, in 1593, and with them captured, besides some French vessels, twelve great Spanish hulks off Portugal, and several other Spanish ships in the West Indies, all of which brought him in more wealth than could be told.‡ In 1594, with five ships, he attacked the *Cinco Chagos*, a carrack much larger than the *Madre de Dios*, almost the largest ever sent from Portugal to the East Indies; which, however, caught fire, at the moment of capture, and, with all its treasure and its crew of eleven hundred men, was lost. In attacking another carrack he was defeated, so that he had to return to England, " having done much

* HAKLUYT, vol. ii., part ii., p. 198.   † PURCHAS, vol. ii., p. 1145.
‡ HAKLUYT, vol. ii., part ii., pp. 199–201; MONSON, in CHURCHILL, vol. iii., pp. 157, 158.

harm to the enemy and little good to himself."* Yet in 1595, out of his spoils, and with a view to winning yet more, he built "the best ship that had ever before been built by any subject," which he called the *Scourge of Malice;* and of this he made much subsequent use.† But we have worthier work to chronicle.

Among the worthiest fighting work done during these years, although we have not much to do with it, it being chiefly carried on by soldiers on dry land, was the war against Spain in Brittany, of which Sir Walter Raleigh was almost the chief advocate. Its first promoter, as it seems, was Sir Francis Drake, who, in November, 1590, wrote to Henry of Navarre, asking whether he would approve of English efforts to oust the forces of Philip II. from the lodgment, which, taking advantage of the troubles in France incident on the War of the League, they had begun to make in Brittany.‡ Henry promptly wrote back to welcome the offer of assistance from "a man so celebrated by fame and noble deeds," as he said. "I have sent a letter to the Queen, your mistress, earnestly entreating for auxiliary forces," he added; "and I eagerly entreat you, most excellent Sir, that you will strengthen my petition before the Queen, as much as possible, by your authority and favour."§ English reinforcements were sent, though in a niggardly way, and apparently without much help from Drake's

* SOUTHEY, vol. iii., pp. 27-33.
† MONSON, in CHURCHILL, vol. iii., p. 189.
‡ RYMER, *Fœdera*, cited in BARROW, *Life of Drake*, p. 381.
§ *Ibid.*, p. 382.

"authority and favour," which, just then, were small at Court.

That help consisted only of land-soldiers, till the autumn of 1594, when, the arguments of Raleigh and others having prevailed so far, Sir Martin Frobisher was sent with a small force of ten vessels, four being Queen's ships and the other six volunteers, to prevent Brest from falling into the hands of the Spaniards. The neighbouring port of Crodon was already in Spanish hands. Sir John Norris, then at the head of the little English army, was ordered to invest it by land; Frobisher to attack it from the sea. The siege, begun on the 1st of September, was hotly continued until the garrison, being forced to surrender, was all put to the sword, and the fort reduced to ashes. But in the last fight Frobisher was wounded in the hip, and he died a few days after he had been conveyed to Plymouth; his death, it is said, being more due to the bad handling of the surgeon than to the wound itself.*

That was the first and last of Queen Elizabeth's naval fighting with Spain on the coast of France. She thought it better to send her seamen to harass Philip in Spanish waters, and best of all to encourage them to take the war into their own hands, themselves defraying the expenses of their privateering enterprises, while, if they were successful, a part of the profits was assigned to her on account of the empty ships which they were allowed to borrow from her navy.

* Monson, in Churchill, vol. iii., p. 158; Camden, vol. iii., pp. 486, 487.

Most of these privateering expeditions, as we have seen, had for their objects the wasting of Philip's and his subjects' shipping off the coast of Spain, near the Azores, and in the neighbourhood of the West Indies. But more distant enterprises were not wanting. The luckless undertaking of Thomas Cavendish in 1591, designed to surpass his former voyage round the world, has already been described. A similar undertaking, also unfortunate, was entered upon in 1593, by Sir Richard Hawkins, Sir John Hawkins's only son. Now about forty years old, he had been well trained by his father in seamanship, and, as his record of his voyage shows, in many other sorts of knowledge.* He had served in the Great Armada Fight, and had been, as he says, a sailor during twenty years. But all we know of him in detail has to do with the voyage which he projected for sailing, as Drake and Cavendish had done before him, through the Straits of Magellan, and round the Pacific Ocean to China and the East Indies.

He left Plymouth on the 12th of June, in the *Dainty*, a new ship built for the work, of between 300 and 400 tons burthen, attended by a bark of 100 tons, and a pinnace of 60 tons. "I luffed near the shore," he says, "to give my farewell to all the inhabitants of the town, whereof the most part were gathered together upon the

* *The Observations of* SIR RICHARD HAWKINS *in his Voyage into the South Sea in* 1593 (Hakluyt Society, 1847)—a work full of shrewd and useful observations on many points having nothing to do with this voyage. A first part was published shortly before his death in 1622. He never issued the second part.

Hoe, to show their grateful correspondency to the love and zeal which I, my father and predecessors, have ever borne to that place as to our natural and mother town. And first with my noise of trumpets, after with my waits and then with my other music, I made the best signification I could of a kind farewell. This they answered with the waits of the town, and the ordnance on the shore, and with shouting of voices, which with fair evening and silence of the night, were heard a great distance off."

Contrary winds made the voyage to Brazil a long one. In the course of it some of Hawkins's men died of scurvy, and nearly all the rest fell sick. Other troubles befel him as he traversed the coast to the south. Near Rio de la Plata, not having men enough to work all his three vessels, he burnt the bark, and a few days afterwards the pinnace deserted him in a storm. The Strait of Magellan was not reached till the 19th of February, 1594. Hawkins passed out of it, and entered the South Sea on the 29th of March. Thence he sailed slowly along the western side of South America. At Valparaiso he captured five small Spanish vessels, the crews of which he treated with rare moderation—moderation for which even the Spaniards blamed him. Had he, they said, like Drake and Cavendish, burnt all the ships he seized, intelligence of his coming would not have been conveyed to other ports. As it was, he deserved to suffer as a coward.

Suffering soon came to him, if it had not come long before, though not from cowardice. Near Lima, three strong ships came out to meet him. From them he escaped; but at the mouth of Guayaquil Bay, or a smaller bay near it, on the 23rd of June, two other ships and a bark approached him. Hawkins saw at once that they had hostile intentions, and were too strong to court a battle with. His sailors, declaring that they were Panama treasure-ships, were eager to fight. "They altogether," he says, "without reason, or against reason, broke out, some into vaunting and bragging, some into reproaches for want of courage, others into wishings that they had never come out of their country, if they should refuse to fight with any two ships whatever. The gunner, for his part, assured me that with the first tire of shot he would lay one of them in the suds, and our pinnace"—a small Spanish prize had been turned into an indifferent pinnace a month or two before— "that she would take the other to task. One promised that he would cut down their mainyard, another that he would take their flag. To some I turned the deaf ear. With others I dissembled, soothing and animating them to the execution of what they promised."

In the end, having the weather-gauge of the enemy, Hawkins resolved to meet them, and he passed out of the bay in order that he "might have sea room to fight." The *Dainty* and the pinnace had in all seventy-five men. The force in the three Spanish vessels was thirteen hundred. As the ships approached one another, moreover, the wind changed and forced the English to leeward. "The admiral," says Hawkins, "weathering us, came down upon us; which, being within musket-shot, we hailed first with our noise of trumpets, then with our waits, and after with our artillery; two for one, for they had double the ordnance we had. Immediately they came shoring aboard of us, upon our lee-quarter, contrary to our expectations, and the custom of men-of-war; and doubtless, had our gunner been the man he was reputed to be, and as the world told him to me, they had received great hurt by that manner of boarding; but, contrary to all expectation, our stern-pieces were unpinned, and so were all those which we had to leeward." The master gunner proved, in Hawkins's opinion, the most boastful and useless man in the world. His guns were out of gear, and much of his ammunition was spoiled by sea-water, through the carelessness of his stowage. He was even supposed to be in treacherous league with the Spaniards. "Whether this were true or no," says Hawkins, "I know not; but I am sure all in general gave him an ill report, and that he in whose hands the chief execution of the whole fight consisted executed nothing as was promised and expected." Thereby the ruin of the English was nearly insured from the first.

Yet they fought bravely through two days and two nights. During the first day, which was Sunday. the enemy was twice driven off; and on the first evening, upon a third attempt being made by the Spaniards to board the *Dainty*, one of the assailants was so disabled that, if he could only have spared a dozen men from the defence against the others, Hawkins says he might easily have taken her. After that the Spaniards dared make no further attack in close quarters. They invited Hawkins—who already had received six wounds, "one in the neck, very perillous; another through the arm, perishing the bone and cutting the sinews close by the arm-pit"—to surrender according to the usages of good war. A few of the English wished to accept this offer. But Hawkins indignantly resented it, and in terms so eloquent, that he convinced even the most wavering. "All who were present," he says, " vowed either to remain freemen or to sell their lives at a price which the enemy would not be willing to pay. Both captain and company took their leave of me, every one particularly, and the greater part with tears and embracings, as though we were forthwith to depart this world, and never see one the other again but in heaven, promising never more to speak of surrendry."

Failing in that, the Spaniards determined to ply their artillery from a distance, trusting to sink the *Dainty* or to exhaust her ammunition. This they did through Sunday night, firing on till an hour before daybreak, when they held off for a few hours, "to breathe, and remedy such defects as were amiss." The interval the English spent " in repairing their sails and tacklings, stopping their leaks, fishing and woolding their masts and yards, mending their pumps, and fitting and providing themselves for the day to come." But for that work the *Dainty* could not have kept above water many more hours.

Early in Monday's fight one of Hawkins's guns carried

away the mainmast of the smaller Spanish ship, and called off the attention of all his assailants. Had he not been "in a manner senseless with his wounds," he might have tried to escape, or at any rate might have got the weather-gauge of the enemy. "But this occasion was let slip," as he says, and no other occasion came to him. The fighting was resumed and continued through all that day and all the ensuing night, until, as on the previous morning, both sides found it necessary to make a few hours' pause. Then they set to work again.

But the English could not work on much longer. By Tuesday afternoon nearly half their men were killed. The other half were all more or less wounded. Their ship too was a wreck. "The *Dainty*," says Hawkins, "had fourteen shot under water, seven or eight foot of water in the hold, the sails all torn, the masts all perished, and the pumps shot to pieces." Hawkins, unless he resorted to the desperate expedient planned by Sir Richard Grenville in like case, had to choose between a conditional surrender or capture without conditions. Believing that he himself had not many hours more to live, he chose the former for the sake of his comrades. Hoisting a flag of truce, he offered to surrender if "life, liberty, and embarcation to England" were accorded to all his comrades. The terms were accepted, the Spanish commander sending his glove as a pledge that they should be honourably observed. The commander was not at fault; but Spanish honour, as interpreted by his superiors, showed itself in eight-and-twenty years of hardship and imprisonment to Hawkins, who did not reach England till 1622. Of the fate of his comrades we are not informed.

Long before Sir Richard Hawkins returned to England his father had left it, never to return. After the failure of his prize-hunting expedition in 1590, Sir John Hawkins had resumed his onerous duties as Treasurer of the Navy. "I account myself most unhappy," he said, in a letter to Lord Burghley, on the 8th of July, 1592, "that it is my lot to follow so unpleasant a service as is the calling upon such excessive payments as do daily grow; for, if it had pleased God to have appointed me to have served her Majesty in any other calling, I am sure I should have made my service very acceptable to her Majesty, and ever stood in your Lordship's good liking and good opinion. But this endless and unsavoury occupation in calling for money is always unpleasant."* In spite, however, of the annoyance that he gave to the penurious Queen and the penurious Lord Treasurer by his demands for expenditure necessary to the maintenance of the navy in an efficient state, Hawkins was too good a servant to be dispensed with. Though considerably over seventy years of age, he continued in office till the autumn of 1595, when he entered on his last seafaring exploit, being chiefly driven thereto, apparently, by a desire to rescue his son if he was yet alive, or, if he was dead, to take vengeance on the Spaniards.

In this exploit Sir Francis Drake was his partner.

* BARROW, *Naval Worthies of Queen Elizabeth's Reign*, p. 89.

Both men entered heartily into a project for winning fresh spoil from the Spanish colonies in the West Indies, which had been not only their own school in fighting seamanship, but also the beginning of England's private and public war with Spain, now more than twenty-five years old. Queen Elizabeth, we are told, readily acceded to the project, and more volunteers than they required clamoured for employment under the oldest veteran and the most daring hero in the English navy.

The project was talked of in the summer of 1594; but nothing was done till the following year. Then, after some months of zealous preparation, on the 28th of August, a fleet of twenty-seven ships, containing about twenty-five hundred men, left Plymouth. Of these ships, six were the Queen's: the *Defiance*, in which Drake went as Admiral; the *Garland*, under Hawkins as Vice-Admiral; the *Hope*; the *Bonaventure*; the *Foresight*; and the *Adventure*. Their mission was to do as much mischief, and seize as much treasure as they could in the Spanish Main.* The voyage was most luckless. The fleet proceeded to the Canaries, and there, in a warlike raid upon the principal island, resorted to in search of food, it only succeeded enough to take in a fresh supply of water. Thence crossing to the West Indies, it reached Guadaloupe on the 29th of September. Next day a straggling bark, the *Francis*,

---

\* MAYNARDE, *Sir Francis Drake his Voyage*, 1595 (Hakluyt Society, 1849), p. 41; MONSON, in CHURCHILL, vol. iii., p. 159; BARROW, *Life of Drake*, pp. 386–391.

was captured by five Spanish ships, on their way to the Isthmus of Panama for the yearly cargo of treasure. Immediately after that, we are told, "Sir John Hawkins was extreme sick; which his sickness began upon news of the taking of the *Francis*."

That, indeed, had worse issue than the loss of the bark and its crew. The prisoners, being put to the torture, revealed the object of the English expedition, and thus in great measure spoilt it. When San Juan de Porto Rico was reached on the 12th of November, it was found to be well prepared for the attack which was intended to be made in secret. "We received from their plants and fortresses, where they planted ordnance," says the chronicler, "some twenty-eight great shot, the last of which struck the Admiral through the mizen, and the last but one struck through her quarter into the steerage, the General being there at supper, and struck the stool from under him, but hurt him not."

While Sir Francis Drake thus narrowly escaped death, Sir John Hawkins was dying. He had been ill for six weeks, and, though his illness was attributed to the loss of the *Francis*, we can easily suppose that it resulted from the unwonted fatigues and troubles of the work to which he had returned after many years of quieter occupation. His long, eventful, and most serviceable life, not least serviceable in those respects which were least admirable, came to an end on the evening of this 12th of November, 1595, when he was about seventy-five years old.

Sir Francis Drake only survived him by eleven weeks. After vainly attempting during a fortnight to capture Porto Rico, he passed on to Rio de la Hacha, which, after some parleying and treachery on the part of the inhabitants, he stormed and burnt wholly to the ground. He then sacked and burnt Santa Marta and several smaller towns on the way to Nombre de Dios. This he easily captured on the 27th of December, and here he halted with the fleet, while Sir Thomas Baskerville attempted to conduct seven hundred and fifty men across the Isthmus to Panama. Baskerville found the rough road and the opposition of the Spaniards too troublesome and returned, after eighty or ninety men had been lost.

The failure, coming after other failures, and after the death of his old friend, is reported to have broken Drake's heart. He and Hawkins had hoped so much from this enterprise; and every hope was being foiled. On the 15th of January "he began to keep his cabin, and to complain of a flux." Each day he became worse, and on the 27th of January he was almost too ill to move. Soon after midnight he started from his bed, talked incoherently, and attempted to dress himself. His friends led him back to his couch, and tried to comfort him. At four o'clock next morning, when hardly more than fifty years of age, he passed out of reach of all comfort, and of all discomfort.

In the Bay of Porto Bello, within sight of Nonbre de Dios, where his prowess had been first largely diplayed, his body, cased in a leaden coffin, was dropped into the

sea, while all the guns and all the muskets of his ships
gave solemn echo to the solemn words of his burial.

> "The waves became his winding-sheet, the waters were his tomb;
> But for his fame the ocean sea was not sufficient room." *

So ran the shortest of a hundred poems written in
his honour, when Baskerville, returning to England
with the fleet, in May, 1596, after having had a tough
fight with the Spaniards off Cartagena, made known to
England the great loss it had sustained. The longest
poem was a fulsome epic by Charles FitzGeoffrey,
styled 'Sir Francis Drake; his Honourable Life's Commendation and his Tragical Death's Lamentation,'—
a poem not so long and not so poetical as Lope de
Vega's scurrilous 'Dragontea.' But Drake's character
was nowhere better reflected than in the sonnet which
he prefixed to a treatise written by his friend and
rival in worth, though not in success, Sir Humphrey
Gilbert.

> "Who seeks by worthy deeds to gain renown for hire,
> Whose heart, whose hand, whose purse is pressed to purchase his desire,
> If any such there be that thirsteth after fame,
> Lo, here a mean to win himself an everlasting name.
> Who seeks by gain and wealth to advance his house and blood,
> Whose care is great, whose toil no less, whose hope is all for good,
> If any one there be that covets such a trade,
> Lo, here the plot for common wealth and private gain is made.
> He that for virtue's sake will venture far and near,
> Whose zeal is strong, whose practice truth, whose faith is void of fear,

---

* PRINCE, *Worthies of Devon*. Most of the foregoing account of
Drake's last expedition is condensed from MAYNARDE. Drake's
will is in *A Selection from the Wills of Eminent Persons*, 1495-1695
(Camden Society, 1863), pp. 72-79.

> If any such there be, enflamed with holy care,
> Here may he find a ready mean his purpose to declare.
> So that, for each degree, this treatise doth unfold
> The path to fame, the proof of zeal, and way to purchase gold."

Drake was dead, and Hawkins was dead, and Frobisher was dead,—all three deaths occurring within a space of sixteen months. The old race of Elizabethan heroes on the sea was quickly dying out. But smaller men could carry on the work they had begun.

And there were great men yet alive,—none greater, in this respect, than Sir Walter Raleigh. Raleigh was not a seaman, but he had caught the spirit of English seamanship, and he was, especially, an excellent advocate of that patriotic resistance of Spain which gave schooling and life-work to nearly every English sailor. And he did more than advocate. While Drake and Hawkins were planning and executing, with such poor execution as sickness and death allowed to them, their last expedition, he was planning and executing a new and famous enterprise. In his Virginia he had tried to rob Spain of its exclusive possession of the wealth of the New World north of Darien. In his scheme for finding El Dorado he tried to rob Spain of its exclusive possession of the wealth of the New World in its southern districts.

This scheme had been growing in his mind for many years. He, like every other Englishman, had been attracted by the fables of the Golden City of Manoa and the Golden Lake of Parima. Columbus had started the fables, or at any rate had favoured the traditions out of which they grew. Vasco Nuñez de Balboa had first been led by them in quest of the glittering phantom, and Pizarro had in following it won the empire of Peru. Two generations of daring and bloodthirsty adventurers—Altinger and Sailler, Nicholas Fedreman and Sebastian de Belalcazar, Hernan de Quesada and Philip von Huten, Pedro de Ursua and Lope de Aguirre, Martin de Proveda and Pedro de Silva, Diego de Cerpa and Antonio de Berreo—had hunted the phantom from place to place until all the northern parts of South America had been brought under the dominion of Spain. Raleigh hoped that where others had failed he might succeed; and he knew that, whether there was failure or success, he could offer no greater insult and work no heavier injury to Spain than by planting the English standard in this most sacred scene of Spanish bigotry and tyranny, whence most of the gold employed by Philip in persecuting Netherlanders and annoying Englishmen and troubling the whole of Christendom, his servile subjects being really the greatest sufferers of all, was being extracted with the help of cruelties that thrilled every honest looker-on with horror.

Therefore he went to Guiana in 1595, and sent Captain Laurence Keymis in 1596. The famous narrative of their achievements, however, need not here be detailed.* It is enough to notice their significance in connection with the great struggle that had been pro-

* I the more readily abstain from briefly noticing these exploits, which would need much fuller notice than my plan allows, as I see that two memoirs of Raleigh, both by competent writers, are forthcoming, in which readers who desire such information will be pretty sure to find it.

gressing now for more than thirty years between Spain and England.

There was a famous episode of that struggle in 1596, when Raleigh shared in a more formidable expedition than any hitherto prepared by England against Spain. Beaten times without number by Englishmen upon the sea, more than held at bay by Netherlanders in their own home, Philip had been steadily gaining ground in Brittany, and his hopes of invading England had been revived thereby. In February, 1594, in the overweening temper that was natural to him, he had instructed his new Viceroy in the Netherlands to destroy Elizabeth's shipping at home. "I am informed by persons well acquainted with the English coast," he wrote, "that it would be an easy matter for a few quick-sailing vessels to accomplish this. Two or three thousand soldiers might be landed at Rochester, who might burn or sink all the unarmed vessels they could find there, and the expedition could return and sail off again before the people of the country could collect in sufficient numbers to do them any damage."* That scheme had been treated as impossible by the Viceroy, wiser than his master. England had been insulted and frightened, however, by a raid of Spaniards from Brittany upon Penzance in that year, and a similar raid had been made upon the same district in 1596. England's danger was much increased, moreover, by the Spanish seizure of Calais on the 10th of April in this

* *Simancas MS.*, cited by MOTLEY, vol. iii., p. 293.

year. Upon that Queen Elizabeth gave her hearty approval to a scheme that had been propounded earlier in the spring for a prompt and vigorous attack on Spain.

No time was wasted in the preparations. On the 3rd of June a fleet of nearly a hundred and fifty vessels sailed from Plymouth. Seventeen of these were Queen's ships; seventy-six were hired vessels and volunteers. The Netherlanders contributed eighteen men-of-war and six store-ships. The rest were pinnaces, fly-boats, and other small craft. Lord Admiral Howard had the chief command at sea. The Earl of Essex, now at the height of his favour with the Queen, was commander-in-chief of the forces to be employed on land. Each of these had charge of a squadron, and two other squadrons were divided between Lord Thomas Howard and Sir Walter Raleigh, while the Dutch contingent under Admiral Warmond formed a fifth squadron. The Dutch crews and soldiers numbered three thousand. From England there went a thousand gentlemen volunteers, about sixty-five hundred foot soldiers, and about as many sailors; the entire force being thus more than seventeen thousand strong.* This was the stoutest armament that had ever been sent out from England since the days of the Crusaders.

It reached Cadiz on Sunday, the 20th of June, and was anchored in the harbour in orderly way, to the

---

* MONSON, in CHURCHILL, vol. iii., p. 160; HAKLUYT, vol. i., p. 605; MOTLEY, vol. iii., p. 381; DEVEREUX, *Lives of the Earls of Essex*, vol. i., pp. 357, 358.

utter amazement both of the townspeople and of the vast number of ships collected under shelter of the fortress. On the following day, the 21st of June, there was a famous battle. Immediately after sunrise, the Spanish ships—consisting of four great galleons, of nearly thirty great war-ships, and of about sixty carracks and other trading-craft well armed—shifted their moorings and set themselves in order for the defence of the town. The English ships weighed anchor and proceeded to attack them. Fighting began soon after five o'clock, and was general from seven o'clock till one, by which time the Spanish force was utterly defeated. Several of their largest vessels fell into the hands of the English, to be ransacked and spoiled by them during the afternoon. The *San Felipe,* the greatest galleon that had been built, the pride and glory of the Spanish navy, was saved from capture by being blown up under its captain's orders. The train was badly laid, however, and before half its company of twelve hundred sailors and soldiers had had time to leave it the gunpowder exploded. "Tumbling into the sea," says Raleigh, "came heaps of soldiers, as thick as if coals had been poured out of a sack, in many parts at once, some drowned, and some sticking in the mud." "The spectacle was very lamentable," it was also said; "for many drowned themselves; many, half burnt, leaped into the water; very many hanging by ropes' ends to the ship's sides, under water, even to the lips; many, swimming with grievous wounds, struck under water, and put out of their pain; and withal so huge a fire, and such tearing of the ordnance in the great *Felipe*, and in the rest, when the fire came to them, as, if any man had a desire to see hell itself, it was there most vividly figured."

That disaster completed the victory of the English. The Spanish ships that were still able to fight made no further resistance. The forts of Cadiz ceased to ply their shot. The Earl of Essex, first to leap on shore, and three thousand soldiers who followed at his heels, pressed up to the market-place, and, fighting at every step, soon broke through all the ranks of men and the hasty barricades that they had constructed. Lord Howard afterwards came up with twelve hundred men and a fresh store of ammunition, and Essex, thus reinforced, then laid siege to the citadel, whither all the surviving soldiers and most of the townspeople had fled for safety. Before ten o'clock next morning it surrendered, and all carnage was stayed. There had been previously no more carnage than was necessary. "The mercy and clemency that hath been showed here, will be spoken of throughout the world," wrote Lord Howard, with proper pride, to the Queen's Council; "no aged or cold blood touched, no woman defiled; but all with great care embarked and sent to Saint Mary's Port, and other women and children were likewise sent thither, and suffered to carry away with them all their apparel, and divers rich things which they had about them, which no man might search for under pain of death." Even Philip II. was forced to admit that the world had never seen worthier proof of good soldiership, both at sea and on land, and of chivalrous humanity among victors. The Dutch auxiliaries, it is said, remembering the cruelty and lust that the Spaniards had practised among their shattered towns and ruined homesteads, were inclined to retaliate; but the English hindered them. One man, found stealing a woman's gown, was sentenced by Essex to be hanged, and only pardoned at the suit of a Spanish ecclesiastic.

The English indeed were too merciful. They did only their duty in sparing the innocent, and resisting the lowest temptations of war; but, if it was right for them to go out against Spain at all, it was right for them to follow this conquest of Cadiz and spoliation of the immense shipping in its harbour, by such further wasting of the military and naval force of Spain as would lead to speedy and sure peace between the two nations. The Earl of Essex, chief hero in the work done on land, and sharer with Raleigh in the chief heroism of the sea-fighting, seems to have wished to do more. Lord Howard, however, was satisfied with the mischief that had already been done; and accordingly, after burying their dead, who were to be told by scores against the thousands of the Spaniards, the allied forces left Cadiz on the 4th of July. After some loitering in Spanish waters, Howard and the main body of the English fleet returned to Plymouth on the 8th of August. Essex, still anxious to do further work, lagged behind, to be taken charge of by the Dutch contingent, and brought to the Downs on the 10th of August.*

"If my pen," said Queen Elizabeth, in her letter of

* The above details are chiefly from DEVEREUX, vol. i., pp. 357-378.

thanks to Howard and Essex, "had as many tongues as the flock of its owner had feathers, they could never express the laud that my soul yieldeth to the Highest, for the great victory which His graceful hand hath given us, and that you, as His instruments, have so admirably, in so few hours, with such valour, order, and resolution, performed so great an action, of which sort, I suppose has not been seen a fellow. You have made me famous, dreadful, and renowned; not more for your victory than for your courage; nor more for either than for such plentiful liquor of mercy, which may well match the better of the two. Never was there heard in so few days so great a gain obtained; which, though I do attribute most to the forerunners, yet I charge you let the army know, both of sea and land, that I care not so much for being Queen, as that I am the sovereign of such subjects, that blast my fame with their worth."

Here our record of the achievements of English seamen under the the Tudors may close. A great fleet of a hundred and twenty ships went out next year, with the Earl of Essex for Admiral, Lord Thomas Howard for Vice-Admiral, and Sir Walter Raleigh for Rear-Admiral, to intercept the annual fleet of treasure ships coming to Spain from the Indies; but it failed therein, and was marked by little save splendid show and paltry quarrelling. In 1598 the Earl of Cumberland led out a fleet of twenty-three vessels with the same object, and, save in some fighting to which he resorted in the Spanish Main, with the same lack of memorable incident. Other expeditions, great and little, there were in abundance.

But the best that can be said of them is that they were pompous and futile efforts to carry on the work that had been begun by Hawkins and Drake. "In perusing them," says their first critic, "I find many accidents to have happened for want of tarpaulin commanders, or gentlemen thoroughly acquainted with maritime affairs. I find punctilios of honour oft insisted on by gentlemen, and the loss of many a good design, when, on the other hand, the tarpaulins observe no grandeur, but, like devils, count themselves most happy that can do most and soonest mischief to their enemies."*

The bluff, dare-devil seamen of the time of Elizabeth had passed, or were quickly passing away.† But not

---

\* GIBSON, cited in the continuation of SOUTHEY, vol. v., pp. 205, 206.

† Lord Admiral Howard did no important naval work after his great expedition to Spain, in company with the Earl of Essex, in 1596. On the 22nd of October in that year he was made Earl of Nottingham. In 1599 was conferred on him the title of Lieutenant-General of all England, "an office," says CAMPBELL (vol. i., p. 399), "scarcely known to former, never owned of succeeding times, and which he held with almost regal authority for the space of six weeks, being sometimes with the fleet in the Downs, and sometimes on shore with the forces." He retained his office of Lord High Admiral under James I., until 1620, when it was transferred to the Duke of Buckingham. He died at the age of eighty-seven, on the 14th of December, 1624. His cousin, Lord Thomas Howard, abandoned seamanship on becoming Earl of Suffolk. The Earl of Essex, as is well known, was executed two years after his last expedition of 1597. The Earl of Cumberland, the other high-born seaman, died in 1605. A new race of sailors had appeared during the last years of Elizabeth's reign, who were "tarpaulin commanders" almost as much as Drake and Hawkins; but their history belongs to the Stuart period. Sir William Monson was, perhaps, the ablest of them.

Ship-building continued till the end of Queen Elizabeth's rule. At the time of her death, in 1603, her navy consisted of forty-two ships, instead before they had done their work. They had helped to save England from the great danger that had threatened it at the hands of ambitious Spain. They had punished Spain for all its wickednesses in America and in Europe. They had led the way to the establishment of a British Empire spreading all round the globe, a hundred times as great as Britain itself, through which were to be disseminated all those blessings of civilization and good government which they, in no small measure, helped to win for their mother country. They

---

of the thirty-four which met the Spanish Armada in 1588. The *Revenge*, famous for Sir Richard Grenville's employment of it in 1591, the *Vanguard*, the *Aid*, the *Bull*, and the galley *Bonavolio*, which appear in the list on page 217, had been lost or disabled in the course of the fifteen years. Accordingly there were fifteen new ones:—

| Names of the Ships. | Tons. | Men. |
| --- | --- | --- |
| The *Saint Matthew* . . . . | 1,000 | 500 |
| The *Saint Andrew* . . . . . | 900 | 400 |
| The *Mer-Honeur* . . . . . | 800 | 400 |
| The *Due Repulse* . . . | 700 | 350 |
| The *Garland* . . . . | 700 | 300 |
| The *Warsprite* . . . . . | 600 | 300 |
| The *Defiance* . . . . . | 500 | 250 |
| The *Tide* . . . . . | 250 | 120 |
| The *Adventure* . . . . . | 250 | 120 |
| The *Crane* . . . . . . | 200 | 100 |
| The *Quittance* . . . . | 200 | 100 |
| The *Answer* . . . . . . | 200 | 100 |
| The *Advantage* . . . . . | 200 | 100 |

MONSON, in CHURCHILL, vol. iii., p. 188.

were not perfect men; but they were heroes. To
understand the men themselves, we must measure them
by the standards of their own times. To understand
the good work that they did, and the better work that
issued from their doings, we must compare the England
of to-day with the England which, under the Tudors,
tore off the shackles of feudalism, loosened the bondage
of priestcraft, and began to be a nation of free men.

# INDEX.

Acre, the siege of, in 1190, i., 17.
Adams, William, i., 290.
Alfred the Great, improvements made by, in English shipping, i., 7.
America, North, discovered by John Cabot, i., 32–35; first English settlements in, i., 39, 40; Sir Humphrey Gilbert's charter for the colonization of, i., 179, 180; Sir Philip Sidney's, i., 209, 210; Sir Walter Raleigh's, i., 200.
Anglo-Saxon ships, i., 4–7.
Armada, the Great Spanish, preparations for, ii., 174, 179, 180, 191, 193, 201, 202; English preparations to resist it, ii., 203–218; its composition, ii., 214, 215; its voyage to England, ii., 218, 219; English fighting with it, ii., 221–239; its flight, ii., 239–241, 244; Philip II.'s opinion regarding its failure, ii., 246.
Ashehurst, Thomas, i., 39.

Barker, Andrew, his expedition to the West Indies, ii., 73–75.
Bartous, the, Scottish merchants and pirates, i., 50–54.
Baskerville, Sir Thomas, ii., 296, 297.
Brendan, St., the fable of, i., 24.
Burrough, Stephen, his north-eastern voyage of discovery, i., 101, 246.
Burroughs, Sir John, his employment under Raleigh and capture of the *Madre de Dios*, ii., 280–284.
Burrows, William, his employment under Sir Hugh Willoughby, i., 92; his quarrel with Drake, ii., 187, 196.

Cabot, John, his birth and early history, i., 28–31; his discovery of North America in 1497, i., 31–35; his second expedition in 1498, and death, i., 35–37.
Cabot, Sebastian, his early history, i., 28; his north-western voyages in

search of Cathay and exploration of North America, 1498–99, i., 31–39; his employments in Spain, i., 42, 44, his north-western voyage with Sir Thomas Spert, i., 43; his return to England in 1517, i., 45.
Cadiz, damage done to the Spanish fleet at, by Drake in 1587, ii., 180–185; further damage done by Essex and Howard in 1596, ii., 302–304.
Callao, Drake's plunder of ships at, ii., 96, 97.
Cartagena, Drake's piracies near, ii., 68–70; Drake's taking of, ii., 168–170.
Cascaes, captured by Drake in 1589, ii., 257, 258.
Cathay Company, the, i., 135.
—— or Khitai, old fables and traditions concerning, i., 25–28; John and Sebastian Cabot's voyages in search of, i., 31–37; Willoughby's and Chancelor's, i., 91–100; Frobisher's, i., 122–171; Pet's and Jackman's, i., 246, 247; Davis's, i., 248–274; Waymouth's, i., 299–304.
Carlet, David, ii., 28, 29.
Cavendish, Thomas, i., 212; ii., 120; his voyage to the South Sea and round the world in 1586–8, ii., 121–136; his second expedition in 1591–2 and death, ii., 137–143.
Celtic ships, i., 2–4.
Chancelor, Richard, his voyage with Willoughby in search of Cathay in 1553, i., 92, 96–101; his visit to Russia in 1556 and shipwreck on the way home, i., 102.
Chaucer's "Schipman," i., 13, 14.
Cinque Ports, origin and work of the, i., 9–11.
Clinton, Edward, Earl of Lincoln, ii., 5, 7.
Clifford, George, Earl of Cumberland, his early history, ii., 248; his share in the Great Armada Fight, ii., 228,

his piratical and privateering expeditions, ii., 248, 249, 260, 267, 281–285, 305.
Cortereal, Gaspar de, i., 106.
Corunna, the siege of, by Drake and Norris in 1589, ii., 253, 254.
Crusaders, ships of the, i., 15–19.
Cumberland, Earl of. *See* Clifford.
Cumberland Island, i., 253–255.

*Dainty*, Sir Richard Hawkins's fight in the, with the Spaniards, ii., 289–293.
Davis, John, his first voyage in search of the north-west passage to Cathay in 1585, i., 248–255; his second voyage in search of the north-west passage in 1586, i., 255–266; his third voyage in search of the north-west passage in 1587, i., 267–272; his abandonment of the work, i., 273, 274; his voyage to the South Sea under Cavendish in 1591–3, ii., 137–140, 143–146; his voyage to the East Indies, as pilot-major of the first Dutch expedition in 1598, i., 289, ii., 146; his voyage to the East Indies, as pilot-major of the East India Company's first expedition in 1601, i., 292; his last voyage to the East Indies, 1603–1605, and death, ii., 146, 147.
Devereux, Robert, Earl of Essex, his early history, ii., 257; his share in the expedition of Drake and Norris to Spain and Portugal, ii., 257; his expedition to Cadiz in company with Lord Admiral Howard, ii., 300–305; his expedition to the Azores, ii., 305.
De Burgh, Hubert, i., 20, 21.
Doughty, Thomas, ii., 83, 87–89.
Drake, Sir Francis, the early history of, ii., 40–42; his employment under Hawkins in 1568, ii., 42–55; his first and second expedition to the West Indies and the Spanish Main in 1570 and 1571, ii., 62; his third expedition to the West Indies and the Spanish Main in 1572–3, ii., 63–72; his employment in Ireland and England, ii., 76, 77; his voyage round the world, 1577–1580, ii., 80–110; his honours and occupations at home, i., 175, ii., 111–115, 158; his voyage to the West Indies in 1585–6, ii., 160–171; his expedition to Spain in 1587, ii., 173–200; his share in the Great Armada Fight, ii., 203, 204, 206, 209–211, 213, 217, 219, 222, 223, 225, 226, 229, 235–239, 244, 245; his plans for a fresh attack upon Spain, ii., 247, 248; his expedition against Spain and Portugal in 1589, with Sir John Norris, ii., 249–259; his correspondence with Henry IV. of France, ii., 285; his last expedition to the West Indies and death, 1585–6, ii., 294–298.

East Indies, the, early voyages to, i., 276–290; Drake's visit to, ii., 106–110; Cavendish's visit to, ii., 131–135. *See* East India Company.
East India Company, the, its formation, i., 290–292; its first expedition to the East under Lancaster and Davis, i., 292–298; its subsequent expeditions, i., 298, 299; its employment of George Waymouth in search of the north-west passage, i., 300–303.
Edward VI., his patronage of Sebastian Cabot, i., 45, 90; and of Sir Hugh Willoughby, i., 95; the state of the navy during his reign, ii., 3.
El Dorado, the fables concerning, ii., 298; Raleigh's search for, ii., 299.
Eliot, Hugh, i., 39.
Elizabeth, Queen, her navy, ii., 5, 7–21, 216, 307; her bearing towards Sir Humphrey Gilbert, i., 112, 178–180, 185, 186, 190; Sir John Hawkins, ii., 28, 37, 39, 40, 43, 266, 293; Sir Francis Drake, ii., 76, 77, 110–114, 158, 174, 175, 204, 206, 210, 211, 250, 256, 259, 260; Sir Martin Frobisher, i., 122, 135, 136, 153, 157, 177; Sir Walter Raleigh, i., 185, 200, 209, 231, 280; the Earl of Essex, ii., 257, 301, 305; her relations with France, ii., 7, 14–16, 18, 148; with the Netherlands, i., 40, ii., 149, 154, 155; with Spain, ii., 18, 27, 38, 40, 43, 112, 148–154, 163; her conduct during the Armada Fight, ii., 202–212, 242.

Esquimaux, Frobisher's account of the, i., 145-149.
Essex, Robert, Earl of. *See* Devereux.

Fenton, Edward, his employment in Frobisher's north-western voyage, i., 156; his expedition towards the South Seas in 1582, ii., 116-120.
Fitch, Ralph, his journey to India, i., 279.
Fitzwilliams, William, Earl of Southampton, Lord Admiral under Henry VIII., i., 76.
France, English fighting with, under the Plantagenets, i., 20, 21; under Henry VIII., i., 54-70, 76-80, ii., 2; under Elizabeth, ii., 14-16.
Frobisher, Isabel, i., 177.
——— Martin, the early history of, i., 120-122; the preparations for his Cathayan voyage, i., 122-127; his first voyage in 1576, i., 127, 128; his discovery of Frobisher's Straits and Meta Incognita, i., 129-133; the results of his voyage, i., 134-136; his second voyage to Meta Incognita, 1577, i., 137-158; his entertainment by Queen Elizabeth, i., 158; his third voyage to Meta Incognita, and discovery of Hudson's Straits in 1578, ii., 155-171; his troubles and employments at home, i., 172-177; his employment under Drake in his West Indian expedition, ii., 162; his share in the Armada Fight, ii., 222, 225, 226, 229, 237; his employment under Hawkins in an expedition against Spain, in 1590, ii., 266, 267; his employment under Raleigh, in a like expedition, in 1592, ii., 280, 281; his fighting with the Spaniards in Brest harbour and death, ii., 286.

Gibraltar, a fight near, in 1590, between English merchant ships and Spanish galleys, ii., 262-265.
Gilbert, Adrian, i., 248.
——— Sir Humphrey, his early history, i., 109, 110; his plans and projects for reaching Cathay, i., 108, 111, 115-118; his employments in Ireland, i., 111-113; in Flanders, i., 113, 114; and at home, i., 114; his plan for colonizing North America, i., 178, 179; his first expedition with that object in 1578, i., 179-183; his subsequent employments in England and Ireland, i., 184-189; his second expedition in 1583, and settlement in Newfoundland, i., 189-195; his homeward voyage and death, i., 196-199.
Gomez, Estevan, i., 107.
Greenland and the Greenlanders, Frobisher's account of, i., 128, 158, 159; Davis's account of, i., 250-252, 257-263, 269.
*Great Harry*, the, i., 71, 72, 78, ii., 3.
*Great Michael*, the, i., 51.
Grenville, Sir Richard, his early history, i., 211; his services and disservices with Sir Walter Raleigh in Virginia, i., 211-215, 231; his piratical employments, i., 213, 215; his great fight with the Spaniards in 1591, ii., 269-277.

Hall, Christopher, his employments under Frobisher, i., 127, 159, 163-167.
Hampton, Thomas, ii., 26, 27.
Hawkins, Sir John, his early training, ii., 24; his first expedition to Africa and the West Indies in 1562, ii., 26, 27; his second voyage in 1564, ii., 28-37; his third voyage in 1567 and 1568, ii., 40-57, 60, 61; his overreaching of Philip II., ii., 152, 153; his work as Treasurer of the Navy, ii., 12, 13; his share in the Great Armada Fight, ii., 203-205, 213, 217, 222, 225, 228, 229, 237, 242; his projects for invading Spain, ii., 259, 265; his voyage in search of Spanish prizes in 1590, ii., 266, 267; his later occupation as Treasurer of the Navy, ii., 266, 293; his last expedition to the West Indies, and death in 1595, ii., 293-295.
——— Sir Richard, his voyage to the South Sea and defeat by the Spaniards in 1593-4, ii., 287-292.
——— old William, ii., 22, 23.

Hawkins, William, his son, ii., 24.
—— young William, ii., 117–120.
Henry VII.'s encouragement of the Cabots and other North American discoverers, i., 31, 35, 39, 40.
—— VIII.'s policy regarding voyages of discovery, i., 41–43, 86; his zeal in augmenting the English navy, i., 46, 57, 60–63, 70–75; ii., 2.
Hore, Master, the voyage of, to Labrador, i., 87–89.
Howards, early connection of the, with English seamanship, i., 48, 49.
Howard, Lord Charles, of Effingham, afterwards Earl of Nottingham, Lord High Admiral of England, his early history, ii., 155–157; his share in the Great Armada Fight, ii., 203–208, 211–213, 217, 218, 220–222, 227–236, 239–243; his expedition to Cadiz in 1596, ii., 301–305; his later history, ii., 306.
—— Sir Edward, his early history, i., 49; his pursuit and capture of Andrew Barton in 1511, i., 53, 54; his appointment as Lord Admiral in 1512, i., 57; his fighting with the French and death, 1512–13, i., 57, 60, 64–69.
—— Lord Thomas, Duke of Norfolk, his fight with Andrew Barton in 1511, i., 53, 54; his share in the Marquis of Dorset's expedition to Spain in 1512, i., 54–56; his appointment as Lord Admiral in 1513, i., 69; his death, i., 75.
—— Lord Thomas, Earl of Suffolk, his services in the Great Armada Fight, ii., 230; his expedition in search of Spanish prizes in 1591, ii., 268–277; his share in Essex's expeditions against Spain in 1596, ii., 301, 305.
—— Lord William, of Effingham, ii., 5.
Hudson's Straits, discovery of, by Frobisher, i., 164, 165; entered by Waymouth, i., 303.

Jackman and Pet, the north-eastern voyage of, in search of Cathay, i., 101, 246, 247.

Java, early trade with, i., 297; visited by Thomas Cavendish, ii., 134, 135.
Jay, John, of Bristol, i., 30, 31.
Jenkinson, Anthony, i., 108–110.
John, King, his care of shipping, i., 19, 20.

Lancaster, Sir James, his first voyage to the East Indies in 1589, i., 280–289; his second voyage in 1601, i., 292–298; his later history, i., 299.
Lane, Ralph, his early history, i., 211, 212; his work as Governor of Virginia in 1585 and 1586, i., 211, 215, 228.
Levant Company, the, i., 279, 280.
Lisle, Viscount, Duke of Northumberland, his appointment as Lord Admiral, i., 76; his victory over the French at Spithead in 1545, i., 78, 79.
Lock, Michael, the career of, i., 119, 120; his friendship with Frobisher, i., 124–127; his quarrel with Frobisher, i., 172, 173.

Madoc, the fable of, i., 24.
Magellan's Strait, passed by Drake, ii., 90, 91; by Cavendish, ii., 122–125; by Davis, ii., 144; by Richard Hawkins, ii., 288.
*Mary Rose*, the, i., 63, 79.
Meta Incognita, Martin Frobisher's, i., 129–135, 145–152, 167, 170.
Michelborne, Sir Edward, his voyage to the East, ii., 146, 147.
Monson, Sir William, ii., 267, 306.
Muscovy Company, the, i., 101, 102.

New Albion, Drake's account of, and its natives, ii., 102–105.
Newfoundland and Labrador, discovered by John Cabot, i., 32–34; early trade with, i., 40, 106, 107, 186, 187; Sir Humphrey Gilbert's settlement in, i., 190, 195.
Nombre de Dios, Drake's first raid on, ii., 64–68; his last visit to and death near, ii., 296.
Norris, Sir John, his expedition against Spain, with Drake, in 1589, ii., 249–259.

Odoric, Friar, his statements about Cathay, i., 27, 28.
Ordnance in Elizabeth's time, ii., 13.
Orkney Islands, the people of, i., 138, 139.
Oxenham, John, his services under Drake in 1572, ii., 77; his voyage to the Isthmus of Darien and Pacific Ocean in 1575, ii., 78–80.

Panama, Drake's land expedition to, ii., 70–72.
Patagonians, Drake's account of the, ii., 85–87.
Pet and Jackman, their north-eastern voyage in search of Cathay, i., 101, 246, 247.
Piracy under the Tudors, ii., 17–21.
Plantagenet shipping, i., 11–14.
Polo, Marco, his reports about Cathay, i., 27.
Pope, Richard, i., 256, 257.
Port St. Julian, Drake's stay and troubles at, ii., 85–90.
Poynings, Sir Edward, i., 49.
Prester John, i., 64–68.
Puente de Burgo, the victory of Drake and Norris at, in 1589, ii., 255, 256.

Raleigh, Sir Walter, his early history, i., 180, 181; his share in Sir Humphrey Gilbert's first colonizing enterprise, in 1578, i., 181–183; his employments in Ireland and in England, i., 184, 185; his share in Gilbert's second enterprise, i., 189; his patent for American colonization, i., 200; his first expedition with that end, 1584, i., 201–208; his second expedition, 1585, i., 211–230; his third expedition, 1586, i., 231; his fourth expedition, 1587–1589, i., 232–241; his employments at home, i., 210, 248; his share in the Great Armada Fight, ii., 228, 249; his views regarding the war with Spain, ii., 278, 279; his privateering expedition against Spain, 1592, ii., 279–284; his voyages in search of El Dorado, 1595–6, ii., 299; his share in Essex's expeditions to Cadiz, 1596, ii., 300–304; and to the Azores, 1597, ii., 305.

Raymond, George, his voyage towards the East Indies and death, i., 280–282.
Revenge, Sir Richard Grenville's fight in the, with the Spaniards in 1591, ii., 269–277.
Richard I., the ships of, i., 15–20.
Roanoke Island, the natives of, i., 207–208; Sir Walter Raleigh's first colony in, i., 218–228; his second colony in, i., 233–243; the later history of, i., 243, 244; its present condition, i., 217.
Rubruquis, his account of Cathay, i., 25–27.
Rut, John, his north-western voyage of discovery, i., 86.

San Domingo, taken by Drake, ii., 165–168.
San Juan de Ulloa, Hawkins's conduct and fight at, ii., 48–56.
Sea fights and naval battles:—
1190. Storming of Acre, i., 17, 18.
1191. Richard I.'s capture of a Saracen vessel, i., 18, 19.
1217. Hubert de Burgh's victory over the French, i., 20, 21.
1512. Sir Edward Howard's fight with the French off St. Mahé, i., 59, 60.
1513. Sir Edward Howard's fight with the French off Brest, i., 67–69.
1545. Viscount Lisle's defeat of the French at Spithead, i., 78, 79.
1560. Sir William Winter's defeat of the French in the Firth of Forth, ii., 14–16.
1568. Sir John Hawkins's fight with the Spaniards at San Juan de Ulloa, ii., 54–55.
1579. Sir Francis Drake's capture of the *Cacafuego*, off Peru, ii., 97, 98.
1587. Cavendish's capture of the *Sancta Anna*, off Mexico, ii., 129, 130.
1587. Sir Francis Drake's fight with the Spaniards in Cadiz harbour, ii., 179–185.

1588. The Great Armada Fight, ii., 214–245.
1590. A battle between ten English merchant ships and twelve Spanish galleys, off Gibraltar, ii., 262–265.
1591. Sir Richard Grenville's fight, in the *Revenge*, with a Spanish fleet, near the Azores, ii., 269–277.
1592. Sir John Burroughs's capture of the *Madre de Dios*, near the Azores, ii., 281–283.
1594. Sir Richard Hawkins's fight with Spanish ships in the *Dainty*, off the coast of Peru, ii., 289–293.
1596. Lord Howard's and the Earl of Essex's fight with the Spaniards in Cadiz harbour, ii., 302–305.
Seymour, Lord Henry, his share in the Great Armada Fight, ii., 204, 211, 217, 231, 237.
Ships, Celtic, i., 2–4; Anglo-Saxon, i., 4–9; under the Plantagenets, i., 11–26; in the time of Henry VIII., i., 46, 70–74, ii., 2; during Edward VI.'s reign, ii., 2, 3; during Mary's reign, ii., 3–5; under Queen Elizabeth, ii., 5–21; Queen Elizabeth's navy in 1578, ii., 10, 11; in 1588, ii., 216; in 1603, ii., 307.
Ship-money, Anglo-Saxon, i., 8.
Sidney, Sir Henry, his speech in favour of voyages of discovery, i., 93, 94.
—— Sir Philip, his account of Frobisher's discoveries and project for accompanying him, i., 134; his project for North American colonization, i., 209, 210; his projected expedition to the West Indies with Drake, ii., 159–162.
Spain, origin of England's quarrel with, ii., 26–28, 38–39; progress of, ii., 43, 44, 80, 81, 111–114, 148–155, 172–174, 194, 199–305.

Spanish Main, Hawkins's exploits in the, ii., 32–36, 46–48; Drake's, ii., 62–72; Barker's, ii., 73, 74; Oxenham's, ii., 78, 79.
Spert, Sir Thomas, i., 43.
Stevens, Father Thomas, his voyage to India in 1579, i., 277–280.
Sumatra, the first English intercourse with, i., 295–297.

Ternate, Drake's account of the king and natives of, ii., 106–108.
Thorne, Robert, his arguments in favour of Arctic discovery, i., 82–85.
Tobacco, introduced into England by Ralph Lane, i., 229.

Valparaiso, Drake's spoliation of, ii., 96.
Verrazano, Juan de, i., 106, 107.
Virginia, Sir Walter Raleigh's first expedition to, i., 200–208; his second expedition, i., 211–230; his third expedition, i., 231; his fourth expedition, i., 232–241; its later history, i., 243, 244.

Warde, Richard, i., 39.
Waymouth, George, i., 299; his north-west voyage, i., 300–303.
Warwick's, the Countess of, Island and Sound, i., 145.
White, John, his services under Raleigh in Virginia, 1587–1589, i., 232–243.
Willoughby, Sir Hugh, his voyage in search of a north-east passage to Cathay in 1553, i., 92, 96–99.
Winter, Sir William, his work as Master of the Ordnance of the Navy, ii., 13; his fighting with the French, ii., 14–16; his share in the Great Armada Fight, ii., 205, 231, 233, 234, 237, 238.
Wolsey, Cardinal, his improvement of the English navy, i., 57, 61–3.

LONDON: PRINTED BY WILLIAM CLOWES AND SONS, STAMFORD STREET AND CHARING CROSS.

*BY THE SAME AUTHOR.*

## I.
## A MEMOIR OF SIR PHILIP SIDNEY.
One Volume, 8vo.

---

This is a very good book indeed. The author has much taste, much sense, and considerable historical insight—qualities which are absolutely essential in a biographer of Sir Philip Sidney. He has further followed an excellent fashion of the day in ransacking the State Paper Office, and his industry has disinterred several documents which throw light on obscure points in Sidney's history.—*Saturday Review.*

In one handsome library volume, this is a Life of Sir Philip Sidney studied afresh, with help from the now accessible State Papers, and clearly presented in good and simple English. In the book we find the grace of a quiet simplicity. The facts are well grouped, the chapters well divided. Distinct references acknowledge every obligation and justify every new statement; but there is no ostentation of research, careful as the research has evidently been. Everything is told in the directest way, and in the simplest phrase.—*Examiner.*

Sir Philip Sidney is undoubtedly the most striking character of an age which, more than any other, has coloured our national history with a romantic hue. Mr. Fox Bourne's elegant and discriminating biography brings into juxtaposition many details which before threw no light upon his character, and enables us to understand more fully the feelings of admiration which he inspired, and the fervent language in which his praises have been sung. The author has evidently written with the deepest interest and sympathy for his subject. The whole work bears the marks of diligent and careful research, and of a sincere desire to ascertain and tell the truth.—*London Review.*

We are glad to have so valuable a memoir of this English hero as that drawn up by Mr. Bourne.—*Westminster Review.*

We thank Mr. Bourne for the pains he has taken, while making use of the larger memoirs and collections of Collins and Zouch, to seek after original documents, especially in that invaluable repository, the State Paper Office. His exertions have thrown additional light on several important points.—*British Quarterly Review.*

We have in the volume before us the details of the active and noble life of Sidney, sought out with great diligence, and told with great ability. No reader will rise from a perusal of Mr. Bourne's labours without a just appreciation of Sidney's character, and certainly not without acknowledging the merits of Sidney's last and best biographer.—*Notes and Queries.*

A distinct view of this famous representative man is an addition to the treasures of English literature, for which all readers will be grateful. Mr. Fox Bourne has given to the public the result of lengthened and laborious researches in a volume which testifies to the care and the zeal with which the writer has studied his subject.—*Morning Post.*

Possessing industry, discrimination, love for his subject, and admiration for his hero's character, Mr. Bourne has succeeded in producing a volume which for pure interest has scarcely been equalled, certainly not excelled, for many a day. The present work is the most complete of the biographies of Sidney. We thank Mr. Bourne for the work, in which we can suggest no amendment, in which we can detect no omission, and which contains much that has hitherto only been known to book-worms—if to them. As an illustration of the inner life of the Court of Elizabeth, it posesses a high value; as a suggestive chronicle of the political movements of the day, it has even more worth; as the history of the life of a *preux chevalier*, it is worth most of all.—*Morning Herald.*

---

LONDON: CHAPMAN & HALL.

## II.
# ENGLISH MERCHANTS:
## MEMOIRS IN ILLUSTRATION OF THE PROGRESS OF BRITISH COMMERCE.

Two Volumes, crown 8vo., with 40 Illustrations.

---

Mr. Fox Bourne, who won his spurs in literature as author of the best memoir of Sir Philip Sidney that has hitherto been written, and then wrote a book not likely to be superseded, here devotes his thoughtful industry to a new labour, and again succeeds so well that the subject upon which he has written he has again made his own. By the judicious selection of his topics, he carries a sketch of the history of British commerce along a chain of lives of men. He never forgets the larger history of a national growth that he illustrates while he is winning our interest in personal narratives which, as he gives them, are compact with incident.—*Examiner*.

To illustrate the history of British commerce by the lives of British merchants, the author sketches, shadows forth, or tells in good substantial detail, some three dozen biographies. Whenever a merchant of note presents himself, Mr. Bourne enters lucidly into his history. These volumes are full of good, honest work, not only of important commercial history, but of capital illustrative and anecdotal matter. They furnish new and interesting chapters in the history of England.—*Athenæum*.

Mr. Fox Bourne, the author of a creditable *Memoir of Sir Philip Sidney*, has applied the industry and research which distinguished that biography to the preparation of a very useful work on the history of British commerce. Out of the vast quantity of material at his service he has collected all the best information he could acquire concerning 'the histories of some three dozen famous merchants whose conduct illustrates the course of English commerce,' and the result is a very entertaining and suggestive book. The De la Poles of Hull head the list, which is closed by Richard Cobden.—*Pall Mall Gazette*.

Mr. Fox Bourne has extracted out of our commercial annals those chapters which possess most human interest.—*Contemporary Review*.

Mr. Fox Bourne's book is both interesting and useful. It is not, strictly speaking, a history of commerce, as any attempt to make it so would have marred the design of the author. It may be described as a succession of vignettes, with a connecting narrative here and there to give it a significance, and weave it into a uniform whole.—*Chronicle*.

The author of this work has done good service by collecting, in the compass of two volumes, the story of the founders and magnates of British commerce. He has made no pretence at fine writing, but has told his story simply and naturally, with just enough of domestic incident to give a life interest in these great merchants of the past. It is a book which should be read by every one having an interest in the mercantile greatness of our country.—*Morning Herald*.

The author of these volumes has rendered an essential service by showing how the exertions of private individuals have given an impulse to the operations of trade, and promoted England's welfare.—*Morning Post*.

Mr. Bourne's handsome volumes are full of anecdote. The book is the outcome of honest work, and we are glad to be able to congratulate Mr. Bourne on the result.—*Globe*.

There is not an event of any importance that has occurred in connection with English commerce but has found a place in this record, and the rise, progress, continuance, or end of any great scheme is graphically related. The style is plain and perspicuous; always free from the ornate incumbrances of an unformed taste.—*Press*.

Mr. Bourne's *English Merchants*, without being a complete history of commerce, gives us a more complete view of its rise and progress than could be obtained in any other way, and whilst thus illustrative of trade as well as national history, the volumes have all the charm of clearly-written, concise, and interesting biographies.—*Manchester Examiner*.

---

LONDON: RICHARD BENTLEY.

www.ingramcontent.com/pod-product-compliance
Lightning Source LLC
Chambersburg PA
CBHW030741230426
43667CB00007B/794